Weather of the Heart

Clockwise from top left: Babushka, Papa (Adolf Lurye), Zeyde (Yefim Lurye) as a young man, Mamma (Olga lourie) and Niura.

Weather of the Heart

A Child's Journey Out of Revolutionary Russia

Nora Lourie Percival

High Country Publishers, Ltd
Boone, North Carolina

High Country Publishers, Ltd
197 New Market Center #135
Boone, NC 28607
www.highcountrypublishers.com
<editor@highcountrypublishers.com>

Library of Congress Cataloging-in-Publication Data

Percival, Nora, 1914-
   Weather of the heart : a child's journey out of revolutionary Russia
/ by Nora Percival.
     p.; cm.
  ISBN 0-9713045-9-9 (softcover : alk. paper)
  1. Percival, Nora, 1914--Childhood and youth. 2. Jews--Russia   (Federation)--Samara--Biography. 3. Samara (Russia)--Biography. 4. Percival, Nora,
1914--Journeys--Russia (Federation)--Samara.
        I.
     Title.
  DS135.R95 P47 2002
  304.8'7304744__dc21

                             2001004638

First Printing: February 2002
First Paperback Printing: February 2003
10 9 8 7 6 5 4 3 2

For my children and grandchildren,
who continue the story here begun,
and in whom the dear dead still have their being.

☙ Acknowledgements ❧

This book would not have been brought to fruition without the support and encouragement of many friends, relatives, and colleagues. The enthusiasm and advice of fellow members of the High Country Writers and the inspiration and generous assistance of my editor, Judy Geary, have been invaluable. I must also acknowledge the many hours of help and the stubborn patience of Schuyler Kaufman and the generosity of Bob and Barbara Ingalls. To all of them I express profound gratitude.

⊰ Contents ⊱

⊰ Foreword ⊱

In all the years this story has been gestating, I have often wondered at its stubborn insistence on being told, its refusal to sink gracefully into the gentle limbo of faint memory. So many times the writing has been put aside, sometimes even out of mind, for months or years; but always it has resurfaced, clamored, persisted. Until at last, the busy years of family and career demands being done, it rose to dominate my days, and finally emerged in words on paper.

It was a long process. Life takes us, moves us, uses us. A husband falls ill, grandchildren are born, the snowdrops and daffodils push up through the heavy mulch of leaves and demand attention to free them to grow. And while we answer the demands of people and plants, of houses and jobs and health and talent, our lives move on to new conditions, pulling us along perforce. While we dream of how we want to shape a life, we have already lived it, and it is gone.

Why then, in the midst of the engrossing now, why this passion to remember, this drive to resurrect the trials and crises of so long ago? Perhaps the need to acknowledge those enormous efforts to survive, to record them on the register of human struggles against dehumanizing forces. So many later catastrophes now overlay these ancient agonies — could they still be relevant? Yet it's always been the same struggle — during revolutions, wars, holocausts, genocides, on whatever continent and in whatever era — always the same struggle of the single human spirit against the massed baleful power of ideology.

In his book *A View of All the Russias*, Laurens van der Post says: "No man is free to commit himself to an honest future until he has first been honest about the past." Though most of my future is now in the past, still this need to explore those desperate days persists. Before I cease to remember, it seems necessary to bear witness, to pass on to my descendants — and to all the other descendants of the people who lived through those overwhelming events — a sense of how it was. So aware of the power of history, I am impelled to show how much it shaped those who shaped and still shape today's young.

We take so much for granted. We see an old church, poised perfectly on a hill commanding the crossroads, its Wren steeple a lovely exclamation point in time. Do we ever think of how this spot was chosen, cleared, who it was that imagined the perfect site? So in our lives, we take for granted what people are, without dreaming of what made them so, what worlds shaped them.

This is the question I want to probe. What happens to people under severe duress, under continuing extreme pressure? Why do some individuals rise magnificently to the challenge, discover unsuspected powers that make them function better than before? While other uncertain souls, terrified in the face of their own inadequacy, with no confidence in their own will, withdraw from the battle and lose the chance to grow into strength, stamp themselves "imperfect" and "useless" and never test the extent of their powers. Their chances of survival are minimal, and if they do live, they are broken and helpless for the rest of their days.

Phyllis Rose wrote in *Biography as Fiction*: "The way people manage to live their lives without prior rehearsal is amazing and insufficiently wondered at." In a crisis situation such as existed in Russia in the second and third decades of the last century, the way life was managed, especially by the millions caught helplessly between opposing forces in which they had no part, seems even more incredible.

Such a revolution is really a struggle between the powerful, such as nobles and wealthy landowners, on one hand, and the poor, tired of living on a bare minimum in an inefficient economy, on the other. Yet the growing middle class was in many ways the chief sufferer in the conflict. The triumphant proletariat tarred the *bourjui* with the same brush as the gentry, although the intelligentsia didn't have the resources of the rich and landed. They were powerless to maintain their status in the new regime, though they had not been exploiters. In fact, many were liberal and welcomed the first steps to democracy; but they suffered as much as the upper classes and lost everything that had been so painfully acquired.

The life one had to live in those years bore no resemblance to anything one might call "normal." A climate of tragedy and terror is unreal because it is unnatural. In ordinary life hunger, death, and fear are occasional traumas, absorbed into the daily fabric of existence. But when they become too large a part of life, the fabric of reality breaks down.

In the decade after 1917 in Russia, civil war, famine, and a brutal campaign of terror created such a climate. What a monk of Cluny wrote in 1040, at another of what historian Barbara Tuchman calls "one of history's ebbs," would serve as an equally apt description nine centuries later: "What can we think but that the whole human race, root and branch, is sliding willingly down again into the gulf of primeval chaos?"

Cut off from their roots, material and spiritual, deprived of family ties and accustomed rituals, people lose their sense of self, and of their place in an ordered universe. They are cast adrift. Trying to remake a life is almost impossibly difficult without the comforting anchors of faith, family, and community.

Now as I approach the end of a lifetime that began in a year of cataclysm (1914), the same unholy wars against the human spirit go on unabated. My generation has been witness to starving war refugees, the dispossessed of the Great Depression, the sacrificed millions of the monstrous holocaust under Hitler, the victims of China's Red revolution, the dissenters tortured in Latin America's political wars, the desperate boat people of Indo-China, and now again the barbaric ethnic cleansing in Rwanda and Bosnia . . . the endless list grows with the years.

In the cause of these and all the other helpless souls offered up to the dark gods of destruction, accounts like this one are minute counterblows struck for humanism— futile perhaps, but necessary nevertheless.

❄ 1 ❄
The Return
Samara, Russia: 1995

I CAN'T believe I'm finally here. After all the years of wishing, really on my way. Over eighty and overweight, on a worn plush seat in a stuffy train that's carrying me steadily eastward across the Russian steppe — in search of a life I escaped so long ago, of a family that was once my world. What can I hope to find of the life we'd shared, filled with alarms and dangers that we'd faced together and survived? The lost faces rise in my memory, crowding around me. Are they the catalyst that sent me on this impetuous quest into an enormous troubled land, where one feels fear everywhere — where even the water can't be trusted?

The monotonous clack of train wheels sings an obbligato to the unending ribbon of landscape that streams by my window as the train chugs through a tedious succession of summer plain and dusty woods. The fields yellow with barley, the weather-beaten villages, a row of fat cabbages in a garden, a flash of blue lake. How Russian it all looks to my American eyes, and yet how strangely familiar.

In the midst of a serene life, with children settling into middle age, and grandchildren growing up into careers, why my obsession to go adventuring into this barely remembered world? Yet here I am, having finally found a tour that includes Samara, being carried east from Moscow toward the city of my birth.

This threadbare seat might be the one in the westbound train that took Mamma and me to the Latvian border all those years ago. Into my old heart creeps the remembered panic of that grim eight-year-old who sat in such a train, rubbing her mother's quivering back and crooning, "Don't cry, Mamushka, don't be afraid! Soon we'll be in Riga, and your cousin will take care of us. And then we'll get on the ship and then we'll sail across the ocean, and then we'll see Papa. Please don't cry, Mamenka, you'll make yourself sick. Everything will be all right. You'll see."

Intent on comforting the hysterical mother who trembled at the thought of facing cruel Red border guards — guards who might at the last moment find an excuse to bar their exit from Bolshevik Russia into a freer air — that child spared hardly a thought for the miles flowing by the sooty train window, taking her away from everything familiar and dear.

Grateful for this quiet interval between the comings and goings of my fellow travelers, I lean back and let the vista wash through my eyes, welcome the memories it calls up. These lush July fields, greens and yellows punctuated by red roof slants of *izbas,* wooden huts that cluster to mark a village, clumps of woods that soon give way to level plain again — these are the landscapes of my childhood. I watch the curious double telephone poles flash by, their tops meeting like the skeletons of tepees — each pole propping the other against the determined winds that scour the steppe — and remember those other fields where the child who was myself sat with Mamma in the grass learning to make daisy chains.

I stir restlessly, weary with long sitting, lick my unbrushed teeth with an ill-tasting tongue. The grungy lavatory at the end of the car is not conducive to thorough cleanups. My breath must be foul, I think, and in an unbidden flash of lost memory feel that eight-year-old self, sharing her feelings and worries, tasting the fetid juices that rose from an ill-fed stomach as she and her mother rode westward on the journey I was now reversing.

Ever since our tour group left Moscow, under the pleasant small talk with visitors popping in from other compartments, my mind has been singing the refrain, "I'm going to see Samara. I'm going back to Samara!" and the haunting question that dims the joy, "Will it be *my* Samara?"

Behind my eyes rise so many dormant memories that may soon bloom into reality after a lifetime in the dusty attic of my heart. For these few quiet moments I savor the anticipation churning in my brain. Tomorrow I will be back in the city I left in 1922, and have never seen since.

What will I find? How much remains of the houses, the streets, the neighborhood that cradled me? I know my river will still be there, the beautiful Volga I've loved ever since I could remember anything. But will even that be the same? How will huge dams and rampant industrialization have changed the river — and the town? In fact, it's only a few years since Samara got its traditional name back, to my delight. During the Soviet years it was called Kuibishev after a local commissar, a change I always deplored.

I turn from the window and smile at Jean Gaskin in the doorway. Jean is a member of our tour group and has become a good companion. She shares my enthusiasm for new places, revels in the fabulous museums, cathedrals and unpeopled palaces of the old world as I do, and savors the double pleasure of sharing our sightseeing.

"Where's Reed?" I ask. Jean is traveling with a teenage grandson. She takes the seat across the little table that hangs below the window, laughing at my question.

"Your guess is as good as mine. Somewhere on the train, I hope. Reed's thing is talking to people. Before we get to Samara he'll be able to tell us all about every interesting person on the train." She sighs and leans back against the doily on the back of her seat. "I feel as if I've talked to everybody on the train too. At least everybody in this car."

I nod. "I feel almost like that even without leaving the compartment. So many heads popping in and out. This trip seems endless. Or is it just that I'm impatient to get to Samara?"

"Of course you're impatient. Actually, to me it seems that all this visiting is making the hours go by more quickly. But you must be thinking only of Samara. Do you really think you'll remember it? You were so young."

I shake my head. "Oh yes, I was seven when we left. So many memories live in my head. If only it hasn't all been torn down. I'm sure I'll remember the places. It's the people I'm afraid are lost." I turn back to the window, my throat tight with yearning. Sensing my mood, Jean opens her book. Worn down by our relentless sightseeing in Moscow and the constant togetherness of group travel, we each feel the other's need for silence.

Soon the constant flow of the passing countryside glazes my eyes, and I shut them to watch the landscape of memory unfurl inside my lids. Half asleep, half thinking, half dreaming, I see the summer fields around the *dacha* the family rented each year, Babushka's house in Samara on the long avenue running downhill to the Volga, and around the corner my own dear yellow house — the house where I was born.

How it wrings my heart, even in a dream, to see the elegant front with its crisp white trim, the balcony above the front door where that long-lost child who was myself played with her constant companion, a stuffed bear named Mishka. A remembered moment of joy leaps into my mind, as Mamma comes out to smell the lilac scent from the ancient bushes in the garden across the street.

"Mmm, it smells so sweet, doesn't it, Mamma? It'll make you feel better, won't it?" Poor Mamma had not been well all winter, and Papa and I had been trying hard to cheer her up. Was that the beginning, I now wonder sadly, of the ill health that haunted her the rest of her life?

The dream of the yellow house fades as sorrow engulfs me. All those who filled my early childhood with love are long dead, and even my generation of cousins are most likely gone. How many people survive the rigors of Soviet life into their eighties?

Jean looks up as she hears my deep sigh. "Poor Nora," she says. "Sometimes I think you're only storing up sorrow for yourself by this hopeless search. What's the use? Going back to where such terrible things happened."

"I was just wondering that myself." How can I make my friend see how necessary this trip has become for me? "Actually I've wanted for a long time to visit Samara. But it was always off limits to tourists. So when it finally became possible to travel freely around Russia, I knew I had to go." I take Jean's hand in both my own. "Even if I can't find any trace of the family, I still yearn to see the place itself, where we all lived together."

Resolutely turning from the painful past, I focus on the view again. It's becoming more varied. The approaching village seems a more substantial one than most. As the train slows down, large villas come into view, set in neat lawns or nestled in wooded grounds.

"Look, Jean, look at those pretty *dachas*. They remind me of the one we used to rent every summer. See that one way back, with the tall linden tree and the little pond?" I point. "That's just like ours was, a sprawling old house with lots of bedrooms and wide shady porches. How I loved our month in the country." I turn to Jean with shining eyes.

She smiles. "You look so happy when you talk about it. Tell me more. What is a *dacha*, anyway?"

"It's what we'd call a country house. Lots of city people in old Russia owned one. Others, like us, rented them by the week or month, for summer vacations. Just like we do in the States. Ours had room for Papa's whole family."

"Not your mother's?" Jean asks.

I shake my head. "No, I never knew any of them except Mamma's sister Xenia. What I think of as my family were all Papa's. His parents and his two sisters, and Aunt Tanya's three children."

It feels so good to talk about them. It brings them so to life. "Everybody looked forward to our holiday month together, living in this informal family way." I look out at the dachas fading in the distance, remembering. "It must have taken them back to the close-knit life of their childhood.

"I loved living together as one family. It was one long funfest for me. I could play with my cousins all day long. And when Papa came up on weekends, that was the best! Papa loved to play." Nostalgia is threatening to overwhelm me.

"All the people I loved and who loved me were there together. Especially Papa. He was the rock I anchored to. At my age, of course, I saw everyone as they related to me."

I ran the list, feeling again the childhood loves I owned. "Mamma was to cheer up, Fraülein was to learn from, grandparents were to be spoiled by — they had the best laps — and cousins were to romp with. But Papa! Papa was to belong to. When he was there, the world was all in place." I shut my eyes, trying to see it all again.

"It sounds wonderful," Jean sighs. "But how can you remember it so well? You were hardly more than a baby."

"I don't really know how much I remember and how much was imprinted on my brain by others. By Mamma in those lonely days in Moscow, when talking about the happy past was one of our greatest pleasures. And later by Papa in America. He used to talk about it when we'd take our walks after dinner or sit outdoors on summer evenings."

I smiled at Jean, a bit sheepish, but anxious to make her understand.

"In fact, some of it may just be stories I imagined, when I would think about Russia in bed at night. I only know that the scene has grown in my memory and my imagination.

"You know how it is, Jean," I confide. "After you grow up you get so involved in work and family that you live totally in the present. But later, when you're older and less absorbed, the past begins to come back more and more.

"After I started trying to understand my Russian life I read a lot about that chaotic time, and I began to create a picture in my head, almost like stories I might have read, of the way it might have been. So I really can't tell you how much is memory, how much may be acquired fact, and how much is probably imagination."

My eyes grow misty as I remember. "But the pictures are so vivid. Was it real? I don't know. But it *could* have been real. It lives in my memory now, valid and complete."

I think about the troubled era I had lived through, wonder how I can make Jean feel it. Her gray eyes are intent, her mouth eager. She is trying to see with me.

"It was a hopeful time. The tsar had abdicated, and the *Duma*, our parliament, was trying to pick up the pieces of a shattered economy. But that summer no one yet had any idea of the catastrophes to come."

"Guess what I found." Reed's voice jolts me back to the world in which I am eighty, not three. Reed Gaskin is the youngest member of our tour group. At twelve, he's already a seasoned world traveler. No language barrier stops him for long.

"Something good to eat?" Jean asks hopefully.

"No, something for you, Nana," Reed says. With eleven grandchildren, I have long been "Nana" to nearly everybody. "I met a lady from Samara in the next car. She's a journalist, and she wants to meet you. I was telling her that you were born there."

"How exciting, my dear." Like everyone on our tour, Jean has gotten involved in my homecoming project. "She might be able to help you."

A journalist from Samara. I'm already on my feet. "Of course I want to meet her! Journalists are the best route to reach people who might know about my family."

Xenia Vassilievna is a stylish young woman with fairly fluent English. Her dark Tatar eyes sparkle at the publicity prospect that has fallen into her lap.

"Please sit down, Madame Percival," she gushes. "I'm so glad you came to see me. Reed told me your wonderful story."

She listens with interest to my hopes of finding traces or at least news of my family.

"Of course I'll be glad to do what I can." She

beams. "You know, you look just like my grandmother."

"Really?" This might be a real break. "I don't know yet who my hosts will be, but perhaps — "

"Oh, don't worry. I'll find you. Let me give you my card, in case there's a problem."

The little square announces "International Public Relations" below her name. The lady clearly knows how to take advantage of opportunities. "We need to arrange an interview for TV and radio, so people who might have known your relatives can hear about you." She details plans and ideas, chatting on and on.

I return to my compartment in a flutter. Maybe it will really happen, I think. Maybe the dream will come to life, and my lost world bloom into being. "Wouldn't it be wonderful?" Jean says.

I ring for the car attendant, Mrs. Markova, to order tea, and Reed says, "The car lady's from Samara too. Maybe she'll know about your street."

Mrs. Markova knows about Komsomolskaya ulitza, where my grandmother's house stood. "Oh, yes, it's in the old section, near where the two rivers meet. I know it well. We used to picnic at a park nearby. The old houses are still there, it hasn't been rebuilt." Now I am in a fever of impatience to reach Samara, and as Reed spreads news of the developments, my fellow tourists keep popping in to join in the anticipation.

Their chatter about new possibilities helps the slow hours to pass. The interest of my new friends pleases me. It reinforces my sometimes shaky belief that my search makes sense. I'm especially grateful to the "Business for Russia" project. This tour includes Samara only because a number of the interns came from there.

Our small group is an interesting mix, a few tourists like Jean and me, two state directors of "Business for Russia" and several business people who had hosted Russians under that program, and are now visiting their interns in return.

As the long evening darkens into night, and we finish up the picnics we had all brought along — there is no food service on Russian trains — the talk dwindles and the intervals of silence grow longer. The accumulated fatigue of four hectic days in Moscow is catching up with us. Mrs. Markova makes up our berths early, and we're all glad to stretch out in them, to read or drowse.

Tired as I am, I cannot make sleep come. Tomorrow I will actually be walking the streets I walked with my parents, strolling along the river as I once did with Nyanya and Fraülein. The thought fills my mind with crowding childhood memories, welling up from the depths where they've been buried all those years ago, when remembering was an agony of longing. This train will pull into the station from which Papa left us and his country, where Mamma and I last saw the dear faces that were my world.

When at last I fall asleep, I dream again, of Babushka's house around the corner from ours, where all the family had crowded together. I see us all sitting around the big round table in the dining room, filling our glasses with tea from the big brass samovar in the middle. "Is there enough hot water for Zeyde?" my grandmother is saying. "He'll be coming home from *shul* soon."

The warm fragrance permeates the room where many voices rise and fall. In sleep my body warms with joy at the sight.

Babushka as usual is gently chiding her complaining daughters. "My dears, there's no sense grumbling. We just have to make the best of it. We're living through a bad time now, but it won't last forever. It never does." Babushka is always trying to keep the family's spirits up. "Zeyde and I've lived through many hard times. We just have to see that the family survives." She turns to me with her sweet smile and says, "Niurochka, where . . . ?"

The sound of her voice is still in my ears as the dream fades away. As my mind struggles back to reality I realize that it's not Babushka's voice but Jean's that I'm hearing. It's morning, and time to get ready for Samara. I rush through my sketchy toilet, only to have to sit waiting for hours, grumbling to Jean in an agony of impatience through the repeated stops and slowdowns. We arrive five hours late, cross and hungry, with no breakfast and late for lunch.

At last the train pulls into a large crowded station. On the roof of an office building nearby, are huge letters spelling out SAMARA. I'm pleased to see how proudly the city displays its restored name. Only days later do I discover that it's not advertising the city but a chain of department stores.

As we leave the train we are overwhelmed to find the station filled with people apparently waiting for us. With them are reporters and TV cameras; we seem to be celebrities. Jean turns to me with a big grin as the media surge toward us.

"I think it's you especially they're waiting for, Nora. How do you suppose they found out about you?"

"Oh, it can't be," I say. "How could they know? I'm sure it's their hosts that they want to interview."

"Maybe it was from Xenia Vas-vas . . . Oh, you know . . . that they learned about the old lady who's returning to her birthplace after so many years?"

"Vassilievna." I supply. "Well, however they heard, it makes a good story, and I guess the media is hot on the trail."

For once I'm glad of the publicity. It may well be the help I need to find news of my lost family. Surely there might still be someone who had known them, or had information about what happened to them. In a flurry of introductions I latch on to Anatoly Semionoff, introduced as head of the state-run TV company. He is as eager to talk as I am.

"We must get your story on the evening news," he says, and proceeds to interview me on the spot. With hope riding high, I supply all the scanty details I have about people I last saw over half a century ago.

Our group is getting a royal welcome, especially those who had hosted interns coming to learn American business methods. Now these Samarans are eager to return the hospitality they enjoyed. "Now we are going to be the hosts, and you will each meet the one who will be yours," the leader says. "We have made many plans for your entertainment."

In a flurry of excited chatter and laughter the gathering breaks up into small groups. The American hosts quickly find their former guests, but the rest of us don't know anyone yet, and must be paired up one by one with the friendly people who will house and feed us for five days. With only bits of common language for most of us, and much translating by the few hosts who have good English, it is nearly an hour before my hostess, Ludmilla, manages to extricate me from the press and take me home for a belated lunch.

The pretty blonde radiates warmth but has no English words to express it. However, her 13-year-old daughter Valeria goes to an English school and carries us over the hurdles.

Through Valeria, Ludmilla apologizes because her husband was not there to greet me, because he is on his way home from a business trip to Holland. "Vladimir has to go out of the country quite often," she says. "He is the principal of a business college, but everybody has to have some business on the side nowadays. Nobody can live on their salary, because of the terrible inflation. He goes to the countries in western Europe to trade. But he promised to be home in time for the opera."

I'm glad to get in a short rest before the evening's festivities. We gather for the performance, an elaborate production of 'The Masked Ball." As I compliment our hosts on the opulent opera house in the main plaza of the old city, Inna, a small dark bundle of energy who runs the English school, interrupts.

"I know it's a show place, but most of us are not happy about it," she says. "An ancient cathedral used to stand in this spot. It was a favorite city land-mark, and everybody was furious when Stalin or-dered it torn down to make way for the new opera house. The older residents resent it to this day."

However unloved, the opera house is a lucky place for me. During the intermission, Inna an-nounces that her husband has a map of the city. "He was able to find your grandmother's street. It's not very far from here. Would you like us to take you there after the opera, or are you too tired? We could go tomorrow evening instead."

"Oh, please!" I don't want to wait one unneces-sary moment. "Couldn't we go tonight?" Russian per-formances usually start at seven so it was still rather early.

"Of course." Inna laughs at my impatience. "It would be our pleasure. It won't be getting dark until at least ten. My husband will drive us."

After the opera, Jean and Reed Gaskin crowd into the small Avtovaz with us. "I've got to be there when you find your old home," Jean insists. "I couldn't miss that!"

It's not far to Babushka's street in the old quar-ter, and soon we find #19 Komsomolskaya ulitza. The house is still there. We park across the street and I stare at the faded tan front of the two-story building, nearly obscured by a tall old weeping birch.

Is this shabby stucco remnant in a ramshackle block really the house I called home for nearly four years? Yes, there's the old stoop where Babushka would take the air after hours in her stuffy kitchen. There's the window of what had been Mamma's and my bedroom. There at the bottom of the hill two blocks down is the Volga, beside which I had walked nearly every day. I always loved to watch the wide river, the dark green hills on the other side, the busy ships and barges moving up and downstream. The longer I look, the more familiar the place feels, no matter how changed. My heart swells as all the memories come flooding in.

"Should we try to get inside?" enterprising Inna suggests. As we leave the car, the old lady sitting on the raised edge of the stoop looks up in surprise.

"She must live there," I whisper to Inna.

"Do you think she might know . . . " Jean says.

"We'll soon see. I'll ask her." Inna goes over and tells my story, while I hang back, uncertain of a welcome. But the old lady looks up and smiles, waving a welcoming hand at me. I hurry over, choked with excitement.

"She never heard of your family," Inna reports. "But when I told her you used to live here as a child, she asked if you'd like to come in and see the inside. I was sure you would."

"Oh, yes," I say, barely able to breathe. "Please." But as I step inside, my heart sinks. There's nothing left of the warm tidy home I'm longing to see again. The five-room flat that took up the whole first floor has been cut up into three or four tiny efficiencies. The one we're in consists of just the hall, with stairs leading to the upstairs flats, one bedroom in front and, at the back, what had been our dining room and is now also a kitchen. None of it has seen paint for decades. None of it holds anything familiar.

Drowning in disappointment, I manage to stammer out my thanks for the old lady's hospitality. But as I turn to leave, suddenly it's as if a sun had broken through the dark. There beside the front door is a window — *my* window! As long as I lived here this deep window niche was my "castle," my special place where I spent endless hours with Mishka, my books and my kitten, where I had taken refuge from the hubbub of a crowded household. Incredibly, it's just the same. Even its faded paint is still blue.

"My window seat!" I cry, and on an impulse get in and crowd my clumsy old body into the child-size space that had been mine so long ago.

All at once, I understand why I made this journey, though knowing that I would not find those loved faces I longed to see once more. Here in this shabby hallway, scrunched up in a scanty space, I've come to the end of my search. On the other side of the planet and of a century, incredibly I've come home and found — myself.

Around me the dear lost faces shine with smiles, the remembered voices ring in my ears, the child I have not been for an endless time is with me, and at least for this one euphoric moment all the lost has been found. This life lived so long ago is the story I know I have to tell, to speak for so many others who have silently endured the loss of all they valued.

≈ 2 ≈
The Scent of Lilacs
Samara, 1918

MY MEMORY begins in sunshine. After months of heavy snow and harsh cold, spring had come at last. On the balcony above the doorway of the yellow house, the child who grew up to be me was serving tea to her dolls and to Mishka the teddy bear, reveling in the soft fragrant air. The scent came drifting from the blind men's home across the cobbled street, where gnarled branches of ancient lilac trees tossed their white and purple plumes over the weathered brick wall of the garden.

The balcony overlooking the street was my only outdoor play space; our house filled its narrow lot. My father's factory lay directly behind it. From the bay window in my nursery I could see the factory and a bit of the river when I curled up in the window seat with Mishka, on rainy days.

Now the gray indoor season was over at last, and I could play on the balcony once more. Happy in the scented sunshine, I wiggled my toes and thought of the outdoor pleasures to come. It had been a dreary winter, with Mama frail and ailing, Papa worried, no tea parties or company. Always there was scary talk about "conditions" and the war — always the war. Now the sun lit the dark corners of rooms and souls; windows were opened to warm breezes, and hearts to hope.

"Mm, smell the lilacs, Mishka." I shared all my thoughts with the bear, my bosom buddy. "It's spring now. Pretty soon maybe we can take our walks by the river again. Last year we always walked by the river with Nyanya, remember?" The peasant nurse had been the hub of my world until a German governess replaced her when I turned three.

That event precipitated the first rebellion of my life. When Mamma explained at the breakfast table that I was now old enough to start my training as a lady, I dug in my heels.

"I don't want to be a lady. I want to stay with Nyanya. If you send her away, I'll go too." I stuck out my small chin the way Cousin Mara did when he was angry.

Papa looked up from his morning paper. "Well, Olya, we seem to have a rebel to deal with." He looked at me, trying not to smile. "Where will you go with Nyanya? You know she's going to another family, to take care of a new baby."

I glowered at Papa. "I don't care. If you send her away, I'll never speak to the governess. Never, never, never!"

"You'll like Fraülein, you'll see," Mamma said placidly. "She'll teach you to speak German. And when you get big, we'll go traveling and you'll be able to speak to people in foreign countries."

That sounded exciting. New places, new things to see, were already an allurement. "Well . . . all right. I guess we can have Fraülein. But I want Nyanya too. I'm used to her."

"Nyanya will come to see you often," Mamma promised. "If you're good she might take you to see her new baby."

"I'm her baby," I growled. And when Fraülein came, it took me all of a week to admit to myself that she told me all sorts of interesting things, and that I liked her. But I never stopped wishing for Nyanya's lap to sit in.

Now on the balcony the thought came again. "Oh, Mishka, I miss Nyanya and our walks by the river." I sighed. "Fraülein likes to walk uptown to look at the shops. That's no fun." The patient bear agreed, as usual.

"I love the river, don't you, Mishka? The big boats and the logs floating down and the hills across the water." Dreaming of the green remembered hills, I leaned over the railing, my straight hair hanging like ash-blond curtains around my face.

I loved to watch the daily parade. Housewives with empty shopping bags on their way to hunt for scarce supplies in the market stalls near the river, boatmen in worn sheepskin coats and felt boots, soldiers on leave, jaunty in their overseas caps and puttees, filled the broad street. I waved at everyone, and passersby smiled back.

"Look, Mishka, there's the officer who waved at me yesterday. There, under the lilacs." As the young man looked up, I smiled and waved, jumping up and down in excitement, my hair bow bobbing on top of my head. His weary face brightened into a grin. He broke off a spray of lilac and, crossing the street, tossed it up into the balcony with a little bow. I clapped my hands in delight and waved the flower until my hero turned the corner.

"Oh, Mishka, he was my prince," I sighed. "Just like Ivan Tsarevich. . . . Mmm, it smells so good!" Returning to my tea party, I presented the blossom to my scruffy yellow friend. "Here, Mishka. You can hold my flower." I tucked it into his armpit. "What a nice soldier. He looked happy, didn't he?" Mishka did not disagree.

"Spring will make it all better, Mishka, you'll see," I promised the bear. "Now Papa won't worry, and Mamma won't be so sad. I heard Fraülein tell Cousin Luba that Mamma was sad because she lost the baby again. What did she mean? We don't have a baby." I paused to puzzle over this, but gave it up with a shrug. "I wish we did.

"Won't it be nice when Mamma is better? She won't have to lie down all the time. Maybe she'll play the piano again . . . I love it when Mamma plays the piano. She'll come for walks with Papa and me . . . and . . . and . . . " My busy little mind was off on another tangent. "Papa said the war is over. Maybe Cousin Luba will go home now."

I was out of patience with the young visitor from Moscow, who mooned about complaining because there were no balls or parties, and all the young men were away fighting. Luba had laughed at me, I complained to Mishka. "She thinks I'm silly because I talk to you, Mishka. Well, *she's* silly too, talking about young men all the —"

My babble broke off as Cousin Luba and Fraülein strolled out on the balcony. They were too absorbed in their own talk to pay much attention to the tea party. Though I was too young at three to make much sense of their conversation, with my later awareness I can imagine how it might have gone, since the upheaval in the government was on everyone's mind and was talked about incessantly.

"I *wish* Mother would allow me to come home," Luba was saying peevishly. "I'm so *bored* here in Samara! There's nothing to *do*, no social life, with Olya always ill and Adolf so busy. All my friends are in Moscow."

"Now, Mademoiselle Luba, you know your mother is only trying to protect you. The Moscow streets are not safe now, there's rioting . . . " Though she would never say it, the governess' face plainly spoke her impatience with the visitor's petulance. "Your parents sent you to us because it's much quieter here on the Volga, and you won't be in danger."

Thin and stiff as a yardstick in her high-necked black frock, the governess looked the epitome of severity. But the flat bosom hid a heart all kindness and concern. "The weather will be much more pleasant now, and we'll be able to get out more as soon as the mud dries up. The Zhiguli Hills are lovely in the spring. Perhaps we can plan a picnic there."

Luba shrugged her indifference to picnics.

"Madame is recovering now from the loss of her B-A-B-Y," with an eloquent glance at me. "She might be well enough for some pleasure. You should make up your mind to enjoy your visit. I'm sure your mother will not let you go home until Moscow is safer and the situation is more settled."

"Oh, Fraülein, *do* you really think things will be settled soon? It seems to be an endless agony. The fighting going badly, the shops getting emptier every day. And now a new government." She flung her hands wide apart. "Do you *really* think the new regime can repair our poor Russia?"

Fraülein's calm assurance was calculated to cool Luba's histrionics. The handsome young visitor, whose eighteen years were more evident in her tall buxom figure than in her petulant self-indulgence, had a flair for the dramatic and enjoyed a show of hysteria now and then.

"We *must* believe that conditions *will* improve." Fraülein brought in a higher authority. "Monsieur Lurye is very confident. You'll see. In a few months things will settle down and life will get back to normal." Fraülein sighed in sympathy, "But I know this is a hard time to be eighteen."

Luba clasped her hands together. "How wonderful it would be. To have fun again. Go to parties and buy new clothes and have beaux. And no war to worry about." She whirled around in excitement, her skirts scattering tiny teacups and cookies. "Do you think we might really go on a picnic across the river?"

I could no longer contain my excitement. I had sat as quietly as I could, so Fraülein would not put an end to the talk with "Little pitchers have big ears," or another of her unfailing supply of maxims. But now I flung myself against the governess in a frenzy of joy. "Oh, can we, Fraülein? Can we really have a picnic in the hills? I *always* wanted to go up there. When Nyanya and I used to walk by the river I looked at the hills and wished I could go there. Will Papa take us, do you think? Oh, I *hope* we can go!"

Fraülein's frown signaled reproof, but a welcome distraction saved me. Mamma's head appeared through the French doors, saying wistfully, "What's going on out here? You all sound so merry. No room for me, I suppose? Is my daughter giving you one of her tea parties?" She caressed my head lightly. "How nice and summery you look, dushenka, in that pretty white dress with your blue sash."

"Of course there's room, Madame." Fraülein moved aside as I took Mamma's hand to pull her out. "Do come out and enjoy the sunshine. It's a lovely day; the sun will do you good. Do you feel stronger today?"

"Yes, yes I am. And you're right. This marvelous warm sun will do wonders for me. And look at Mishka, with a lilac in his arms. Where did you get the flower, darling?"

As I told my romantic tale, Mamma edged out onto the crowded balcony. "What were you saying about a picnic?"

"I suggested to Mademoiselle Luba that it might be possible to plan an outing in the hills across the river, and the idea excited the child. Do you think we might, Madame? I'm afraid our quiet life is perhaps a bit dull for a gay young lady from Moscow."

"Do you think we might, Olga?" Luba added.

Luba's urging was hardly needed. The invalid was quite ready for some enjoyment. For Olga Nicolaevna happiness was still a barely explored territory. Though born to plenty and privilege, she had been a neglected child. Those desolate years had left traces in a sadness that lurked beneath the surface of her quiet face.

It was this very air of melancholy, I learned years later, that had first intrigued Adolf Yefimovich Lurye. In America Papa would reminisce about their meeting as we lounged on the front porch on warm summer evenings.

"I longed to chase the shadow from those pansy-brown eyes," Papa confided. "and to bring a smile to that mouth. I was a new entrepreneur then, launched in Samara society by the widow Ratner, from whom I had bought my factory. One of her friends was Mamma's Aunt Zoya, who was much taken with me. I was the newest eligible bachelor in town. She sent off an invitation to Olga, then arranged a series of parties for her. From the first dinner, I was enthralled. Zoya was thrilled to see the instant rapport between us. Soon I was a constant visitor."

"'What makes Olga Nikolaevna so serious . . . so almost sad?" I asked Zoya once when we were alone.

I could see that Zoya was happy to encourage my interest. "I'm afraid the poor girl had a very unhappy childhood,' she told me. 'My sister died when Olga was born, the third daughter in three years.'

Zoya's voice grew harsh. 'My brother-in-law was un-interested in these disappointing babies. He wanted sons.' She sneered. 'So the girls were farmed out, each to a different relative.'

"My heart hurt for the orphan baby," Papa would say, stroking my hair as I stretched out on the bench, my head in his lap.

"'Little Olga unluckily went to his mother,' Zoya continued bitterly. 'She was a Victorian marti-net who had long forgotten, if she ever knew, that children need love to flourish. She certainly didn't teach her son much about love. Nikolai was the cold-est fish I've ever known.'

"Zoya told me the whole story. 'Olga was raised by servants, without playmates, without tenderness. Only iron discipline. I remember when I first met her. She was about twelve then, I think. She was tall and spindly, with enormous eyes, timid and with-drawn. Yet something in her seemed to be searching — trying to reach out but not knowing how. Like a young plant in stony ground, stretching up to find sunlight. Her only joy, I suppose her consolation, was her music.' Zoya felt my interest, my instant sympathy. 'Did you know she's a talented pianist?'

"I hadn't known it. I wanted to know every-thing about her. Thinking of my own cheerful child-hood, threadbare but so rich in family joys, I could imagine the desolation of the lonely child.

"'Her *only* joy? How terrible for her!' I said. 'No wonder she finds it so hard to smile.' Already a re-solve was forming in my mind to devote myself to making her happy — to bring a sparkle to the shad-owed eyes, smiles to soften the reticent mouth.

"Your mother was so beautiful, and so sad. What began as sympathy soon bloomed into love. I remember . . ." Papa's blue gaze was far away, see-ing a distant past. "I would stand watching the river, leaning on the rail of one of the Volga steamers on which I spent half my time, buying raw materials and visiting my customers at towns up and down the river. I would look at the water and dream of those soft eyes that enchanted me. I hardly knew her, yet I missed her terribly. I would write her postcards whenever I had a free moment — usually every day, sometimes more." He would laugh at the thought of his romantic obsession. "One day on my way up the Volga to the Trade Fair in Nizhny, I wrote her three cards, the last one at midnight.

"I made up my mind to make her my wife and devote myself to making her happy. Instead of thinking about the problems of bluing production or where to find new markets for my violet-scented soap, into my mind would intrude entrancing pictures of the life I would have with Olga," Papa would confess, smiling shyly. "I've always been an ambitious man, and I can't deny that Olga's beauty and elegance, and her dowry too, would be of real help in my career. But I felt that the promise of happiness I offered her would be a fair exchange. I was proud that I now had the means to offer a worthy home and a solid future to a daughter of wealth. The yellow house provided a surprise bonus when I acquired the factory in 1911 . . . "

"'You know my house is included in the sale,' the widow Ratner informed me during our negotiations. 'The property runs through the block from street to street. It's all one parcel.'

"'But it's your home!' I ventured. About to become a proprietor for the first time in my life, I felt trepidant enough without an extra obligation.

"Mrs. Ratner quickly reassured me. 'No, no! What do I need with a whole house, now I'm alone? I'm going to Moscow to live with my son the actor. He's doing so well at the Moscow Art Theatre; he'll never come back to Samara. Don't worry, it'll all be in the same mortgage.'

"For an ambitious young bachelor like me, it was a perfect arrangement: a home close to my business, a place where I could entertain my new friends, a house to bring my bride to.

"Handsomely redecorated by my Olga, it was a gracious home. The main living space was upstairs. From the little entrance hall a long staircase rose straight up to an elegant drawing room dominated by Olga's grand piano, a long narrow dining room with a sunny breakfast corner, the big master bedroom and, at the back: your pretty blue nursery, Nora, with a sleeping alcove for your governess. Only the kitchen and the service areas and storerooms were on the ground floor."

Years later in America I got to meet Papa's lady bountiful. She was the mother of Hollywood star Gregory Ratoff. Papa told me the story one summer evening, when he was expecting a visit from her. He always spoke of her as the source of his success.

And Olga? I already knew her side of the story. It was the one I asked for most often during the hot Moscow nights when we couldn't sleep. Mamma would lower her eyes and a soft flush would rise on the sallow cheeks. "From the beginning I was overwhelmed by his admiration," she confided shyly. "I thought Adolf Yefimovich Lurye was the most charming man in the world. I couldn't believe that he had chosen me, when he could have *anybody.*" She sighed, thinking of that lost happiness. "I thought I would never be lonely any more. I would have my own husband, my own home, my own children. After twenty-five years, I would finally belong to someone."

It was easy now for me to imagine them in love, how under Papa's tender tutelage Mamma began to bloom. She would listen as he poured out his hopes and feelings and worries, and learned to open her own shut-in heart and to share her dreams and early sorrows with him.

"I was always frightened, Adya," she confided, "when I lived with my grandmother. She was so strict, so quick to get angry. I could never do anything right. I was always being punished. Shut up in a dark closet, or locked in my room." She shuddered at the memory.

"When Grandmère said I was to go home to Father, I was so happy. But it turned out to be another disappointment. Father had remarried. There were four more children. The last one, Yevgeni, was finally the son he wanted. His darling. He paid very little attention to us older ones. His wife resented us too. We were the stepchildren. She spoiled her own and was quite unkind to us."

Papa would kiss the hand he was holding. "Now it will be your turn to be spoiled," he would promise, his heart aching for the rejected child.

"But there was one great joy," Mamma would go on, leaning back against her lover's shoulder, savoring the new delight of being held close. "Even though I didn't get the real home I was longing for, I did get to know my sisters. Especially Xenia, the eldest. She was so kind to me, almost a mother. But for such a short time. She went away to school, became a teacher in Moscow until she married. She lives in Tashkent now, so far away. How I would love to see Xenia again."

"So you shall, dushenka," he said. "When we are married and settled, you will invite her for a visit." He laughed with pleasure at the thought of inviting his wife's guests to his home. Olga gazed at him in wonder. This marvelous man had transformed her life. He would create a whole new future for her.

"Go on, Olya." Adya understood that the greatest gift a lover can give is to listen. "Did you go away to school too?"

"Oh, yes. My father provided all the luxuries for us. It was only the necessities, like love and attention, that we were deprived of," she said bitterly. "I went to finishing school in Lausanne, then to the conservatory in Dresden.

"I was happy then. Switzerland was so beautiful, the teachers were kind. And Dresden! My dear, it must be the best place in the world to study music. It filled my life." Eyes shining, she felt again the high excitement of applause. "When I played in recital, the response of the audience was like food to me."

"And love, dushenka? Was there no room for that in your life of music?" he teased gently.

Olga looked up shyly, then in a burst of feeling threw her arms around him. "No, my dear one, never any room till now. You are the first." She leaned back to smile into his eyes. "I'll tell you a secret. I never really believed I would have anyone to love, that anyone would love me. At the conservatory, and later in Moscow at the university, all around me students would be falling in love, talking about love. But I was outside. I never thought it could happen to me. Then I met you — and you *loved me.*"

So they dreamed and planned, and finally the dreams came true, and they settled down happily in the yellow house. Olga spent her bridal year and some of her dowry furnishing it with beautiful things. Marriage was good medicine for her damaged ego. Her days were filled with laughter and love. Soon a baby daughter arrived to expand the magic circle. The childhood shadows began to fade.

Then the miscarriages began. The first pregnancy had been prompt and uncomplicated; but the second one ended tragically when, catching her heel on the carpet, Olga plunged down the long staircase.

The fall must have caused some structural injury as well, because the next two pregnancies miscarried spontaneously in the fourth month. The last one was especially devastating because the hemorrhaging went on for nearly two months, sentencing Olga to a bedridden winter. The drain on an already delicate constitution fed her disposition to melancholy. Her husband had to work hard to keep up her spirits, just when the war was putting a big strain on his own. He came home most days worrying about the growing problems of shipment and supply that were plaguing manufacturers all over the country. Yet he couldn't talk about them with his wife, he had to be gay and funny and optimistic.

But today the spring sun on the balcony was a tonic, and Mamma now resolved to be happy. She embraced the idea of a picnic as an elixir. "What a lovely idea. We'll plan a picnic as soon as Papa has time to take us. I'll speak to him this evening. He's been working so hard lately. It will do him good to take a holiday."

"Oh, Mamushka, what fun. I *hope* Papa will say yes." The child wanted instant assurance. "Can I go ask him *right now?*"

Fraülein at once assumed her censor's role, before Mamma in her pliant mood might allow a rule to bend. "Not '*can* I,' '*may* I,' Niura. Of course you may not." The quiet voice was inflexible. "Your father has made an absolute rule that you must never go into the factory. It's filled with chemicals and vats and machines, very dangerous for a child. You must wait until your Papa comes home."

Unsquelched, I turned to more available pleasures. "Come and play the piano, Mamushka. You
haven't played in so long!"

Mamma's face lit up at the idea.

Later that afternoon as Papa came through the
gate from the factory he caught the faint notes of a
piano. Was Olga playing again? he wondered, his
heart lifting at the thought. Upstairs, the strains of a
Chopin "Impromptu" led him to the doorway of the
drawing room. His wife was at the piano, her dark
eyes glowing with pleasure. Luba and Fraülein were
relaxed in easy chairs. His child, her crisp white dress
vivid against the soft mauve of her mother's tea gown,
sat on the floor leaning against the piano bench,
stilled by the melodious flow. In the ebbing daylight
the scene had the quality of a "Dejeuner sur l'herbe,"
radiating the same happy air.

The weary man stood still in the doorway. The
lines around his blue eyes softened as the music
and the peace flowed over him; his tired shoulders
relaxed. At thirty-five he was an attractive figure. His
matinee-idol looks and well-cut clothes were a ve-
neer over a primal energy that showed in his buoyant step, his flashing smile. Yet recent tribulations
— the loss of the longed-for son, Olga's frail health,
the strains of keeping his factory running amidst
the dislocations of war and upheaval — had cast a
pall over his normal verve.

The "Impromptu" ended. Mamma looked up and
saw her husband in the doorway. Suddenly, Papa
was bombarded from all sides by plans for a picnic
and demands for his approval. In this happy glow a
veto was unlikely. "I suppose I could steal a day away
from the factory. Pavel can manage. Yes, we'll go next
week. If the good weather holds."

He swept me into his arms, tossed me high as

I squealed in delight. His eyes danced as he warmed to the project. "We'll rent a launch, shall we, Niurochka? Make a day of it? We haven't had a real outing since last summer." He sank into his big arm-chair, with me snuggled in his lap.

Playing idly with Papa's curly mustache, I thought happily about summer. "Are we going to the dacha this summer, Papa?" I remembered the hot summer days in the country, when I ran barefoot in the grass and chased butterflies, swung lazily in the porch swing, went wading with my cousins in the pond under the big willows. "It's so much fun there. Will we go, Papa?"

Papa smiled. My effervescence annulled his anxieties. "It does look as though things will get bet-ter now. I see no reason why we can't go. I must remember to write and rent the dacha, and talk to the family."

The lovely weather held. Balmy days sent us outdoors to stroll along the esplanade by the Volga. The green vistas, the busy wharves where the river steamers tied up, the big freighters sweeping around the wide Samara Bend on their way to the Caspian Sea, or beating back upriver. It all delighted me. I watched the log rafts floating down from the great forests of the north, chained together in queues sometimes a mile long. Little log huts on the rafts housed the loggers during their long trip downriver, as in a floating village.

I'm sure our young family made a charming picture on our Sunday strolls. The tall dark woman with an elegant air and shadowed eyes, the hand-some man with crisp brown hair and brilliant smile, and the skipping blonde child between them, being swung across puddles and potholes with a gay "upda" from Papa. On his other arm he escorted his young cousin with her "Moscow ways."

One day he went out on the balcony after breakfast. One look at the shining morning and he shouted, "This is the day for our picnic." and sent us all rushing to get ready. Papa rented a launch, and we set off across the river just as he had promised.

The Zhiguli Hills, their dark evergreens laced with white birches, were fluffed with the tentative green of the first leaves. The broad Volga was receding into its banks after its annual outburst over the low riverside meadows. Buttercups opened in the sunshine along the shore, while old snow still crouched in the north faces of the highlands. Signs of renewal helped wash away the gloom of the harsh winter.

"Today," Papa announced, "I'm going to forget all my troubles. I won't even think of the *volost* committee and its crazy rulings." He put his arm around Mamma's slender waist, as they stood in the bows. "Today I refuse to be annoyed by the endless *skodkas*, the meetings I have to hold to make even the smallest decision. I won't puzzle about where there might be some raw materials to be had. Today I'm going to enjoy myself!"

Olga smiled at her husband's enthusiasm and her child's excitement, and fell in with their mood. "And today I won't think any sad thoughts. I'm just going to breathe this lovely air and enjoy myself too. Every minute!"

Even Luba refrained from comparing the country outing to her worldly Moscow amusements and gave herself up to the enjoyment of the day. Fraülein smiled and curbed the urge to edify. And I beamed at everybody and jumped for joy.

The launch carried us briskly through the busy river traffic, scooting boldly across the bows of a lumbering barge riding low under its load of early fruit from the south, so close that the ladies shrank back nervously from the expected collision. I shrieked with excitement, while the launch captain roared with laughter at the success of his maneuver.

On the farther shore lay a good-sized village where Papa engaged a light buggy to take us up into the hills. He soon spotted a clearing in the pinewoods, opening onto a bluff overlooking the Volga. We sat on the edge of the headland to admire the bird's eye view of river and city. Papa and I kept up an enthusiastic chatter.

"Look, Niurochka, there's the dock at the end of our street. Our house is just beyond that clump of stores. See, to the right of the church steeple."

"Look, Papa, you can see around the bend. Look how the river turns back."

"The Volga makes a big curve here," Papa explained. "It doubles back in a wide turn, like a great tongue. When we get home I'll show it to you on the map. They call it 'The Samara Bend.'"

"Look at the dock, Papa. See all those soldiers marching onto the big ship? Where are they going, Papa?" I had never seen such a large military group. Papa's face lost its smile. "They are going to fight, Niurochka. They are going to the war."

"The war?" Somehow the word scared me. "What's a war, Papa? Is it bad?"

"It's a very bad thing, darling. It hurts people and makes them unhappy. We are having a war now, and I hope it will soon be over."

I could see Papa didn't want to talk about the war. He turned his face deliberately away from the dock. "This is a perfect place for our picnic," he declared.

I know he was worrying about Mamma. I could see her beginning to droop. He quickly made her comfortable on blankets and cushions. Fraülein, with Luba's help, spread the picnic on the grassy bank, while I ran around among the clumps of tiny wildflowers that dotted the grass everywhere, shouting with delight.

The charm of the secluded clearing held us in its spell. Long after we had finished our lunch of cold *pirogi* and a variety of tasty *zakuski*, we were loath to leave, though the sun was beginning to sink toward the hills.

"Oh, Adya," Mamma sighed, reluctantly getting up to go to the buggy, "what a lovely spot you found. Up here we're so far above the troubles down below. There's no war here, no rationing, no illness, no inflation. If only . . . "

Papa smiled at her indulgently. "I know how you feel, Olechka. There's magic here. We'll come back, I promise. But we must hurry now, to get back across the river before dark."

Over the years I've done a lot of reading about this period in history, trying to understand the causes of the cataclysm that struck our lives, and what it must have been like before. It began in the spring of 1917 , when the disaffected liberals in the Duma, led by Alexander Kerensky, took matters into their own hands and forced the tsar's abdication. They set up a constitutional democracy and promised reforms. It was an optimistic time, the romantic moment of the revolution. The country was in euphoria. The failures of the old regime were discarded — those of the new still undiscovered. Even cautious observers were pleased; the more optimistic waxed eloquent. "The sunshine of freedom flooded men's souls, " wrote one.

The growing middle class, to which our family belonged, had hopes for a new economic stability. Like most of his business friends, Papa backed Kerensky, believing that a democratic regime would stimulate prosperity. As a liberal, he also had faith that the plight of the poor would now be addressed.

The lower classes dreamed too, of a life above the starvation level at which millions had been kept by the tsar's corrupt bureaucracy. The Samara Gazette *had printed a story, early in the century, which was quoted for years as a horrible example of the evils of heartless bureaucracy, and of people's patient acceptance of those evils. An eighteen-year-old teacher in a village school earned seven and a half rubles a month, out of which she paid three for a tiny room. One winter they forgot to pay her for two months, and she silently starved to death.*

Such abysmal poverty, which kept so many on the cutting edge of disaster even during prosperous times, was what had created the revolution. In 1917 people believed that such tragedies must no longer be tolerated. Hope was in the air — a strong wine. But in November a Bolshevik coup d'etat led by Lenin and Trotzky toppled the young democracy. Kerensky fled the country, and the rest of his government was arrested.

Anxiety filled the once optimistic middle classes. But a number of anti-Red generals were gathering forces to fight the dictatorship, and it was widely believed that it would soon be overthrown. In Samara, far from the ferment in the political centers, Moscow and Petrograd, it still seemed possible for normal life to go on.

I remember that last summer month at the dacha that the family rented each year, a sprawling villa with wide porches and gables sprouting in all directions. Built in the old country style, of weathered boards in a herringbone pattern, surrounded by lilacs and hawthorn, the place seemed as enduring as the towering trees that sheltered it. It had rooms enough for Papa's whole family, who all loved spending a month together.

Aunt Sonya, Uncle Pavel and Papa had to work all week, but they came up every weekend. We were only a couple of stops from the city on the local train. Though new regulations were making things difficult at the factory, Papa did manage one week off as well as some long weekends, brief times of perfect contentment for me.

Mamma would listen to the chatter and easy camaraderie, but I think she didn't really know how to join in. I know the others didn't mean to shut her out. My father and Aunt Sonya, in fact, were always trying to include her in the fun — but it seemed that she had never learned the comfortable give-and-take of siblings. Now I realize that she couldn't break through the wall of reticence she had built so strong. Though she knew it was irrational, she didn't know how to enter their charmed circle.

Happily, I had no such problems. The best part of my holiday was playing every day with Tanya's two boys, Mark and Aaron. Like all Russian children, they were never called by anything but their pet names. Ara was just my age; but it was Mara, a year older, whom I loved most. I had already admitted privately to Mishka that I planned to marry Mara when we grew up. We mostly ignored the boys' sister, baby Sonya, who was too little to play.

The halcyon days slipped by. The cousins played hide-and-seek among the trees, picked raspberries and currants from the tangled bushes out back, from which Babushka made delicious jam, and chased dragonflies across the sunlit fields. We giggled at Baby Sonya as she toddled unsteadily across the lawn, tripping over the bulging roots of ancient larches. "Don't be so smug, only two years ago you were just as rickety," Aunt Sonya reprimanded us.

We rowed with Papa on the pond shaded by trailing willows and lordly elms, and swung drowsily in the porch swing on hot afternoons, while the grownups drank tea and discussed the latest news from Petrograd.

I can imagine them on a windless day in late August, when the leaves hung drooping and still. The family was gathered on the wide veranda, sheltering from the scorching sun around the big table that held the indispensable samovar and the remains of afternoon tea. Papa, as usual, was reading the paper and every few minutes commenting on the latest news from Moscow. Mamma was resting in a chaise, with a pile of lisle stockings beside her. Every now and then she picked one up to reweave a worn heel or toe; her meticulous darning was practically her only domestic accomplishment. But in a few minutes the effort grew too great, and her hands lay idle in her lap again.

I was in the porch swing, absorbed in what the grownups were saying. Listening to conversations was a passion with me; they formed my ideas of the world, and I filed away in my busy head whatever I could absorb.

"I don't see how the new government expects to bring back stability?" Papa was saying. "All these unrealistic reforms. Do they really think that people can be trusted to discipline themselves and deprive themselves for the general good? It just doesn't work that way." Papa waved his hand at Tanya's husband. "Pavel can tell you. If he or I aren't always there to keep an eye on them, most of my workers get careless, slow up, even spoil a batch sometimes. *They* certainly don't care whether production goes up or down, as long as their wages are paid."

"But Adya," Sonya broke in. "That's just the point Lenin has been making. They don't care because it's *your* factory and not theirs. When the workers share in the ownership, they *will care*. Lenin says we must all join together to bring the country back to a sound economy. At least they've ended the war."

Papa had small patience with Sonya's enthusiasm for Lenin. "The man is dangerous. For nearly thirty years he's been obsessed by the proletarian revolution, and I don't trust a man with an obsession. He only sees what proves his point. My friend Arbatyeff was talking about Lenin only last week."

Sonya snorted. "What does he know?"

"He knew Lenin when he was named Ulianov, when he studied in Samara. He even practiced law in our town, did you know, Papa? Before he was exiled."

"I've been hearing about him too." Zeyde usually had the latest gossip from his cronies in *shul* and at the cafe, and lately the gossip was more and more about Lenin. "He comes from a very respectable family, actually. The Ulianovs were from Astrakhan, but they were living up the Volga in Simbirsk when Vladimir Ilyich was born. His father was the inspector of rural schools." He took a sip from his glass of tea. "Young Lenin was a serious, devout student until his older brother was executed. Some assassination attempt, I think. After that Vladimir became very radical. Absolutely incorrigible—"

"Well, wouldn't you? If they shot Adya?" Sonya routinely took the opposing side to her father in any argument. "His brother was just a *boy,* a student. I don't think it was even a serious attempt. A few years of exile would have been punishment enough."

Shocked, her sister Tanya looked up from her lapful of diapers. "Surely, Sonya, you don't approve of assassination! Nothing justifies killing people in cold blood. Since Tsar Alexander was assassinated, the authorities have had to be very harsh. Can you blame them?"

"Order must be maintained if we are to have a stable society," her husband added. Pavel was inclined to be a bit pompous at times. "Look at the mess we're in now. This breakdown in authority." He smacked his fist into his other palm. "People must be controlled!"

Sonya could stand no more. "What do you mean, authority? Control?" she flared up. "It's because the authorities made such a botch of everything that we are in this mess. Getting us into a war when we were totally unprepared. Sending soldiers off with nothing to fight with. Leaving farms and factories without enough workers to keep them going. The terrible stories we hear." She glared at Pavel as if holding him personally responsible. "One surgeon reported that only every second man in his corps had a gun when they went into battle. Every second man!"

"Impossible." Tanya was incredulous. "How could they fight?"

"The men were ordered to take the weapons of those who fell. Imagine such a thing. No wonder soldiers were running away by the thousands. Lenin says —"

"Please, Sonyachka." Sonya's rising indignation was interrupted by her father. "These stories about bureaucrats are all very well. But the new regime is just as bad as the old." Zeyde, always for the underdog, cast himself in the role of defender of the old order, now that it had been kicked out. "Look at that terrible 'Order Number One.' It's destroyed all army discipline, demoralized everybody. Imagine calling on soldiers to ignore their officers and elect their own regimental committees. That's what began the 'melting away' from the front that you're talking about. Now we're going to have more trouble. Since the tsar and his family have been sent to Siberia, I'm afraid they're in danger."

"They were not safe in Tsarskoye Selo," Papa said. "There's less civil unrest in the east."

Sonya had less faith in the ruling powers. Her voice rose with her emotions. "After the thousands the tsar sent into exile, isn't it fitting that he's getting a taste of his own medicine? I'm sure they'll have them out of the country before winter comes — just wait and see. But anyway, I don't think it hurts to show him a little of that life, when he sent so many people to endure it."

"Sonyachka," her mother said quietly but very firmly. The family listened when Babushka spoke. "Nothing is helped by revenge. The tsar did many wrong things. And the tsaritsa must be a very foolish woman, to have listened to that terrible Rasputin. But they *are* parents, after all. They shouldn't be made to suffer this way. The family should be allowed to emigrate. They have relatives all over Europe." She spread her arms eloquently. "It doesn't help anyone to shut them up in Siberia."

Several heads nodded in approval at Babushka's simple logic. Her son patted her hand and said with a smile: "You should be running the country, Mamushka. You would do it without hurting anybody."

Pavel hooted. "Sure. And everybody would lie down together like the lion and the lamb. Tell that to the Germans! The cruelties — "

"Pavel!" His wife's voice stopped him abruptly. All eyes instinctively turned to Fraülein, in her tactful place by the door. But her thin face remained composed and the yarn ball she wound kept growing steadily fatter. She had shared enough of her employers' lives to make her sympathies as much Russian as German.

It was Olga who spoke up to rebut Pavel's chauvinism — a rare event, since she hardly ever joined in political talk. But now she sat up in indignation. "Such generalizations are absolutely useless, Pavel.

When I was studying in Dresden at the conservatory, I lived among the Germans. They're no different from any of us. Some people are capable of terrible cruelty — here in Russia as much as in Germany. But most people, everywhere, are . . . are just people like us." She suddenly heard her own raised voice and stopped abruptly.

Lying back dispiritedly against her cushions, Olga went on. "That's what's so terrible. We're all at the mercy of the people who make wars and revolutions, the people who want power. *We* are the ones whose lives will never be the same. What will our future be, when . . . oh, I am so afraid." She covered her face, trying to stifle her sobs.

Papa was at her side in an instant. He cradled her in comforting arms, while I jumped off the swing to hug her knees. "Dushenka, darling, don't be afraid. Things will be better. Wait and see. You have a whole family to love you and take care of you.

"No matter what happens in the world, we'll make a good life for ourselves. We are strong, we'll survive. When the fighting comes to an end, when men get back to their farms and jobs, things will soon straighten out. You'll see, Olenka." Papa's superb confidence in his ability to deal with whatever life brought had been nourished in a hard school, and was unshakable.

Sonya had no patience with unrealistic optimism, but as she opened her mouth to refute it, Babushka raised her hand. "Enough politics for today. We are not going to solve the problems of the world around this samovar. Sonya, pour a fresh glass of tea for Olya, it will do her good. Pavel, more tea? Have this last hard-boiled egg. Here's a little babka, children; finish it up." Her world was tilting precariously, but Babushka would keep it steady with hot tea and a bite to eat.

Papa quickly took the same tack. "Come, children, let's go for a row on the pond. It's cooling off a bit. It's too nice to be moping about on the porch. First one to the boat will be captain."

Papa kissed the top of Mamma's head and went racing off, while we children followed, shouting: "I'll beat!" "No, no, me!" "I want to be captain!"

The others soon dispersed in various directions. Only the grandparents were left sitting around the deserted table. Zeyde sighed and got up. "I need to stretch my legs a little. Come, Betya, let's go for a little walk before you disappear into the kitchen again."

As the old couple strolled arm in arm down the path under the lengthening shadows, Babushka gave voice to what had been troubling them all.

"I think there are hard times ahead for us, Papa. We learned how to deal with hardship, you and I, how to survive. Our children too, they know how to meet trouble, how to make do. And we all have each other, thank God. But I worry about Olga. She is so soft. She has no experience with hard times, she always had servants and money to buy — "

"The worst is," Zeyde took up her thought. After nearly forty years together, they walked in and out of each other's minds at will. "She's never before had people to turn to for comfort. She doesn't know how. Even now, she is so alone inside — "

"I know. That's the worst. Adya will take care of his family, I'm not worried about that. But nobody can give Olga the strength she needs to meet the calamities that are bound to come. Her weakness will put an extra burden on Adya."

"He is strong, he'll help her. As long as she has Adya, she'll be all right."

❧ 3 ☙
Autumn Gales and Griefs
Samara, 1918

IT WAS very quiet in the cellar. The low storage room had no windows and no outside door. The monotonous dripping of autumn rain over the gutters and the occasional rattle of withering leaves in the wind were only shadows of sound, like the muted voices of the family gathered around the dim light of the kerosene lamp set on a packing case. On my cot in the corner where I'd been put to bed, I listened to the talk droning on, first one low voice then another feeding it, as if they could hold at bay the panic that might descend with silence, as the lamplight held back the dark.

Fraülein, as always, was knitting socks. Mamma had brought her mending basket, but was not even pretending to darn in the uncertain light. Papa was sprawled in an overstuffed chair, trying hard to be gay and funny. Half aware, half dreaming, I stared up into the cobwebbed beams. Sleep could not find me in this strange shadowy place, where chairs and cots and buckets of water were crowded in among the storage shelves and packing crates.

Mamma was talking wistfully about our summer at the dacha, only a few months ago, when war and revolution were worries but not yet calamities. Yet every happy memory led somehow to the doleful present and the menacing future. Things had not "straightened out" as Papa had confidently predicted. Far from it. The troops had come swarming back from the front to take sides in the civil war that was now fragmenting the country into hostile factions. Even Papa's stubborn optimism was shaken by the news of violence and terror that came closer day by day.

Now the talk was not of trouble far away in Petrograd — or Moscow, where the capital had been moved — but here in Samara. A provisional anticommunist government had been set up in our area. Conservatives, Cossacks, even Czech deserters clashed with Bolshevik forces in Volga villages, and they were not winning. Today there had been a report that Red troops were advancing on Samara. Tonight at least half the city's families were sheltering in their cellars from the dreaded first rush of armies in battle heat.

What is going to happen to us? I wondered, my head spinning with overheard rumors of burnings and lootings, of casual shootings and wanton destruction by the mobs — military and civilian — that ranged through the countryside unrestrained. All my life I had loved to listen in on grownups' talk; now my curiosity only fed my fears. My feverish imagination pictured soldiers overrunning the city. I saw them as a human tide pouring into the streets, like the Volga did in spring when it rose over its banks, flooding the low places and sweeping away anything in its path. They would smash windows, kick old ladies out of their way, steal whatever they wanted, ravish women (I wondered what "ravish" meant; It was an intriguing new word that kept turning up in people's talk), and shoot anybody that tried to stop them.

They might shoot Papa! I suddenly realized. All at once the swarm of amorphous dangers crystallized into one overwhelming threat. Papa might be hurt. I could not imagine him dead. In my sunlit life death was not yet a reality. But any risk at all to Papa was more than I could bear.

Though I smothered my sobs in the pillow, Papa heard, and had me in his arms at once. "What is it, dushenka, little soul, what is hurting you? Tell Papa. Did you have a nightmare?"

"Oh, Papa, I'm afraid of the soldiers. They might hurt you."

"Me? Never!" Papa's merry laugh banished the brooding shadows. "Do you hear this?" he asked, carrying me into the lamplit circle. "She's afraid for me. Not for herself. A real heroine."

Settling back in his big chair, Papa cuddled me close, tucking a warm shawl around me. "Don't worry about me, dushenka. Nobody's going to hurt your Papa. We just have to stay here quietly until things settle down. It won't be long, you'll see."

But Mamma too was overwhelmed by her fears. "Oh, Adya," she sobbed. "How can you be so unrealistic? Our whole world is collapsing, and you say 'things will soon settle down!" Her voice was rising toward hysteria. "Life will never — "

"Olya, you're not to talk that way." Papa cut his wife short with unusual sharpness. "Life *always* settles down after a time of troubles. Here on the Volga our history is full of such times. Have you heard of Stenka Razin, Fraülein?" As he turned to the governess, I guessed he was really trying to divert Mamma and me with a story. "He's an old folk hero in these parts, a famous Cossack chief who led a peasant revolt about three hundred years ago. Razin captured several Volga cities, even Samara, before the revolt was put down."

"I heard about him, Papa. Nyanya used to sing a song about him."

"That's right, darling. There are many songs and legends about him. But he was only one of many warriors who fought over this land. Our Volga has always been at the heart of trade routes, and our black earth is rich and fertile. It's vital to anybody who wants to rule Russia. Over the centuries this town has seen many upheavals, but it's always managed to survive."

Mamma found ancient history uncomforting. "That's true, Adya, but this is different. Now the revolution — "

"We'll live through the revolution too, Olya." Papa would not allow her to sink into her natural pessimism. "I myself have already lived through many kinds of trouble, but I've managed to survive, even when it seemed impossible. I remember when . . . "

I snuggled down into my warm cocoon of lap and shawl. When Papa said, "I remember when," I knew a story was coming. Papa told wonderful stories. Panic retreated into the shadows beyond the lamplight, the gusts outside sounded less menacing.

"I remember when I worked for my uncle in the lumber business. I had to go deep into the northern forests to buy standing timber. One freezing day, we were traveling through heavy snow. We had only one horse, just the driver and me in a light sleigh. So we couldn't go very fast, and night came on before we reached the lumber camp." Papa's eyes were seeing far beyond the lamplit walls to the majestic forest shimmering in moonlight, the branches of spruce and hemlock bending low, heavy with snow. He saw firs towering above them, and white birches shining among the dark evergreens.

"The woods were beautiful, and so still — until suddenly we heard a howl. Other voices answered, and in only a few seconds four or five big gray wolves were running behind us. The driver whipped the tired

57

horse, urging her on, but the wolves were faster —
and hungry."

"Oh, Papa." My eyes must have been like saucers. "Did you really think the wolves would eat you?"

"Well, it had been a hard winter, and they were
probably desperate for food. They certainly wanted
to eat our horse. Once they had her, there was no
way we could escape on foot. We had no guns, only
the driver's whip. I can tell you that for a few minutes there, I was pretty sure it was the end of me.
They were gaining on us pretty fast." He stopped to
take a long breath.

"What happened, Papa? What happened then?
How did you get away?" The suspense was not to be
borne one more second.

Papa smiled. Once more he had managed to
make the family forget their immediate danger.
Mamma was quiet, enjoying my excitement. She had
heard the story before, but she still felt her husband's
terror — and relief. Even Fraülein was leaning forward, eager to hear the outcome.

"We were lucky. We were already near the camp,
and they were expecting us. So when they heard that
howling, they guessed we were in trouble, and rode
out to meet us. They were well armed, of course, and
started firing even before they saw us. Boom! Boom!
And the animals howled and ran away. You can imagine how glad we were to see our rescuers. So you
see, dushenka, something always turns up."

I drew a long relieved breath at the happy ending. "Oh, Papa, that was an exciting story. I like scary
stories. But . . . " I thought for a long moment. "But
I guess I like them because there's nothing to be
afraid of *really*. I knew the wolves wouldn't eat you,
because they didn't. But now — well, this is a different kind of scary, because now I don't know how it's
going to turn out — so it's really scary."

Papa's own life offered ample proof that something always did turn up. Born Avrom Yefimovich Lurye in a *shtetl* near Minsk, where his parents struggled to keep afloat with a tiny dry goods store, he had come far by grabbing the coattails of every passing opportunity, and often making one. Only fifteen when he managed to shake the rural dust from his heels, the ambitious boy was determined to find a richer life than Ula's threadbare existence offered.

His uncle owned a lumber business. In those days the law forbade a Jew to own land, but Uncle Shmuel circumvented it by a stratagem widely in use. He bought forests and property for his sawmills by paying an illiterate peasant to act as nominal owner, using his name to legalize transactions. A well-grown boy and a charmer, Avrom badgered his mother to speak to her brother about taking him into the business. Then he set himself to absorb all he could about the larger world of commerce. Within ten years he had parlayed his drive and social talents into a successful career as a sales agent, progressing from lumber to a line of chemical products that took him all over central and eastern Europe. The Russian name Adolf was given to him at the passport office, as was customary.

The next step up came to him unsought. One of his customers, Simeon Ratner, who owned a small chemical products plant in Samara, took a fancy to the enthusiastic young salesman; so did his wife. They had become good friends by the time Ratner fell victim to cancer. His widow — grateful for Adolf Yefimovich Lurye's sympathy and help with her affairs — offered to sell him the factory on surprisingly easy terms. She could not run it, and her only son was a rising actor with the Moscow Art Theatre who had no interest in the family enterprise.

So before he was thirty, Adolf Yefimovich had acquired a thriving business with a comfortable home included, had brought his family to Samara and installed them in a nearby apartment. He was able to help one sister with a dowry and the other with dental training. Then he was ready to take a wife and settle down to prosperity. His was truly a life compounded of opportunities. He could hardly be blamed for considering himself a child of fortune.

This time the tide of battle ebbed away southward and the threat of occupation seemed to be averted, at least for the moment. For a week, nothing happened. After three uncomfortable nights in the cellar, the family went back to sleeping in our beds and to an uneasy "normalcy." It was normal only in the most relative sense.

First we lost the servants, one by one. The housemaid went home to her mother in the country. One night the cook's husband turned up, an army deserter, and she fled with him to the hills. The laundress just stopped coming, without a word. The family concentrated on trying to manage from day to day. Only Fräulein remained, loyal as ever, determined to help "her family" through this hard time. Always calm and efficient, Fräulein was the rock on which we all leaned more and more. She knew she must soon go back to Germany. Russia was not the place for foreign governesses any more. But making her way through the war-torn border areas in the west was risky. So she lingered, knowing she was badly needed, hoping against hope that conditions would improve. In the meantime, she quietly took over the marketing, cooking and washing, while Mamma made stabs at tidying the house and tending to me. Mostly my distraught mother played the piano by the hour. It seemed to be her talisman against terror.

I was the one who had the least trouble getting "back to normal." The problems of caring for a family in crisis, of finding ways to run a factory without workers or materials, of trying to prepare for a threatening future and the loss of all one's usual comforts — these miseries were not in my lexicon. I considered things much improved, since I was back in my own cozy room and the weather was sunny and warm, so I could play on my balcony.

Next week was my fourth birthday, the first with a new birth date. The old Julian calendar had been reformed to make Russia conform to the Gregorian system of the west. As a result thirteen days were lost. Papa explained it all to me several times. I was rather pleased by the idea of having my birthday officially rearranged. It made me feel quite important, and I looked forward eagerly to the occasion.

Alas, by the time the birthday week arrived Red troops were once more headed for Samara. The town again wore the hushed air of impending doom. But I had been promised a party, and I had Papa's assurance that I would have one.

Yet the natal day did not start out like a holiday. Shortly after breakfast, I saw that Papa had a visitor. They talked for a long time in the library, while Mamma and Fraülein came and went, casting anxious glances at the closed door. As he was leaving, the man wrung Papa's hand and wished him luck, then checked the street before slipping away. Papa reacted with only a frown to the worried faces of the women, and shut himself up again. But soon he called Mamma in, and they talked for a long time before going into their bedroom, where they could still be heard in earnest conversation.

Fraülein distracted me by calling me into the kitchen to help get the party ready. Carefully hoarded sugar, an egg or two and even a little butter came out of hiding. With the last nuts and raisins, a real cake could be managed. Happily picking the meats out of the nuts Fraülein was cracking, I was too lost in anticipation to dwell on the strange events of the morning. We hadn't had a party in so long, or any fun at all. Today would be a special day, reminding me of so many others — days with visitors coming for tea and cake, flowers in the drawing room, and nothing to worry about.

And it *was* a lovely afternoon, after all. The whole family came. Babushka brought a jar of her own raspberry jam for the tea, and Aunt Sonya had found a few real bonbons somewhere. Even the cake turned out remarkably well, considering the skimpy ingredients. Everybody brought gifts, a picture book from Aunt Sonya, a game from the cousins. Aunt Tanya had made new clothes for one of my dolls, and Babushka had knitted me a blue sweater. There was a warm dress from Mamma. Papa produced a small gold bracelet, which made me feel very grownup.

After the cake the cousins romped and shouted. We were busy with hide-and-seek and blindman's buff and hardly noticed that the grownups soon took their tea into the library, leaving Fraülein to keep order.

When it was time for the guests to leave, the goodbyes were strangely fervent. Everybody hugged Papa so hard and whispered so many little messages, assuring him that he was not to worry. Only then did it dawn on me that something ominous was in the wind. After all, my grandparents lived only around the corner.

As soon as the guests had left, Papa's packed suitcases appeared in the front hall with his hat and coat. Fraülein came in to announce that the *droshky* was waiting. Papa hugged me hard and held me close for a long moment. I felt the familiar rough tweed of his coat scratching my arm.

"I have to go away on a trip," he said, "and I have to rush to catch my train. It may be a while before I can get back. You must be a good girl, dushenka, and take good care of Mamma."

With a last quick kiss for his wife he was gone. Mamma, eyes brimming, shut herself in her room. Fraülein set about clearing up, finding one chore after another to keep me busy and the tears at bay.

We were just finishing up the dishwashing when the front door banged. Papa's hearty "Where is everybody?" sent us all rushing into the front hall.

"You didn't go." I shrieked as I threw myself on him. "You're not going away."

"No. I didn't go." Papa's grin widened at my excitement. "But only because I missed the train. I will have to go tomorrow. I should have left much earlier, but I couldn't spoil your party."

While I hung on the arm of Papa's chair, he admitted that he hadn't really arrived too late. "The train and the station were so crowded I couldn't get near enough to even try to board it. My only chance will be to arrive hours beforehand and try to bribe my way on past the hordes of refugees and 'baggers.'"

"Baggers?" Mamma asked.

"They come from the big cities, where food is getting really scarce. After the harvest failed in the north, people have been getting desperate. Here in the Volga basin we had our usual good crops. So they come here looking for food and drag it home on the train in long cloth sacks. The station was full of them and their sacks."

"So many?" Olga shook her head sadly. "There must be so much suffering in the big cities now."

"Yes, and a lot of profiteering too." Papa pulled me into his lap as he explained. "Many of these people speculate with the food and trade it for manufactured goods, which are scarce in the country. Then they trade these goods for food, and so on. Always at a profit, of course."

"But all this must make traveling conditions difficult."

"It certainly does. Between the baggers and the refugees, who are all lousy and diseased, we're ripe for an epidemic of some sort. But don't worry," he hurried to reassure us as the saw the fear rise in Mamma's eyes. "I'll be fine. You know I *never* get sick. Only you must be careful not to let Niurochka play with any strange children or go near any beggars."

I was playing with Papa's mustache while he talked and thinking, I won't be able to do that after tomorrow.

"Papa, why can't we go with you? You'll be so lonely without us, why can't you take us along?"

He laughed at the idea. "I wish I could, dushenka. But it's going to be a long hard trip. I don't even know where I'm going, exactly. I just need to get out of Russia till things quiet down. Mamma could never stand such a trip."

"Then take me," I said. "I'm strong. And I could take care of you."

"But then Mamma would be all alone. You wouldn't want her to be lonely here by herself?"

"Oh, Babushka could take care of her . . . and Aunt Sonya, and — "

"I'm sorry, darling. It just can't be. But I want you to take care of Mamma for me, and not let her get sad. I'll come home just as soon as it's safe, but now I must go, and alone." He set me down and got up. "Let's just enjoy this extra evening together, and not think about tomorrow."

What a mixed-up bittersweet time those bonus hours were. To have Papa back when we'd scarcely begun to miss him was a special present. Yet in all our thoughts ran the mournful refrain, "He's going away tomorrow." I could see that poor Mamma needed all her courage to restrain her tears and not spoil her husband's last few hours at home, and I kept grumbling to myself, "I wish I could go with him."

It was only years later that I learned just how dangerous Papa's situation was. It was a chance encounter earlier in the week that had prompted his decision to leave. He was uptown, futilely searching for replacement workers, when he ran into an old business acquaintance. Pyotr Ivanovich Arbatyeff was a member of the *zemstvo,* the local governing body that lately, in the breakdown of central authority, had assumed almost total control over citizens' lives and property. Most members of the provisional government had fled to Omsk with the Czech Legion and joined the counter-revolutionaries under General Kolchak, or had been arrested as *"bourjui,"* as the middle classes were now disdainfully categorized. The city's administration was now largely in the hands of unprincipled opportunists and inexperienced peasants and laborers, though a few conciliators still managed to keep their posts, striving somehow to control the chaos.

"Adolf Yefimovich, you're still in town?" The old man was shocked to see his friend. "You should have left long ago. Surely you've heard what's been happening in Saratov, and all over the area?"

"No, I can't say that I have. I've been spending all my time trying to keep the factory running — though it seems pretty hopeless. But why shouldn't I still be here?" Adolf asked, puzzled.

"Oh, my goodness! Forget about the factory. It's going to be confiscated anyway. The *zemstvo* received a directive two days ago to nationalize all private enterprises. 'Expropriating the bourgeoisie,' they call it. You're in great danger of arrest, or worse. And you know how trigger happy the Reds are. Your name has sometimes been linked with the anti-communist group. Anyone who owns a factory or a large business is automatically considered a capitalist."

Adolf couldn't believe his ears. "Shoot me just because I managed to buy a small factory? But I started out as poor as any peasant."

"Please, Adolf Yefimovich, don't try to make any sense out of these crazy times. There isn't any. Just get yourself away until this wave of killings is over. It's the only way to survive, because any tipsy soldier can put a bullet between your eyes and ask questions afterward — if ever."

"But my family? How can I leave — "

"The Bolsheviks usually don't bother women and children so much — at least in the cities. It's the businessmen and public officials who are in danger right now." The old man glanced fearfully around. "I must go. I shouldn't be seen talking to you. It's not wise." The caprices of the new rulers created a climate of paranoia among those who had most to lose, who saw betrayal lurking around every corner.

Adolf raised an inquiring eyebrow.

"Nevertheless," added Arbatyeff hurriedly. "You've always been a fair man, and you've helped me a time or two. I wouldn't like to see anything happen to you. Russia will need men who can run things, when all this frenzy quiets down. The best thing," he repeated, with a hurried look over his shoulder. "The best thing is just to go away for a while. Go east — things are quieter there — and go *soon.* God go with you." And he scuttled around the corner.

Adolf's head was spinning. What to do? How could he leave his family — a frail wife, a small child, aging parents. Everyone had always depended on him, the strong one, the manager. But what good would he be to anyone if he was dead? He had never before been political, but now his standing in the community marked him as a member of the hated "bourjui."

He realized with a start that he was still standing where Arbatyeff had left him. Automatically he turned in the direction of home. In his mind's eye rose a vivid picture — his wife a despairing widow, prostrated with grief and fear, his daughter a pitiful orphan starving in the streets, his parents broken by sorrow. Surely the worst risk for them all was for him to stay. He was already realizing that his precious factory — the enterprise he had worked so hard to build, was trying so desperately to keep afloat — was gone. He had been steeling himself to accept its loss. But to leave his family — to abandon them to face heaven knows what hardships without him . . . How could he?

In times of trouble, Adya always went to his mother. It was her strength the family turned to in need. She was the one who had kept them going in hard times, and still held them together.

Babushka spent most of her day in the kitchen now, trying to concoct adequate meals out of the ever-shrinking supply of food, performing miracles of ingenuity to tempt Zeyde's failing appetite. She heard her son's news with unexpected calm. Pouring two glasses of tea from the faithful samovar, she sat listening to the unhappy details, nodding her head gravely as he described Arbatyeff's advice and his own quandary. She was not surprised by any of it.

"We've already heard some of this — this confiscating order, the terrible news from Saratov. Your father and I were planning to come over this evening and talk to you about leaving. We think it's the only way to save your life."

"But Olya, and the child? If only I could take

them with me. But there's so little time. And I don't know where I'm going." Papa's usual level-headedness had for once deserted him. His mother led him patiently to a rational decision.

'You must go east, as Arbatyeff said. It's the direction that has the least fighting. And you have to get across the border, out of Russian territory. Of course it would be better if you could take your family with you, Adya. But I don't believe Olya's health would stand a trip across Siberia, let alone the kind of life you might have to live. Where will you go, do you know?"

Her son shrugged gloomily. "I won't know till I get there. Manchuria, maybe."

Babushka nodded encouragingly. "Darling, you're strong and you learned long ago how to get along, wherever you found yourself. I am not afraid for you. But Olya is different. She has been so ill, and her stamina is so low. She needs to stay near the family, where we can help her. And if anything would happen to her out there, how could you manage, alone with a small child to care for, among strangers? No, you must go alone."

Babushka reached out and covered her son's hand with her own. "You know we'll take care of Olya and Niurochka. We'll just wait here together until things settle down, and then you can come home. It can't go on being so crazy forever."

Papa got his optimistic nature from his mother. She was a realist, but in spite of a life filled with vicissitudes, pessimism was impossible for her.

So his going away was decided. Even Olga, though terrified at the prospect of being left alone, came to see that he must go. He was making plans to organize his affairs and be ready to leave in a week, but early the next morning he had a visit from Arbatyeff.

"Why haven't you left?" his friend demanded as soon as the library door closed behind him. "I came by to see if I could help your wife, and you're still here. Adolf Yefimovich, I warned you — "

"I'm leaving, Pyotr Ivanovich," Adolf assured him. "I'm getting everything arranged for my family and I will be ready to go on Tuesday or Wednesday."

"Forget it." The old man shook his head, disgusted. "You'll be arrested long before then. They are already making up the list of suspected anti-communists to be liquidated, and you're on it. I would say you have two days — three at the very most, but you mustn't wait till the last minute. Nobody can be sure just when — " He grasped Adolf's arm. "Go today! Go at once."

Adolf hesitated. Arbatyeff's urgency was making him understand that his safety was now numbered in hours, not days. "We're celebrating my daughter's birthday this afternoon. I couldn't spoil that. But I will leave right after the party," he promised. "I am really grateful for your concern, Pyotr Ivanovich."

"You needn't be. I am really thinking mostly of our poor Russia. She is losing so many of her best people in these wanton days. If I can save one or two for her, I must do it."

Next morning Papa left for the second time, and didn't come back as I secretly hoped he would. Now alone, we settled down to a strange half-life of waiting — for what, no one knew. How we missed Papa and his cheerful smile, his ready talent for turning glum into gay!

I would sit in my window seat, looking at the river and trying to imagine where Papa might be now, how his trip might end, when he might come home. He was all alone now, and I thought sadly how lonely he must be without his Niurochka and his Olechka to love him.

I'm sure his Olechka was thinking the same thoughts. Alone in their bedroom at night, her heart would go out to her husband in his lonely exile, without family or home, without the factory he was so proud of. A lifetime of struggle and success had been snatched away overnight. She yearned to comfort him, yet dreaded the possibility that he would find other comfort. Adya was a man whom women would always rush to console. She wanted to write to him, to tell him she loved him, but where was he?

And Adya, cramped in his corner of the crowded compartment for interminable hours that stretched into days and weeks as the ramshackle train slowly chewed up the eastward miles, what were his thoughts? His mind must have been a turmoil of anxieties. Would he manage to elude official notice and escape beyond Bolshevik control? Each time the train stopped, often for hours, each time officials came through looking at papers, he steeled himself for arrest or questioning, though he had managed to get all the papers he needed to validate his trip.

Would the train, which kept breaking down and seemed barely able to negotiate the narrow passes of the Urals, even manage to complete the journey that was taking him three thousand miles from all he loved? How would his family endure the coming hardships without his strength and ingenuity to shield them? In what alien city would he finally settle, how would he spend the lonely months — maybe years — that must pass before he could hold his wife and daughter in his arms again? Would he ever again live the life he had achieved and had rejoiced in? His body chained in unaccustomed inactivity, his imagination leaped ahead to probe the unfathomed future, or ranged homeward to relive his happy history in Samara, to wonder how his city was faring, to touch in thought the loved ones he had left there.

Though the year was rapidly falling toward winter as bright October faded into gray November, the first snow was late in coming, and the thermometer stayed above freezing. The water level in the Volga sank until shallows and sandbars stood revealed like momentary islands in the stream. Autumn fogs drifted over the city veiling the dingy streets and the downcast people who haunted them.

The town lived in anxiety over fuel scarcity as well as the looming occupation. By now, no one really believed any more that the conservatives could stem the Red tide. Though local clashes ebbed and flowed, the Bolshevik grip on the country was inexorably tightening.

Just when the passage of one uneventful day after another was beginning to ease the tension, Red troops appeared in the streets. After the weeks of trepidation the undramatic reality was almost a release. There was no turmoil, no fighting in the streets; not even any gunfire. Like the fog the Red tide simply flowed in and inundated the town.

One day the thoroughfares were practically empty, citizens waiting tensely behind locked doors. The next there were soldiers everywhere, in uniforms marked with the red star, going from house to house, taking a census of the number of rooms, inhabitants and facilities.

In a few days they came to our house. When the loud knock sounded, Fraülein looked fearfully at Mamma, who clasped her hands convulsively, took a deep breath, and nodded. The unbolted door opened to a tall young officer with a patch over one eye and surprisingly correct manners.

"Lieutenant Ivanov to see Comrade Lurye," he announced.

"I am sorry, Gospodin Lurye is away on a business trip." Fraülein started to shut the door, but the lieutenant was already inside.

"Then I will speak with his wife. My business is official. Comrade Lurye," he addressed himself to Olga, correctly gauging her family status. "I have to notify you that your husband's factory is being transferred to state control, effective immediately. As soon as he returns from his trip he is to report to the *zemstvo* for formal notification. Also, we are taking a census. My men must come in to count the rooms in the house and list all conveniences. With your permission." With a slight bow he opened the door to two soldiers waiting outside. "How many people live in this house?"

Nothing more happened for about a week, except that soldiers came and ripped out a bathtub from every house that had one, commandeered for the military hospital. The tubs were left by the curb to be picked up. There they stayed all winter, covered with snow, of no use to either patients or householders. Happily for our family, the yellow house had two bathrooms. The unsuspected second tub in the servants' attic was left intact. We lived quietly behind our bolted doors, managing on stored supplies and Fraülein's market forays.

Mamma spent many hours playing her piano and visiting her house. Sitting in the airy rooms with their long windows and blue velvet portieres, rooms filled with the elegant French furniture and oriental rugs that she and Adya had chosen with so much pleasure on their honeymoon trip, she would lovingly finger a Dresden figurine on the mantel or the Meissen clock, as if to memorize their delicate curves and tender colors. She tried to fill her memory with the gracious setting of her brief married life. Each object became a symbol of the happy years spent there, of a life she was sure was gone forever.

Perhaps sensing my mother's fears, I too looked at our house with a new pleasure and love. Though I had always wanted to be with the grownups, now I loved to play in my pretty nursery — where the row of solemn bisque dolls sat primly on the cushioned window seat, the small painted table was set for tea, and Mishka in his own little chair sat waiting to listen to my troubles.

Darling Mishka. He had been my best beloved ever since my Aunt Xenia had brought him from Tashkent. That visit had been such a happy time. Though I was not even three at the time, I still remembered it. I loved playing with Xenia's daughter Asya. I envied my cousin her curly black hair and soft brown eyes like Mamma's, and wished I had a sister like her. We were only three months apart in age, very different in coloring yet with the same features — Aunt Xenia called us "Snow White and Rose Red" — and were both named after our grandmother Annette. Mamma glowed with joy to see again, after so many years of separation, the older sister who had been almost a mother to her.

Aunt Xenia told us stories about her exotic eastern home in Turkestan — a place half-European, half-Asian, where people roofed their houses with mud in which wild poppies grew, so that in the blooming season the city suddenly turned red. Among the presents she brought us was Mishka, a tawny stuffed bear who captured my heart at once. Ever since then he had been my inseparable companion. My pretty French dolls sat ignored in a row while I dressed Mishka in my own baby clothes, entertained him with tea parties, and slept curled around his chubby back.

I clutched the bear for comfort now, as we waited for the next development. The slow days went by, unreal and lonely. Then suddenly we were invaded. The lieutenant must have been taken with the yellow house, and decided to commandeer it as quarters for his group of seven junior officers. However, he kindly allowed us to choose one room for ourselves.

Mamma was terrified at the prospect of those "savages" camped in her sanctuary but was also unexpectedly stubborn about leaving the house to them. "This is our home," she decided with surprising courage, after a discussion with her in-laws, declining Babushka's invitation to move in with them. "This house is all we have left. I *have* to try to hold on to it till Adya returns — if I can."

I remember how she and Fraülein, with me helping and hindering, moved the most necessary and most valuable things into the nursery at the back. Though small, it was strategically suited to be our stronghold because it was farthest away from the main living areas. Uncle Pavel installed a stout bolt on the inside, and we made ourselves as comfortable as three people can be in one crowded room. Mamma carried some of her most precious things to Babushka's for safekeeping, just in case.

Many of Mamma's initial fears proved groundless. Our non-paying guests were not abusive, indeed were usually polite; some of them were even kind. Occasionally they brought home scarce food — meat, fresh vegetables, once even some almost-coffee — and asked Fraülein to prepare it in return for a share in the meal. But mostly they ate at the officers' mess.

We were never molested or threatened. In a way we were even protected. Sometimes one of the soldiers would romp with me. I often ventured out of our room as I got used to them. He would ride me on his knee or bring me a rare treat of candy. After many months of hard living and brutal fighting in the field, the men seemed to revel in the sense of home that the house radiated, even with its real life so disrupted.

Even so, the situation grew more and more tense. The young men were merry and boisterous, and used the house as if it were their own. Their evenings were spent in carousing, with plenty of vodka, any number of guests — military comrades and complaisant local girls — and dancing far into the night to an accordion or a couple of balalaikas.

As soon as our own supper was cooked, Fraülein would bolt us into our little refuge, bracing for another night of revel. We listened to the drunken laughter and the loud voices. Mamma cringed when a scuffle ended in a crash, or a toast in the tinkle of shattered crystal. We clung together nervously when heavy boots came toward our end of the corridor. Our nights were passed in exhaustion and our days in despair over the fresh havoc we found on emerging from our citadel each morning. Mamma's helplessness to protect the house must have been a constant frustration, a rising rage.

Other developments brought matters to a head. The *zemstvo* announced that all dwelling space was to be apportioned equally, a national policy designed to cope with the swarms of homeless. Adding in the thousands of refugees who had poured into the town from the war zones, the troops already quartered there, and the starving peasants arriving daily from the north, something like sixty square feet was all that could be allotted to each person in Samara.

My grandparents lived on the parterre floor of a three-family house, halfway up the avenue that ran down a long hill to the river. Aunt Sonya, not yet married, lived with them. But it was obvious that three people were not going to be left in sole possession of an entire five-room apartment. Obsessed by the fear that strangers would be assigned to some of her rooms, while the rest of the family would have to share their homes with other unknowns, Babushka launched a campaign to convince Tanya and Mamma to fill her extra space and keep the family together. We had already started to bring objects of value to store at Babushka's; but my mother could not yet quite reconcile herself to abandoning her house.

Then, as November neared its end in a heavy snowfall and a sharp freeze, Fraülein at last made up her mind to go. Rising anti-German feeling was making her position too risky. Babushka, meanwhile, was becoming frantic, because her friend uptown had just been forced to house three refugee families — people who didn't understand indoor plumbing and had already stopped up the toilet, causing a bad overflow and a terrible stink.

The morning after Fraülein's decision was made, Mamma emerged to find the debris of a wild party, with vodka poured all over her piano, and the center of the drawing-room rug burned through, where some drunken soldier had tried to start a bonfire. That was the last straw. After her hysterics subsided, she and Fraülein came to the inevitable conclusion.

"There's really no use staying here to protect the house," Mamma had to admit. "I can't do anything to stop their destroying it. In fact, it's very likely the place will be burned down before they're through. Even if it isn't, nothing of value will be left whole. Winter is here, and I can't keep up the fires or find coal, so we'll freeze." She turned to Fraülein, her eyes filled with despair. "Now you must leave, and I don't even know how to do anything — not even cook."

"I wish I could stay, Madame." Fraülein had long since become a friend rather than an employee, but in spite of the harrowing months they had shared, her formal habits were ingrained. "But I absolutely agree that there's no sense in your trying to live here. You should go to the Luryes, for your sake and the child's as well as theirs. They'll take care of you and you will help each other. Even if you don't feel entirely at home with them," she added. "It will be much better than here among strangers.

"And after what the Reds did to the Volga Germans around Saratov, I know I must leave Russia while I can."

Mamma turned her tear-wet face to the governess. "Yes, of course you must go home. There's really no other choice. I'm grateful you've stayed this long. And we must leave too. I really can't bear to watch this ravaging of my house. Every new boot scrape on a table, every shattered figurine, is such an agony. You know, I had no idea I felt so strongly about my things." She sighed wearily. "Of course I couldn't manage here without you for even a day. I am so poorly trained for a hard life, so ignorant — "

"Poor Madame." Fraülein patted Olga's hand in an unaccustomed show of sympathy. "I'm afraid no one is trained for the life this unhappy country will have now. You'll have to learn to be strong, and not give way. For your child's sake, and for your husband, who depends on you to survive until he can come back."

"Yes, I know." She gave another great sigh and got up, gathering purpose and determination like skirts around her. "We must think how we can move what we can save. Will you be able to help me do that before you go, dear Fraülein? It's the last service I shall ask. Do you think we can manage it today?"

77

As I tried to choose the few toys and books I could take with me, and resign myself to leaving all the rest, I thought about all the changes in my life since that birthday less than two months ago. Still acutely missing Papa's presence, I now had to face the loss of Fraülein, who had shared every hour of the day with me for more than a year. How strange it would be when Fraülein was not there any more.

Was I sad to leave the yellow house? No, I decided, it wasn't home any more. Papa wasn't there, it was filled with strangers and noise and mess. Mamma was always nervous and afraid and I didn't know how to help her.

I shut my eyes and remembered the days when it was home. I hadn't known then how much I loved it all. I pictured myself coming into the big bedroom for the morning ritual, where my parents would be sitting up against their big square pillows in their high carved bed.

I would curtsy and address them politely in German as Fraülein had drilled me, "*Guten morgen,* Papa, *guten morgen*, Mamma. *Moechte ich die schluesseln haben?*" Prim in my white dress with the eyelet ruffles, my blue satin sash and matching hair bow, I would get my good-morning kisses and the keys for Fraülein.

From that world of happy days and tranquil nights, memory called back laughter, sunshine, music, comfort, loving voices, learning and play, everything ordered and secure. All gone in a few calamitous weeks. Would it ever come back?

Grateful for the snow-covered streets, Mamma and Fraülein spent the day dragging sled-loads of clothes, linens, food and whatever valuables they could move, around the corner and up the hill to my grandparents' house, while I carried my own small burdens behind them.

As we rounded the corner of our street on the final trip, Olga noticed along the waterfront the ragged peasants in their sackcloth and birchbark shoes, dragging their grimy bundles as they streamed ashore from a riverboat. Refugees from the war-ravaged villages, they were crowded aboard every steamer, sleeping all over the decks, carrying all they owned in their pathetic sacks.

Now I am a refugee too, Olga thought gloomily, with my life in bundles and my home lost. Yet there was no comparison. She still had shelter, food, people to care about her. As we came up the hill, we were welcomed by a relieved Babushka and Zeyde. Before the short daylight had faded we were settled in. Pavel was taking Fraülein to the station to wait for the next train west. The little back bedroom now abandoned, life in the yellow house had come to an end.

As the housing crisis deepened, the family closed ranks again. Aunt Tanya, with husband Pavel and their three children also moved in with her parents. They took over the large parlor which, partitioned with portieres and blankets, housed all five. Yet the ten of us, stuffed into a modest apartment designed for three, counted ourselves lucky. All around us we saw families forced to share life's intimacies with total strangers.

❧ 4 ❧
Dog Days and Decline
Samara, 1919

EVEN WHEN the hot weather came, it didn't feel like summer. Until now the word had meant delight: a month in the country; river outings and forest picnics; the fairs that came to put up their tents and booths in the big empty block by the river; rolling a hoop or bouncing a bright painted ball, with Nyanya or Fräulein or Papa to play with. But this year the season was not worth the name of summer. Except that the days grew hot and dry, the nights mild and airless, it was no different from winter. Nobody wanted to play or go anywhere or do anything just for fun.

Sometimes, waking in the night in the bed I shared with Mamma, after a dream about Papa and our happy days in the yellow house, I would lie drowsily wondering which was the dream and which the reality. Maybe I'm still asleep, I'd think wishfully. Soon I'll wake up and it will be morning, and I'll be back in my own bed in my own blue room at home. Fräulein will come in and say briskly, "*Guten morgen,* Niura, time to get up now."

I'll jump up and run into the big bedroom. Papa

and Mamma will be sitting up in bed, and I'll jump in with them and get a big hug from Papa . . . Then the ache of longing for that hug would grow too real. I would know then which was the wishful dream and which the painful reality — the stuffy little bedroom at Babushka's, the hot narrow bed, and no Papa.

I'm sure my mother's thoughts often echoed mine. Between sleep and waking, relaxed in bed, the small warm back cuddled against her own, Olga too drifted on a river of time, hoping to escape into dreams of the lost past. She was penned in this strange parenthesis in which they all lived now — each tentative day leading only to another of the same succession of small mean shifts for survival.

She had grown up solitary in a world of plenty that she had accepted as a given. Now she was at the opposite pole: in the midst of close family living (though in her heart she still felt alien), yet with all the physical substance of life in jeopardy. The short years of happiness and security with Adya had vanished like a girlhood daydream in the harsh winds of adult living. Though my memories of that time are fragmentary, it is easy to imagine the rest and produce something like reality.

On a scorching day in early summer Mamma and her sister-in-law Sonya were sitting on her bed in the crowded room where she and I now made our home. Once it had been Sonya's room, but now she slept on the daybed in the dining room. Though she had insisted she didn't mind being displaced for the sake of her brother's family, Mamma still felt guilty over usurping her space.

Both women were busy with the mending and patching that was now the only way to keep the family decently clothed — a task not calculated to raise the spirits. Olga's state of mind had been steadily deteriorating. She tried to thwart her depression by giving voice to her feelings.

"Nothing seems real any more," she mourned. "Adya, our home, all my lovely things — even my dear piano. All gone. Everything that gave me a real life, like other people. Adya is thousands of miles away in Manchuria. Except for Niura, there's nothing left of it all. In a way, there's nothing left of me."

In my "cozy corner" — a sanctum I had fashioned by pushing boxes and packages around to make a little private den for myself and my few salvaged toys — I lay listening with my head on Mishka's stomach, my book forgotten.

"That's ridiculous, Olya." Sonya the pragmatist — though like all the family she was tolerant of Olga's dark moods up to a point — had small patience with such futile self-torment. She bore her own sorrow stoically, keeping at bay memories of her dead Kolya — memories she could not yet deal with — by concentrating on each day's trials.

"I know this is a difficult time for us all, but it won't last forever. We just have to get through it as best we can. That makes more sense to me than longing for what's gone. I know you're used to comforts and servants, but — "

"Oh, Sonya, you don't understand. That's not what I mind losing, it's just . . . " Olga searched for words to try to make the other see. She needed Sonya to understand. Of all the relatives now crammed into Babushka's apartment, only with Sonya did she feel an affinity that her starved spirit so longed for.

"You know, my dear, how lonely I was as a child. My grandmother only took care of me as a duty; she never loved me. I was separated from my sisters. . . . Well, this is the same way I felt at that time — not really a part of the world. I didn't seem to belong anywhere. I used to imagine my life was a story I was reading. Something out of Gogol or Tolstoy, probably," she added with a forlorn attempt at grim humor.

"Even in my student days at Lausanne, or at the university — even in Dresden at the conservatory, where I was really happy — I still had some of that sense of not being really connected to the world." She closed her eyes to the old pain.

"Only when Adya and I were married, when I had a real family life that belonged to me, and that I belonged to — it was only then that those unhappy feelings faded away. But now . . . " The long lashes rose again. Olga's luminous eyes were swimming in unshed tears. "Now all that life is lost — and I feel so bereft — now I find myself drifting back into that terrible nowhere, where I lived so long. And I don't think I can bear it." She bent over her darning, covering her face as the tears fell.

Sonya's thoughts raced, seeking a way to snatch Olga back from a limbo she only dimly glimpsed. Her own life had been lived so entirely in the real world. As her brother began to succeed and send money home, she emerged from a village childhood into the larger world of the university, into a profession made possible by her brother's support. All of it was a reaching out to life, to the savor of challenge, to the struggle as well as the rewards. Like her mother, she knew her own strength and believed it would suffice for survival. Though the death of her fiancé was a blow terrible to endure, she knew it would not break her.

A beautiful woman, Sonya was unconcerned with her looks. The soft chestnut hair that curled around a delicate oval face, the rosy mouth, the golden brown eyes, no longer merry, that still looked bravely out at the world, gave no hint of her iron determination to deal with life, whatever it brought. The doubtings and shrinkings of a fainthearted spirit like

Olga's were like a foreign country to her. But Sonya was devoted to her brother and had learned to care about her sister-in-law, even though their personalities were so opposite.

Though she sensed that this time her habitual "Things will be better soon," would just carom off the wall of Olga's despair, instinct also told her that she had to find a chink in that wall somehow. Only brutal frankness, she decided finally, would do it. Sonya set her chin and squared her shoulders.

"Olya, you are being absolutely unrealistic," she began. For her that was the severest possible charge. "*How* can you say you are not connected to real life? Life now is more real than ever — now that every day is a new challenge, just to survive. What could be more real than searching for food for the family, fuel for cooking. In a few months there'll be the heating too. Keeping us all healthy with no medicines, trying to keep everything from wearing out, nothing to buy in the shops. No money to buy with anyway, with inflation eating up all its value. All these problems are *real.* And you *have* to deal with them, for your child as well as yourself. And for Adya, who will not stay in Manchuria forever. And for all of us."

Olga sat unmoving.

"Listen, Olya. Please! We all have to work together, to care for each other, to manage somehow. That's the only way we'll all survive. Each one of us has to do what we can to keep the family going. We depend on you as you do on us. We *do* care about you. We do need you."

Olga looked up at that, surprised. "*Need* me? Need *me?* But I'm so useless. I don't know how to do anything. Can't even take care of my own child properly. Remember when I tried to warm some kasha for Niura in the wall heater? I tipped it over and burned my hand. And I wasted the kasha too."

Passionately, bitterly, she catalogued the list of her inadequacies. "All I can do is darn socks and play the piano. A lot of help that'll be to the family — even if I had a piano any more."

Having to leave her beloved instrument behind in the yellow house was still an unhealed wound. She'd gone back a few times to play on it at first, but it was deteriorating so rapidly under the ravages of careless thumping and spilled drinks and plain neglect that she soon gave the visits up as too painful. "I'm just an extra mouth to feed, a burden on everybody. You'd all be better off if — "

"What nonsense!" Sonya exploded. She had listened long enough. "Come on, Olya. Let's get out of this hot room and go out for a breath of air." Action was always a good way to end an unsatisfactory talk. "We'll walk down to the river. If there's any breeze, we'll catch it there. And the exercise will do you good."

At once I popped out of my corner, where I'd been getting more and more depressed by the conversation, but afraid to say anything for fear of being shooed out of earshot "Me too, Aunt Sonya? Me too, Mamma? I love to walk by the river."

I was forbidden to go alone to the busy port, and these days it was hard to coax Mamma to take me there, or indeed anywhere.

Mamma had to smile at my fervor. "You remind me of Papa, dushenka. He loved it too. 'Our Volga,' he used to call it. He used to talk about it so often, and read about it. He traveled on it so much, you know; it was like home to him."

Sonya nodded; she too knew the magic of the river. "I know. I felt it too, when we first came here to live. There is such a power, a . . . a living force in a great river." She paused to marshal the words to express feelings not often examined. "In old Mother Volga above all — the life-giver, and the roadway. When you think how for countless ages she has poured her waters through the heart of Russia . . . "

I was fascinated. "Tell me about it," I begged. "Tell me the story of the Volga."

As we strolled down the hill both women, smiling at my eagerness, gladly turned their weary minds to recall what they knew of romantic river lore.

"'This old wild rich brown silent river,' a poet once called the Volga," Mamma recited, dredging up a line read long ago. "Adya told me it turns yellowish after the Kama flows into it. And in the spring, when it floods its banks, he once saw whole forests swimming in it."

"Nightingales sing in the forests beside it. I've heard them on summer nights," Sonya reminisced, wistfully recalling delicious evenings on the river with Kolya.

"The first spring we were married, your Papa took me with him to the Caucasus," offered Mamma, lightly smoothing my hair as she brought back the dear memory. "The river was in flood, and in low places the flat-bottomed steamer would sometimes leave the current and float over low fields and meadows. And at the Gates of Samara, where the river narrows and runs fast between the hills, the wind brought us the fragrance of millions of lilies of the valley. They grow wild all over the hillsides — it was heavenly."

"How beautiful!" I was enraptured. "Will we ever go down the river, Mamma? I wonder where the Volga goes."

"All the way to the Caspian Sea," Sonya replied. "It's very long — two thousand miles and more. It's one of the longest rivers in the world."

As we reached the waterfront, we stopped to drink in the river's beauty. The afternoon sun gilded a path across the dancing wavelets, a tentative breeze freshened the sultry air. A kind of radiance hung over

the scene that began to ease our hearts. Sonya un-
buttoned the collar of her muslin blouse and pushed
up her sleeves with a grateful little sigh as I skipped
ahead, savoring the simple joy of movement. Even
Mamma's eyes seemed to brighten a little, as if mir-
roring the sparkle on the water. One tonic at least
was still free and ours for the taking.

"Don't get too far ahead, Niura," Mamma called.
"I want to keep my eye on you."

The scars of revolution and general neglect and
decay were evident along the waterfront, in broken
windows, peeling paint, and the unhinged doors of
abandoned warehouses, though the port still bustled
with commerce. Fish, lumber, grain, hides, meat,
wood — anything produced or needed by the Volga
towns and countryside — came in or went out through
the transportation center at Samara.

Traders haggled outside the boatmen's tavern,
a hangout of the iron-muscled *burliaki*, the men and
women who wore out their lives pulling barges up
the river, straining to the cadence of their mournful
songs. Smoke from the steamboats wafted acrid over
the piers. Stevedores yelled and whistled. The white
decks of the big side-wheelers glinted with reflected
sunlight.

Sonya was looking across at the bustling com-
mercial street between the river traffic and the uptown avenues. "The famine in the north must be easing," she noted. "There aren't nearly as many baggers
around. Remember last winter, when they were all
over town?"

"It was terrible," Olga agreed. "They brought so
much infection with them, typhus, diphtheria — even
cholera." She spoke the dread word fearfully. "There's
still so much disease around, especially in the schools.
Niura wants so much to learn, she keeps asking about
going to school."

"But she's not even five yet."

"I know, but she can read quite well already, and is always asking questions. I can't even think of sending her at seven if things don't improve." She paused to caution me as I was hanging over the ballastrade to watch the fishing boats below. "If she got sick, if anything happened to her — "

"You're absolutely right, Olya." Sonya refused to let the other's thoughts run down such dark paths. "Why couldn't you teach the child yourself? She's certainly ready to learn, and she needs something to occupy her mind. Besides, it would give you something interesting to do — something useful."

"You know, I've been thinking that." Olga nodded. "She's so eager and curious, I know it's hard for her to be shut up with me. It would help us both to fill our days, and that's what we need. We should get out more, but there's such danger in the streets . . . "

Sonya's soft eyes darkened with grief as she nodded wordlessly, shaken once more by the frightful memory she worked so hard to keep shut away. By the time the date set for their wedding had come and gone, Kolya had been dead for nearly two months. Sonya felt again the staggering shock when the telegram arrived from his parents.

Sheer chance had brought her fiancé to the gates of Kazan University just at the moment when a street clash erupted between the local Reds and Whites. He was doing postgraduate studies in surgery at the medical school and had just left a lecture. Engrossed in his textbook, he stepped into the street directly into the path of the wild blade swung by a Cossack on the gallop, dashing to rescue a comrade from a Red detachment.

By the time the melee moved on and Kolya could be carried into the school infirmary, he had lost a lot of blood and his wound — a deep one in the shoulder

— was muddied and septic. His colleagues struggled to repair the damage, to stop the hemorrhage, to save some function in the half-severed muscles. But their scanty store of antiseptics and his malnourished body were puny defenses against a massive gangrenous infection. When the erratic telegraph service finally carried the news to his parents and from them to Sonya, he had already been dead for almost a week.

Living as they were in a time of almost daily catastrophe, Sonya took her own loss, at least outwardly, with a stoic acceptance at which her family could only wonder. She shut her grief away in her heart and impassively went on with her work at the dental clinic.

But in the long nights, when the distractions of work and family life failed, she mourned her hopes of a future with Kolya. All his brilliant promise, all the long years of training for a life of service to the sick, all their dreams. Everything had been wiped out by one random stroke by a stranger. As she lay in her narrow daybed, Sonya's nerves prickled with longing for the touch of Kolya's cheek, his special smell, his whispering voice as they would sit embracing on that very daybed, talking of their love and their plans. The lost dreams turned in and festered.

In only a moment Olga become aware, in the sudden silence, of what her careless remark had triggered. "Oh, Sonya, my dear, forgive me. How could I be so stupid — "

"Don't be silly, Olya." Sonya refused to be coddled. "Of course you can't watch every word, just in case . . . " She took a deep breath and forced herself to continue. It was time to speak of it. "We can't go on hiding away from facts, even when they hurt. I had to face it — and I did. My hopes died with Kolya, but I am still alive and I must go on living, even without hope."

"You are so strong, Sonya." Olga deeply admired her sister-in-law, seeing in her the qualities she felt she lacked and wished for herself. "You are like Adya, a survivor. You not only manage to face your own grief, you give us all strength too. I've wanted to say this for a long time. I know how you spend yourself on the family. You've done so much to help us all — to help me especially — to keep going." Olga's eyes, turned on her companion, were filled with admiration and pity — pity for them both, for all the young women whose lives had been shattered by the vast impersonal cataclysm of the revolution.

"I wonder if I could bear the total loss of hope," Olga mused. "But maybe it's even harder when there is hope, when you're kept dangling by possibilities. I do believe Adya will come back from Harbin, that we'll be together again, have a home again. But the months go by, and I wonder how many more months will it be — how many years — and could I bear to wait that much longer? I sometimes think hope only keeps us from letting go of the past and facing what is to come, the way you've managed to do. I'm so afraid things will get worse before they get better, and I won't have the strength — "

"That's not the way to be strong, Olya." Sonya had learned the techniques of survival in a hard school. "You must just take one day at a time, then you'll find a way to get through it. When hopes can't come true, they must be put away until there is a chance for them. Otherwise hoping and longing only weaken you.

"We are all in the same boat after all, just trying to stay alive until this storm is over. It seems to me, my dear, that we've gotten caught up in history that's being rewritten, and whether we like it or not, we're all part of it. It's too strong for us. We just have to drift with the current until it quiets down; we have no other choice. But we *can* fight to keep from capsizing, and that's what I mean to do. I'm convinced the future will be better, and very different from the past, and I want to see it."

Determined not to let the pleasure of the day slip away, Sonya resolutely turned the talk to a lighter vein. "Look how gay the esplanade looks today, Olya. Look at Niurochka playing with that baby in the carriage. The summer weather has brought the strollers out, just like it used to, remember?"

"Oh, yes, I remember." Olga's face relaxed a little and her eyes lit up at the memory. "It was so pretty here then, with the streets clean and everything tidy and fresh, the women in pale summer dresses and the men so elegant in their white linen suits. We had silk parasols, mine was a lovely lilac . . . We were always laughing . . . "

Sonya smiled at the memory. "Oh, yes. We used to take walks here when you were first married. Before my parents moved to Samara, when I stayed at your house. We had so much fun that summer. You were carrying Niura . . . "

The contrast between past and present darkened Olga's eyes again. "Oh, Sonya, do you really think it will ever be gay and pretty here again? Do you think some day people will have enough to eat and homes to live in; that life will be comfortable — and fun?"

"Of course it will." Sonya said. "Terrible things have happened, and maybe more will happen, but it can't go on forever. Nothing does. Life must get back to normal some day."

"Ah, but what day?" Olga wasn't buying hope so cheaply. "And will we be able to survive until that day?" She looked at her young in-law with sudden sympathy. How unfair this terrible time is to the young. she thought, turning her head so that Sonya wouldn't read the pity on her face. They've been robbed of the years that should be their happiest ones. They are only just beginning to live. At least I've had a little while to be happy, to be in love, to be young. At least I have Adya's letters to comfort me, to give me hope.

How well I remember the magic effect of Papa's letters, especially when the first one came, after many weeks of silence. Mamma's dejection had deepened with each day that passed without any word. Not knowing where her husband was, unable to write and tell him that she had left the yellow house. Olga had her first news of him almost by accident. The last time she went to play her piano, she'd found his letter stuck in the front hall mirror. It had been mailed in Manchuria over three weeks earlier. She rushed home with it, her face wreathed in smiles, her step brisk and her voice bright with enthusiasm.

"I have finally arrived in Harbin," he wrote. "I plan to stay here until I hear how things are going at home. It was a terrible trip, with long delays. Often we stopped for many hours in open country, with no food and no way to buy any. No heat in the cars, and really bad sanitary conditions. Sometimes we had no water all day long. Getting across the border was complicated. I know now that I was right not to subject you to such a journey.

"There is a large Russian colony in this city, and I'm sure I can find a way to make a living and send money home soon. I am well and comfortable, only worrying about you and missing you all. Please write me at once, for I'm sure letters must take a long time now. I hope this reaches you. Remember to date all your letters."

Since then my parents had kept in touch as regularly as a disorganized postal service permitted. He wrote of his life in the large industrial city, and of the new friends he had found among the Russian émigrés. Every month he sent home money that went far toward supplying our family's needs, since his fairly stable Manchurian currency bought large amounts of devalued Russian rubles. His life sounded pleasant and successful — a far different life than his family's in Samara.

Although he couldn't put details in his letters at the time, we later learned how, with his usual enterprise, he established himself in Harbin as a commission agent. He also traded in lumber, putting to good use his early training in the business. Now and then he acted as a civilian quartermaster for General Kolchak, one of the White military leaders struggling against the Red advance into Siberia.

Like the trains, the mails were totally undependable. Letters took weeks to go even short distances, and many never arrived at all. By numbering their letters to each other, Papa and Mamma at least had some hint when one went astray, so their exchanges were a bit less confusing.

For us that year of 1919 was a hard one to live through, a time of great uncertainty. All our nerves were rasped raw by the daily tensions of dealing with one small crisis piled on another, while the constant threat of new catastrophe lay coiled under the surface of the days like a serpent in a dark pool. Even we children lived in an aura of anxiety. No one had the energy or the means to shield us from the constant strains of daily living. Life was a confusion of glowing promises and dismal disappointments as all sorts of new programs were reported by the authorities, only to fall victim to the bungling of ineffective committees and inadequate means.

The biggest worry was lack of fuel; it aggravated everything else — transport, home heating, light, food preparation, production of needed goods, even local services like schools and hospitals. Everything suffered from the severe shortage of coal and oils. And in a vicious cycle, the breakdown in railroad service made it harder to distribute the fuels that were available, which added to the problems even more.

The family lived in constant fear of disease. Shortages of soap and disinfectants abetted the vermin that traveled with the refugees and spread the germs of typhoid and typhus, smallpox and cholera — all the ancient plagues that follow history's violent turns.

Schools were hotbeds of infection, to say nothing of the social plagues of untrained administrators and intimidated teachers, who had to work in cold and dirty classrooms, with hardly any school supplies. No careful parent would risk exposing her child to their dangers. Mamma shuddered at the mere thought.

Even the small comforts that might have lightened a dreary existence were disappearing. Tea was now being made from apple and berry leaves, coffee from grains. Matches and salt became luxuries, meat and eggs a rare holiday treat. A kerosene famine darkened the long winter evenings, especially in the north.

Many ingenious devices came into use to conserve the precious fluid. Sonya brought home the latest idea. Instead of a lamp, an oil-filled bottle could be fitted with a thin wick threaded through a cork. It gave off a feeble unstable light, but used the kerosene very slowly, and made it possible to move about in a dark house.

The dining room had become the family gathering place. Around the big round oak table with its resident samovar we children studied and played games, the women mended and folded laundry, Zeyde read the paper and Mamma wrote her letters to her husband. It was the hub of the family wheel.

In the evening the grandparents would sit listening to the day's news, brought home by Sonya
from her clinic and by Pavel from his bureau. Tanya
would share the day's tribulations with her husband
and, perforce, with everybody else. Olga might have
Papa's latest letter to read aloud, or report on the
children's progress in arithmetic — she was now
teaching Tanya's two boys as well as me. Mara and I
would be playing checkers on Sonya's daybed in the
corner, with Ara noisily coaching and his father periodically shushing us all. Baby Sonia, nicknamed
Sosu by her brothers, would be on her mother's lap,
half asleep. She always cried now if she was put to
bed alone, so Tanya had to rock her to sleep before
putting her down, to keep her from disturbing the
precarious peace of the crowded household.

Fear of house searches, looting and arrest kept
people in a state of nerves that was even worse than
deprivation. Home was no longer a sanctuary, even
though most households were seldom raided. Kept
off balance by anxiety, and with all the accustomed
habits of life being overturned one by one, people
existed in a state of continued shock.

Since everybody worked for the state, every enterprise was controlled by political commissars, rather
than experienced managers. Production was no longer
dependent on demand but on arbitrary quotas. Under such conditions, problems followed one another
faster than one could cope with them, and used up
all one's energies. In an economy where money was
rapidly losing any value, the hoarding of negotiable
possessions became a fine art. Survival now required
all sorts of new stratagems and tradeoffs. How grateful Olga was now for Fraülein's practical advice as
she began to trade small valuables rescued from the
yellow house for necessities that money would no
longer be able to buy.

In the summer of 1919, however, the worst of these depressing developments were still to come. Most people believed that times were bad only because they had no basis for comparison. They had no idea how much worse things could get. While I skipped ahead, the two women strolling along the river relaxed in the sunshine and let the day's sparkle lighten their spirits.

Olga's eyes were on the summer green of the hills on the farther shore. I'm sure they made her think of the farms and dachas, the woods and fields the family used to visit. I knew how she longed for those idyllic summers, for the blooming countryside that had seemed to pour health and vigor into our winter-weary bodies, for my mind was running in the same channel.

Impulsively, I came running back to say, swinging on Mamma's arm: "Oh, I wish we could go to the dacha this summer."

"If only we could," my mother sighed. "How marvelous it would be. The good country air, fresh vegetables and milk, fresh — "

"Why can't you go?" Sonya demanded. As usual, she immediately grasped the possibilities. "Oh, I don't mean rent the dacha. I know you can't do that. But what about the Karsavin farm, where we always got our vegetables? Couldn't you take a room there for you and Niura for a few weeks? It shouldn't cost much. The child could have good fresh milk, and it would do you both a world of good. You're both getting so thin and pale." She was delighted with her new idea. "Really, Olya, you should find out about it right away."

Mamma stood still and stared at her sister-in-law in wonder. "What an idea, Sonya. Where would we get the money?" But the delicious notion rooted in her mind. "I suppose I could pay them with something they could use," she ventured. "A coat or some shirts or — maybe my brass candlesticks, or — "

"Of course. There's sure to be something they want. Karsavin comes to town with vegetables every week, doesn't he? Go and talk to him at the market. You could stay for at least a month." Sonya's mind raced on, planning a holiday for her brother's family that she herself would have enjoyed — a thought that never occurred to her.

For once it proved possible to realize a dream. Farmer Karsavin was quite receptive to the idea; he had always been a friendly sort in the old days. His sons' bedroom had been standing empty for years. Now he was glad of the chance to get a return in tangible goods instead of the devalued currency the government paid for his requisitioned crops — payment that was usually delayed, when he got it at all.

By mid-July I was romping in the flowery meadows around the old farmhouse, helping to feed the chickens and ducks, making friends with the old cow and the sway-backed horse that were the only stock left, my cheeks turning rosy again.

For my mother too the country was an elixir. The simple life of the peasant household was like heaven after the endless futile shifts to maintain the illusion of gentility that occupied people in town. Unbelievably, life here seemed to go on just as it had for centuries. The homely farmhouse seemed almost untouched by recent cataclysms. Its unpainted walls were mellow with weathering, there were carved blue shutters on the small front windows, their bright geraniums framed by white curtains. Strips of home-woven matting crisscrossed the worn painted floors. One corner cupboard held the best rose-sprigged china, the other the traditional icons that had been handed down in the family for generations.

Marfa Karsavina's heart was as ample as her bosom, and she lavished on her guests — she would not think of us as boarders — the same fussy mothering she gave every living thing in her enclave. "Have another potato pancake, *gospoja*, do. You're so thin." She turned to me with a smile. "Come along, Niurochka, I've got to bring these slops out to the piggies. You can open the gate for me."

The well-tended Karsavin acres had been a model for the local farmers, and the chief pride and joy of their possessors, who seemed as unmoved by the shifting winds of revolution as the ancient lindens that towered over their farmhouse. There had always been bad years and good. They endured the bad ones and enjoyed the good ones with the same patience, serving the land like loving children. Their fields of buckwheat and barley, the long rows of potatoes, cabbages and sugar beets, the old trees in the orchard bending under their wealth of apples and plums, the bright borders of sunflowers — all proclaimed their loving care.

Most of their own large brood had fallen victim to infant disease or childhood accident. Both their surviving sons had disappeared into the maw of the army during the war years — perhaps dead on some border battlefield or fighting with the Red troops on the steppe — no one knew. Yet the couple went about their lives as they always had. Their strong horses had been "requisitioned" for the troops, their fat cattle to feed the starving townfolk. Most of the crops they could coax from the soil went to the government food committees that passed through the countryside like locusts, seeking sustenance for the cities. But the Karsavins kept on working, managing as best they could with the poorest remnants of their stock. Whenever danger threatened, they ingeniously hid the last rooster and hens, the few piglets they had left, the seeds for the next crop.

Like all successful farmers, they lived in dread of the threatened collectivization program and took advantage of the growing power of barter whenever a chance presented itself. To earn a warm winter coat or a pair of elegant candlesticks for the pleasure of housing and feeding a young mother and child was a welcome opportunity.

I remember how I reveled in country pleasures, eager to be active after the boring months in town. At home they were always saying No.

"Don't go far, it's not safe."

"Stay in the house, the streets are all full of rioters."

"Don't make too much noise, Zeyde isn't feeling well."

"You can't go to school, you might catch something there."

"Not today!"

Here I was free. I could run in the fields chasing butterflies, pick armloads of wildflowers, make daisy chains, play with the animals, wade in the duck pond, stir the batter for the *blinchiki,* help shell the peas, chase the chickens until the old rooster chased me, nipping at my legs. There was never an end to new delights — and I felt so safe.

After days filled with sunshine and fun, I would drop off to sleep in the deep puffy featherbed. I had grown fast in the past year, and skinny on the inadequate diet. Now Mamma would look at me with pleasure instead of worry. "You're getting so rosy and plump, Papa will be so happy when I write him."

It was the fresh air, good farm food and plenty of milk still warm from the milking that was doing it. Though the Karsavins' old cow had long since gone dry, Mamma made a trade with a neighboring farmer, who still had a couple of milkers. For one of her husband's fine English shirts, we got a steaming pail full every morning for two weeks.

The happy interlude on the farm also eased my worries about Mamma. Since my father's departure, I had taken over his concern for her frail health and low spirits. At Babushka's I could not miss seeing, young as I was, how steadily loneliness and the daily hardships were draining those vulnerable spirits. As Mamma visibly drooped and retreated into melancholy, I felt increasingly responsible for keeping her in good spirits, yet less and less able to manage it.

At the Karsavins' this burden lightened perceptibly. On the farm it was almost impossible for Olga not to feel cheerful. The blooming countryside fed her starved appetite for beauty; the wild poppies, sweet peas and yellow locoweed rioted in the fields, while skylarks rocketed up into the fragrant air and bees droned thirstily over the blossoms.

Here she was at peace. Resting and reading in the hammock under the lindens, sitting in the grass teaching me to make daisy chains ("Look, Mamma, I'm a princess. And you're the queen."), petting the old deaf dog who had attached himself to her and lay with his head on her foot or slept under her hammock for hours. Her appetite sparked by good fresh air and food, her sleep quiet and deep, she was steadily gaining in health and serenity.

"I feel better and happier than any time since you went away," she wrote Papa. "And it's good for Niura too. She's been growing so fast this year, like a beanstalk. You'd hardly recognize her. It's wonderfully peaceful here, so quiet and beautiful. For these few precious weeks I can imagine that all the shocks and worries of this past year happened to someone else, in another time, another world.

"If only we could stay here forever!"

⚜ 5 ⚜
The Muffling Snow
Samara, 1920

" . . . and summer's lease hath all too short a slate."

HOW BRIEF those golden days were! Though the memory faded, through the years it would well up at unexpected moments — from a field of daisies, at the smell of fresh country milk, in a Shakespeare sonnet. All too soon Mamma and I had to return to our city life in a crowded home, with meager food, summer chilling into fall, and heating fuel hardly to be found. That was the winter when Samara's tree-lined boulevards were shorn, first of branches, then gradually of their smaller limbs. When scrap wood ceased to exist at all, when keeping warm seemed even more critical than keeping fed.

I turned to books to fill the long hours before Babushka would permit a fire to be built in the big Russian stove. As our dinner cooked, its heat spread through the back of the apartment and created a semblance of the cozy home we used to have.

Tears were running unnoticed down my cheeks as, lost in my favorite story, I leapt with terrified Eliza across the tilting ice to the sanctuary of Ohio. Wrapped cozily in a down quilt, curled up in the wide windowsill by the front door that felt like my own windowseat at home, I was deep in the Russian edition of *Uncle Tom's Cabin*. I was living in a world far from my own chilled and hungry one, a world where people overcame insuperable problems and the last page brought happiness. Or at least an end to sorrow. Not like Samara, where life only got steadily worse and harder to bear.

Arrived at last at the farther shore, and the end of the chapter, I came to myself with a long satisfied sigh, and wiped my wet cheeks and sniffly nose on the corner of the quilt. Purged by vicarious terror and comforted by the resolution of one more crisis, I felt reassured that people *could* survive catastrophe, that separations *could* end in reunion. In sympathy with storybook sorrows, I gave my tears freely, though I faced my own trials with stubborn determination not to give way.

Ever since reading had opened numberless new worlds, all filled with radiant possibilities, between the covers of books, it had absorbed me more and more as my real world became sadder, dingier, and more circumscribed. My true life now lay in the library, and its shelves full of marvelous stories. Now that I was going on six and had Mara to go with me, I finally managed to convince Mamma that a walk of two blocks in broad daylight did not pose a terrifying hazard.

Every few days I went back for more books, reading my way right across the children's fiction shelves, except when I backtracked for a return visit with an old favorite. I couldn't decide which satisfied me more, the thrill of discovering an unforgettable new story, or the joy of returning to familiar places and friends I had grown to love.

How pleasant it was to transport myself to sunny Mississippi with Uncle Tom or to a London garret with Sara Crewe or to the fairyland East of the Sun and West of the Moon. To weep over a dying Little Eva or Toinette's Philip and his lost Mammy. It eased my own pent-up longing for Papa, ending with happy tears over some sweet reunion or homecoming.

In a life so constricted by social breakdown and crisis, at an age when my mind was hungry to learn and stretch, it was hardly surprising that it took only a few months for me to progress from beginner to bookworm. Once Mamma had taught me my letters from newspaper headlines, and shown me how they were made into words in my picture books, there was no stopping me. Each book was a new gift of places, happenings and feelings. I couldn't wait to start the next one, the next adventure in a great world where nothing was gray and eventless, where all impossibilities became conceivable.

My mother was amused to discover that my pet books all seemed to be American. It was true that Russia had long enjoyed a vogue for English and American fiction in translation. Dickens, Hawthorne, Mark Twain were almost as widely read as Tolstoy and Dostoyevsky. But for a child of my age, just beginning my acquaintance with books, it seems remarkable that my favorites were almost all set in the United States, especially the antebellum South. What drew me there? Mamma wondered.

Was it because these foreign settings and characters were, oddly, so familiar that I found them so appealing? It was in stories like *Uncle Tom's Cabin* or *Little Lord Fauntleroy* or a Victorian tale of New Orleans called *Toinette's Philip* that I touched lives and experiences I could best relate to. Intrepid children surviving social upheavals (as I hoped I would), lost relatives finally found or recognized (like Papa), bereft wives and mothers enduring loss and loneliness (like Mamma and Aunt Sonya); everyday people whose world was suddenly turned upside down but who met catastrophe with grace. These stories best satisfied my need to hope. Though I loved the fairy tales and fantasies all Russian children were raised on, stories Nyanya had told me as far back as I could remember, I could not really see myself as Ivan Tsarevich riding his wolf. Just now I needed more plausible escapes from my narrow world.

Still half in Ohio I stared out the window at the fat snowflakes, falling as if to conjure up the scene I had just left behind. In the white air, the drab familiar street was transformed. The leaning figures hurrying to shelter were only half-visible in their pallid camouflage. The blizzard muffled everything, transmogrified the deteriorating city into a Snow Queen's fairy domain.

In this insubstantial world everything real seemed suspended. Somehow the enveloping snow made a buffer. Like Kay in the Snow Queen's palace, I had a strange sense of being sheltered by the elements, insulated for this moment from the cold, the hunger, the infection, all the enemies people battled in order to stay alive one more day, one more year. Just as the snow blanketed and masked the city's scars, it also seemed to quarantine its people from their woes.

Pure illusion! And I already knew it. The family had come to this winter, now gripping us in earnest, through a year of trials the like of which we would not have dreamt even a year ago. Trials which, alas, would not be neatly resolved at the end of a chapter. The best anyone could do now was to learn how to live in this nightmare world, how not to be overwhelmed.

The conversations I eavesdropped on these days were apt to be so discouraging that it was no wonder

I retreated to my books. "Sonyachka," Babushka worried one evening as she bustled about her kitchen, "you must find out when we can get the next allotment of stovewood. We've got less than a week's supply left."

She glanced anxiously up at the firewood stored on the flat top of the tall brick stove that filled a quarter of the room. I too glared up at the wood that had usurped my favorite winter reading place, so warm and private. But since stovewood had become precious no one dared leave it out in a yard or woodshed. It would disappear the first night.

"And we need kerosene," Babushka went on. But Sonya just laughed.

"Kerosene. You're dreaming. They cut the allotment in half again, and you can't even find that. Pavel did say they expect a shipment in next week, but till then . . . "

Sonya and Pavel, the two wage earners, were the ones whose contacts served as ears for news of scarce supplies. Sonya also concerned herself with the family's health. Once in a while she could bring home a priceless bar of soap or some alcohol or aspirin from her clinic, or take one of the family in to get their teeth looked after.

With so many problems to deal with at the same time, it helped that each adult in the household took on a particular responsibility. Babushka performed miracles of improvisation to make the inadequate rations go around. Tanya, her aide-de-camp, scoured the markets and every possible source of supply. "I found a farmer with potatoes to sell," she might announce triumphantly as she returned from a foray. "He's going to bring us two sacks tomorrow, for a silk blouse I promised him. He said he wants it for his wife's name day."

Tanya also took charge of us children, except

when Mamma gave us our lessons. She found it hard to control Tanya's unruly boys. Both were lively fellows whom privations had seemingly done nothing to tame. Even I, who always went along with Mara's shenanigans in blind loyalty, was becoming a handful for my gentle mother. But we were all bright children and learned easily. It helped her to convince herself that she too had a productive role in the family's struggles, something she found hard to believe.

Sonya and Babushka were always trying to reassure her. "You help in your own way, like the rest of us," her mother-in-law would chide when Olga lamented her ineptitude. "Never doubt your usefulness. We need it, and we need you."

But the rampart against my mother's depression was never secure for long.

Beyond the basic problems of trying to keep fed and warm, clean without soap, healthy without medicines, there was the daily spectacle of the refugees, who were everywhere. Starving, freezing, collapsing, dying in full view of the townspeople. Along with the frustration of being powerless to help, there was resentment against these unfortunates who crowded in to compete for scarce supplies, and the unadmitted guilt over having food while others starved, being warm while others froze. These added traumas, beating on the shattered psyches of a people enduring repeated blows with no respite, helped destroy many an unstable mind, break down many a frail constitution, such as Mamma's.

She came home one day close to hysteria. She had gone out to look for her friend Karsavin at the market, hoping to get some fresh vegetables. "I never even got to the market," she sobbed. "The streets were full of refugees. They crowded around and looked so angry, maybe because I was wearing my fur coat and they were all in rags. One fell down right in front of me, just collapsed right on the street. I didn't know what to do, I was so afraid of them.

"And then some wild boys began to follow me. They tried to pull my purse away. I was terrified." She caught her breath raggedly. "I ran to the boulevard, where there were lots of Samara people and . . . and the boys didn't follow me. I just came home as fast as I could."

After that she would never go out alone, and rarely even with others. Only in the house did she feel any measure of safety.

In addition to the general tribulations, each family had its own special trials to endure. For ours it was my grandfather's worsening health. For years we had all taken his troubled digestion for granted, like Mamma's melancholy or Tanya's occasional migraines. Just something to put up with, a nuisance, not a danger. But in the past year, Zeyde's condition had deteriorated. It was no longer just a matter of avoiding foods that gave him dyspepsia. Now he could hardly eat anything without bringing on violent pain and colic. Since delicate foods, which his invalid stomach might have tolerated, were impossible to get, his only defense against pain was to give up eating — a rejection of life that drove Babushka frantic.

Poor Zeyde, always the most patient of men, tried to endure his trials without complaint. But no one at the table could help noticing his flagging appetite and Babushka's endless efforts to tempt him to eat.

"Just try a little of these mashed turnips, my dear," she would coax. "Or a little bread? Dunk it in your tea, it shouldn't be so hard. You must eat something!" she would finally scold, her patience at an end.

Zeyde would look at her with his gentle smile, pat her hand. "Stop fussing at me, Betya. I'm just not hungry today. You think I'm a baby to be coaxed, like Adya used to coax Niurochka?"

It was an old family joke, Papa's tricks to get me to eat the vegetables I had always tried to avoid. "Take just one spoonful for Mamma," he would say, and make a mark on the edge of his newspaper. "Now just one more for Babushka." By the time he'd been around the family, his tally would be sizable, and my plate at least half empty. How could I refuse to eat without disloyalty? "Now just one more bite for Papa." He always saved that for last. Or he would convince me that eating lots of carrots would give me curly hair, my heart's desire.

So long ago, those carefree days when you could worry about a finicky child — or curly hair. The same thought would be in all our minds as Babushka gave her husband a little hug of apology; but she managed to whisper in his ear, "You really must eat something, you know. You need nourishment to get better."

Yet we all knew that Zeyde's problem was not going to be fixed by a little nourishment. Whether it was only a chronic inflammation, an ulcer, or something much worse, clearly its treatment required medicines and delicate foods that just weren't to be found. The milk and custards and fine white bread that he might have succeeded in digesting were almost unheard of this year, with all food supplies dwindling steadily, and what there was of the coarsest and poorest quality. What could anybody do? Babushka wondered in dismay. She who was always so resourceful could now see no way to reverse Zeyde's gradual disintegration. I suspect she sensed, perhaps without ever framing the thought in words, that the problem was too big for anybody's ingenuity.

I came to understand something of its magnitude much later, when I began to research this period of Russia's history. By 1920 the country's entire system of food production and distribution was collaps-

*ing under the stresses of war, terrorism, collectiviza-
tion and drought. Less than half the pre-war area
was under cultivation and half the railway lines and
equipment were out of operation more often than in.*

*The new regime, in its eagerness to court the
peasants, had speeded the downward plunge. The
large productive estates had been expropriated and
put into the hands of the landless muzhiks who used
to work them. But most of them did not have the know-
how to farm efficiently or organize production. Giddy
with their new power, they were determined to steer
their own course. They formed land committees and
defied the Bolshevik authority that tried to apply the
principles of military communism to agriculture.*

*In dividing up the acreage the peasants frag-
mented the former productive holdings into tiny plots.
Parceling out animals and machinery, and smashing
and burning whatever they couldn't use, they soon had
to revert to ancient primitive methods of tilling the soil.
Though substantial farmers like the Karsavins went on
managing their land as well as they could, they ac-
counted for only a small part of the total acreage. Soon
the "breadbasket of Europe" couldn't even feed itself.*

Pavel was the family expert on the new regime
and its doings. He had managed to secure a post in a
local bureau of supply, where he heard everything
and brought home every rumor. "When they were so
desperate to feed the cities and the army," he explained
when the women complained of the growing shortages,
"they prohibited free trade in food and made farmers
sell everything above their own needs to the state markets, and at a fixed price. Of course this price was far
below what they could get on the black market. And
they were paid in devalued currency. When they were
paid at all. Naturally the muzhiks balked at giving
up their surplus for nothing."

That was why we could buy it, or better still trade for it with real goods.

"But now they're sending armed factory workers to the villages to force the peasants to deliver food." Pavel continued his lecture. "And they've organized committees of "Poor Peasants," the lowest, least productive muzhiks in the village, to force the rich kulaks and the efficient peasants like Karsavin to share with them."

"Poor Karsavin," sighed Olga, thinking of her lovely days on the farm.

"Of course this class war in the villages is a disaster for agriculture. The productive peasants are fighting back by growing just enough for their own needs. Now there are threats to confiscate the land if all the fields are not sown. This will probably break the strike, but it's too late. The plunge in production won't be reversed. So while they fight each other, we starve," Pavel concluded grimly.

As if things weren't bad enough, the disruptions of civil war added significantly to the damage in the Volga valley, where different White groups were fighting to overthrow the revolution. Fierce Cossacks from the river towns along the Don, trying to regain their ancient independence, joined counterrevolutionary armies under Kolchak, Krasnov, Denikin and other tsarist generals. Even the Czech Legion of deserters from the Hapsburg armies, trapped inside Russia after the armistice with Germany, joined the Whites in an effort to get home. All these anticommunist groups were desperately trying to stem the Red advance.

Some of the generals tried to set up military dictatorships in the areas they occupied. In 1918, the Czech Legion had supported a provisional government formed at Samara by former members of the constituent assembly of the Kerensky regime. They fought with the forces of General Kolchak and were pushed eastward by the Reds to Omsk in Siberia. It was this exodus that had partly prompted Papa's flight.

By 1920 most of the White groups were on the run, and supplying their needs from each area they occupied as they moved east or south. Red Guards and bandits roamed the countryside, adding to the general chaos. Thousands of horses and cattle and poods of grain (the Russian pood is a weight of just over 36 pounds) were carried off by these bands before they were finally destroyed by the Red armies or driven into oblivion on the Kirghiz Steppe. In the shifting flow of battle, the Volga towns were still uncertain which side would finally be their master.

To all these ills was added the treachery of the weather. All year the people had watched it with anxious eyes. Spring and summer were hot and dry, the crops meager. When autumn came and went with little rain, winter crops had to be sown in parched soil. The old-timers shook their heads and muttered darkly. Since time immemorial the fertile "black earth" provinces had suffered periodic famines during times of drought; this year, the signs of coming disaster were unmistakable.

The peasants, living from day to day in economic bondage, were ill prepared to weather bad years. With a chronic lack of government programs to secure those most vulnerable against crop failure, famines had regularly decimated the villages. "What a country!" Ivan Bunin wrote in The Village in 1910. "Black loam soil over three feet deep! But what of that? Never did five years pass without famine. The town was famous throughout all Russia as a grain mart — but not more than a hundred persons in the whole town ate their fill of the grain."

Not every drought year was severe, but in the 20th century there had already been serious famines

*in 1906 and 1911, and back in 1891 and 1892 the
disaster had been great enough to require relief from
America.*

The Luryes had moved to Samara just too late
to have experienced the 1911 famine, but they heard
about it from friends and neighbors who, as things
got worse, spoke fearfully of that dreadful time.
Drought and famine were becoming the chief topics
of conversation around the family dinner table.

"I don't know what will happen," Pavel was saying gloomily. "It's clear that the next drought is coming, and it's bound to be worse than the last, because now there are no reserves and no stability.
The whole area's already living on minimum rations,
and even these have to be shared with the cities, the
army and the damn bureaucrats." He waved a hand
in a vague gesture of disgust. "I hear they've even
requisitioned the grain that the peasants tried to hold
back for next year's seeding. What stupidity!

"Those 'Iron Broom' food collectors and their
precious regulations. Meanwhile, nothing whatever
is being done to protect against famine, even with
warning signs everywhere around us."

Poor Babushka didn't need Pavel to tell her
that she faced impossible odds in her struggle to
save her husband. Famine years had always carried
off the frailest babies and oldsters, those without the
strength to survive at a level of bare subsistence.

"How am I going to find something digestible
for Zeyde?" she complained to Sonya one gray morning. "Anything we can get in the shops is barely edible. It's all spoiled with substitutes and poorly processed. The flour is so coarsely ground, and so badly
winnowed, it's like baking sawdust. And it's full of
indigestible additives — to make it go farther, I suppose. The bread is too sour for even healthy stom-

achs to tolerate." But still the determined wife would not give up. She marshaled all her resources to do battle for Zeyde.

Now and then one of the packages sent regularly by her son would filter through the undependable mails with some precious staples. Papa's trading was going well, and he had invested the funds he had brought with him to good advantage. Babushka reminded him in every letter to send the white flour, rice and milk powder that Zeyde needed.

Eggs, butter and milk were in very short supply, but with four children in the family and Pavel handily installed in the bureaucracy, it was possible to get occasional rations. Babushka saw to it that Zeyde got a share without unduly depriving us.

For produce we depended on farmers like Karsavin. Our old ally came by regularly now that he wasn't permitted to sell in the free market. He would bring a big bag of potatoes or turnips, a nice fat cabbage or cauliflower, his biggest cucumbers, a bunch of beets, a bag of early apples or plums. As scarcity set in Karsavin, like most of the farmers who used to come to market, tried to keep regular customers supplied, earning in return some quick cash or tangible goods of value.

Now, facing the prospect of a hungry winter after a scanty harvest, the family turned its energies to stockpiling food, a Herculean task when we already needed all our ingenuity just to put food on the table from day to day. But Babushka was adamant. "We have to put aside everything that will keep and eat perishable stuff as much as we can," she dictated.

Olga, Sonya and Tanya nodded; the four women were having a council of war. "We must save as much as possible for the cold months. There won't be any fresh vegetables. This is going to be a terrible winter, and we must be prepared."

"They were saying at the clinic last week that we'll be getting part of our wages in firewood," Sonya contributed. "That will be a big help — if we actually get it," she added cynically. Her early faith in the "new democracy" was increasingly strained by daily disillusion.

"Pavel said his bureau might do that too," Tanya volunteered. Maybe he will be able to get us a stock of flour and oil too. He knows some of the supply commissars. And if we keep getting Adya's packages, we ought to be able to get through the winter. Certainly by spring things should get better." She turned to her mother wistfully.

"Don't you think?"

"Who knows?" shrugged realistic Babushka. "We simply have to try to manage, one day at a time. But we must absolutely stock up for the winter, come what may. Next time Karsavin comes we'll ask him about buying double amounts of potatoes, beets, carrots, anything that won't spoil."

"But that's just the trouble," Tanya said. "Karsavin didn't come last week. We always depend on him, and it's hard to get much from Ivanov. We didn't buy so regularly from him in the old days."

"Well, maybe Karsavin was sick," Babushka theorized. "I'm sure he'll be back this week. When he comes by we'll try to arrange for him to bring us a sack of potatoes and as much as he can spare of the other roots. Now, Sonya, about medicine — "

"Mama, please don't ask me to talk to Comrade Abrashin about getting aspirin for Papa. I can't get it myself any more, and I *really* don't want to be under obligation to him." Hot color flushed Sonya's cheeks as she vainly strove to keep a touch of panic out of her voice.

"I understand how you feel, darling." Her mother patted Sonya's hand, then frowned. "But we've *got* to get something to help your Papa, somehow. He has so much pain at night, he hardly sleeps at all anymore. Sonyachka, couldn't you just try?"

"I don't know how I can, Mamushka. Abrashin bothers me constantly. He's always trying to ingratiate himself. You know I can't *stand* him. He's an evil man. As long as I do my work, as long as we have so few trained dentists and so many patients, I hope he won't make trouble for me even if he *is* the new commissar. But once I go to him for a favor . . . " Sonya shuddered. "I'm afraid of him, Mamushka. I promise to see what I can do on my own to sneak out a little paregoric or aspirin. But please . . . " The council of war ended on a gloomy note.

Sonya's silent struggle against the commissar's thinly veiled campaign, to coax her to secure advantages for herself or her family with her favors, was one more unwelcome burden for the helpless family to bear. But the worst was the dread of a hungry winter to come, the fear that the future would prove even worse than the intolerable present.

When Karsavin had not appeared for three weeks, Olga made a desperate resolve. She would go to the farm and see what food she could bring back. This would mean hours of waiting in a station teeming with refugees, squeezing into a crowded train, walking two miles at the other end, convincing the Karsavins to trade a good food supply for warm clothes or a piece of furniture, and getting the farmer to drive her and the food back to town. Or else she would have to find a way to get the heavy sacks back to the station, on to the train, and home, on her own. For a woman with so little self-confidence, who lived in fear even in the safety of home, this was an act of enormous daring. But with the family's anxiety mounting day by day as the means of survival became scarcer, she screwed up her courage and resolved to do her part, whatever the cost.

I was startled by the vehemence of Mamma's goodbye hug — Mamma, whose normal caress was a butterfly touch on my cheek, a whisper of a kiss on my head — and at the tears I saw welling up in the mournful eyes.

"Why are you upset, Mamma? You'll be home tomorrow, won't you?"

Mamma nodded mutely, stifling her fear that this might well be a final farewell. The turmoil and tragedy she saw everywhere in the city, the clamoring crowds in the empty shops, the whole threatening world she now lived in, terrified her. She was unarmored against it and shrank instinctively from any unfamiliar contact. This time, however, she felt compelled. The food was vital to them all, and Olga, the one who knew the Karsavins best, was the logical one to get it. She went as a condemned man to his doom. But she went.

Tanya put her on the morning train. Fortunately, the local trains were less crowded than the through express. Still, no one was surprised when she didn't get back that evening. We hardly expected it. But as the next day wore on, we grew anxious. The trip was a short one, only two stations on the local, but the decrepitude of the system made even such a simple schedule uncertain.

The family had accepted Olga's decision with many misgivings and only because the need was so urgent. Besides, the mission's success might well depend on her friendship with the Karsavins. In the evening Pavel went to the station, but came back alone. The following day Tanya met the morning train, but came back alone. The morning train had been canceled.

By late afternoon both Tanya and Pavel, with the three older children, were at the station, staring westward to catch the first glimpse of the engine. I'd insisted on going along, and then of course the boys had demanded equal rights. Sonya was still at the clinic, working late as she did almost every night now. Poor diet and rampant infection had sent dental decay skyrocketing.

The boys and I were bewildered by the press of people on the platform. We clustered around the adults, shrinking in alarm at the violence we sensed in the crowd. Nobody protested Uncle Pavel's orders to stay close and not wander. Even the intrepid Mara had no stomach for testing his father's authority this time.

Finally the evening local came puffing slowly down the track and into the station. As the motley collection of cars crawled by, Pavel suddenly caught a glimpse of Olga frantically trying to pull a heavy sack to the edge of a freight car doorway.

He shouted "Olga," as the train halted, but the departing crowds pressed close and shut out his view. Fighting his way through the throng, he grabbed Olga with one hand and her sack with the other, and managed to drag her out onto the platform before the boarders scrambling for places could push her back inside.

By the time Pavel had elbowed a path for us through the crowded platform Olga was exhausted and on the verge of hysteria. She collapsed on a bench outside the station, gasping for breath, her heart pounding. She held on to me as though she'd feared she never would again. Pavel shrugged off her thanks and took charge of the precious sack with its hard-won addition to the family larder. It contained onions and a large cabbage.

The exhausted traveler was in no condition to answer questions until, with Aunt Tanya and me helping her, we finally reached home. Then the family gathered eagerly around the samovar. Though the tea was made only of apple and blackberry leaves, it was hot and comforting. As her fears and forebodings faded in the warm safety of home, Olga gradually revived, buoyed by the interest of her audience, who waited to hear the story of her adventure.

"Karsavin is gone," she reported. "I was lucky to get anything at all. The train broke down at the first stop, and it was nearly evening before I finished the two miles to the farm." She drank thirstily. "There I found only Marfa, gathering up her icons and crying while she packed. She told me how the local Poor Peasants' Committee had accused her husband of holding back his produce and selling it privately. I just sat there in shock."

"Oy, vey," Babushka said, clasping her hands in distress. "Go on, Olechka."

Olga took a deep breath. "Marfa readily admitted that he was. That's how we got food from him. 'You know it's only what every farmer is doing,' she said. 'It's the only way we can live. But the Committee wants our land, and this was the easiest way they could get it.' She started weeping again at the awful prospect.

"Finally she told me the whole story. 'As soon as the food collectors from the cities heard the accusation, they arrested my poor Karsavin. Then they grabbed whatever they could find. They call it confiscation. And now they're taking the farm and turning us out.'

"Though she was terrified, the poor woman was determined to save her husband. She went alone to plead his case before the local soviet. 'But they didn't even know where my poor Karsavin had been taken. They said most likely he'd been sent out of the province. They tried to help, but they don't dare go against the orders. All they could do in the end was give me a few extra days to find a place to go and to move.'"

Around the samovar, the shaken family sat listening without comment.

"So I stayed all next day and helped her get her things together," continued Olga sadly. "She's going to live with her sister in the village. At least she'll be there if her sons come back looking for her. Or if by some stroke of luck Karsavin should come home. But nobody really expects to see him again."

Babushka bent her head into her propped arms, hiding her dismay from the children.

"It was terrible!" Olga's eyes were swimming in tears as she remembered. "All she kept saying was 'Forty years we've been together. How will he get along without me?' They've always worked side by side, in the fields, in the house, always together. And losing her home and furniture. I know how I felt when I had to leave my things behind. And this was the home of a whole lifetime, and how many family lifetimes before that? I felt so sorry for her, and so helpless. I couldn't bear it."

Worn out, she looked despairingly around the circle of faces. The others nodded in sympathy. Standing in the crook of her arm, I patted my mother consolingly.

"But how did you get the onions, Olya?" Pavel couldn't wait to find out. "If the collectors took everything . . ."

Mamma brightened a little, reminded of her success. "That was a real surprise." She shrugged. "Of course I didn't think she had anything left, but almost as we were leaving she suddenly remembered that Karsavin had kept a store hidden under the floor in the barn. She'd forgotten it when she checked everywhere else. She ran out and uncovered it — it had a lot of straw over the slats — and we found two sacks of onions and one of turnips. Naturally she wanted to take them to her sister, but she thought they could spare one sack, in exchange for my wool skirt to give her sister."

"Your skirt, Olya?" Tanya exclaimed, shocked. "How could you do that?"

The family stared in amazement as the modest Olga, still wearing her coat, stood up and opened it, revealing herself in blouse and petticoat. "I wanted the onions," she said, sitting down and taking up the story again.

"The sister's husband moved Marfa's things to the village in his cart, and took my onions to the train station at the same time. He gave me the cabbage too, and said he would try to bring us some potatoes or whatever roots he could find, for winter storage. They want a clock, he said. They've never had a clock." she finished, between tears and laughter.

As Olga ended her recital, the listeners looked at each other with anxious eyes, each asking the silent question: What will become of us? Stories like the Karsavins' were heard almost daily now. Pavel was the first to find his voice.

"We might as well face it, we are all going down. Now there's no safety even within your own walls, when harmless peasants like the Karsavins are being destroyed."

"Hush, Pavel." Babushka hissed. "That's no way to talk in front of the children — " And Sonya, her amber eyes flashing black, declared at the same moment, "Nonsense. We will find a way to survive. While there's life — "

"Life." Pavel snorted. He was beyond caring about the children's ears. "You call this life? Everything's crumbling. It's not just hunger. We are being attacked from all sides, even from inside. All the things that make us civilized, that make us human, are being undermined. Families are breaking up, people are forced to abandon their principles, their best instincts."

"How can you say that, Pavel?" Tanya raised

shocked eyes in denial. Less exposed than her husband and sister to the venality of the world, she pleaded, "We're still the same, we care — "

"A lot you know about it, shut up in the warm kitchen with your mother," Pavel's eyes blazed cold fire. "Do you have any idea what a jungle it is out there? People are becoming animals. Cruel greedy animals."

Sonya, eyes on her stricken sister, contradicted him hotly. "No, no, Pavel, she's right. I'm out there too, and I know there are still good — "

"Oh, sure." Her brother-in-law'a last inhibitions gave way in a rush of fury. "You should be the last one to talk. You who's got that Abrashin slobbering over you day after day. How many women do you think there are out there, abandoned or widowed or spinstered by all the killings, or just tired of waiting for their own men to return? Women afraid of the future, striking up liaisons with the new bosses for a bit of security. How many men are grabbing the coattails of those in power to pull themselves up any dirty way they can? How many young people are turning their backs on homes and families, losing themselves in pleasure or debauching themselves for food, for an hour of security, or just to forget? I tell you — "

"That's enough, Pavel." Zeyde's voice, seldom heard now in the family's arguments, was surprisingly compelling. "You are wrong. It's true that many weak people these days are unable to bear their trials, many are taking easier roads to survival. But you're forgetting the strong people, Pavel. The good people, who have not abandoned hope. They will keep their principles as long as they live. And there are many, many of us."

Pavel started to interrupt, but Zeyde gestured him to silence.

"Yes, we live in a time of despair, but it's not the first time. We Jews have known despair before, many times — and hunger too — but we've endured it, and without losing our humanity. We are not animals. And with God's help we'll live through these trials too. And if we die . . . " His mild eyes rested on his wife's face. "If we die, it will be as we've lived." The quiet voice suddenly rang out strong and prophetic, "Not like animals."

Listening to such conversations, I sensed, though I could not fully understand, the dangers around me. Awaking in the night, I would hear my mother's muffled sobs and feel her body quivering. The grownups understood all too well but were helpless to find any remedy — for Mamma's growing hopelessness, for the continued impossibility of Papa's return, for the tightness of Sonya's pretty mouth and her growing shortness of temper, as she faced the unwelcome advances of the commissar. Though she had managed thus far to ward him off, Sonya could not vent her anger and disgust because her job was the family's lifeline. The tensions were perhaps most evident in Babushka's battle for patience as she watched her family suffer but could not "make it better" for them as she had been doing all her life.

I was able to deal with this frightening new life only by insulating myself with things to do, by building a busy cocoon of books, study and activities, of safe impersonal facts. Along with my cousins, with Mamma as teacher, I learned the rudiments of arithmetic, geography — which I loved — and scraps of grammar. History was largely ignored; it was difficult ground for Olga. The past had become irrelevant, the present was inscrutable, the future inconceivable.

The library provided an unfailing supply of stories through which to escape to brighter worlds. I was also making new friends, two sisters who lived in the upstairs flat. Irina, the younger, was nearly six like me, but it was in the elder, Sofia, that I found a thirst to know that matched my own. When I found a French grammar left behind by Cousin Luba, Sofia and I set ourselves to learn French, convulsing our elders by our efforts at conversation.

At least for the children, on whom worries sit lightly, there were still ways to have fun. My unsquelchable energy demanded active expression to offset my sedentary life. Mara, an even more enterprising child, could always lure me from my book to share a small adventure. He'd find me in my "cozy corner" and nudge me, finger on lips to command quiet. "I'm going exploring," he'd whisper. "Let's go." If I was reluctant to tear myself away from my story, he knew how to tempt me: "We could go down by the river." That prospect never palled.

We two conspirators would creep out stealthily to avoid adult notice, especially Ara's. He always wanted to tag along after Mara as he'd done all his life. But we knew he would whine if we climbed too high or ran too fast, or ignored him, as we were apt to do. Even worse, he would probably tattle when we were scolded for our truancy, to avoid his share of the punishment. So it was our standard policy to keep Ara in ignorance of our excursions and sneak out without him whenever possible. Despite repeated warnings about the dangers of the streets, we two had an uncontrollable need to challenge that larger world, and an unbounded confidence in our ability to succeed.

When we managed to escape, we'd run up the hill to wander the broad avenues leading to the central city, near Mara's old home, or climb trees in the unkempt parks, or explore the riverside. We'd hang over the stone railing of the esplanade to listen to the rough talk and mournful songs of the boatmen and the dockhands below.

We still had our old playthings: balls to toss and hoops to roll outdoors, dominoes, lotto and cards indoors; and in winter, our sleds. On the hard-packed snow we went flying down the long hill toward the river. Mara was getting old enough to envy the big boys who started 'way back at the top of the hill and built up enough momentum to carry them right out onto the frozen river, competing to see who could go the farthest.

I found the idea terrifying. The only way I could stop myself was by steering into the thick wall of snow, often six feet high, that was piled up between road and sidewalks each time the streets were scraped after a new snowfall. This made the road passable for the carts and sledges that brought goods down to the dockside warehouses. These snow ramparts lasted all winter, getting fatter and higher after each new scraping, until the spring thaw rotted them. Then a new river would run down the hill to join the Volga until the walls disappeared.

I would back snorting out of a cave of snow, the white haze in my eyes tinged rosy by the cerise silk scarf my mother wrapped around my head, under my old fur hood. Tucked tight around my ears and brows to keep out the stinging cold, the scarf stayed snug when I turned my head. The stiff lambskin hood left one ear and cheek exposed to the biting cold.

In spite of our inadequate diet, I was growing fast. The little rabbitskin fur coat Papa had bought me when I was three had long been outgrown. Mamma had salvaged it to line the black wool coat, clumsily remade from a topcoat of Papa's, that I now wore. It was long and stiff and plain, and even the knowledge that it had once been Papa's did not make me hate it less. But it did keep me warm enough to play outdoors on sunny days during the long winter months, when the thermometer often stayed below zero for weeks.

I was glad I could still wear my dear old bonnet and muff of curly white lambskin. It was a reminder of the time when clothes were pretty and fun to wear, not dingy hand-me-downs or makeovers. Grownups' clothes were patched and shabby too, but at least they had originally been made to fit and be attractive. Children, who kept growing into different sizes and needed whole new wardrobes, fared the worst, and usually looked like scarecrows. Without enough needles, thread and patterns, and only faded re-used fabrics in odd shapes to work with, even experienced dressmakers couldn't do much except cover bodies for warmth and decency.

So the year of 1920 muddled along, between creeping calamity and "normal life," except when the dark wings of disaster brushed too close.

Afterwards people said that the fire was probably started in the night by refugees who had crept in for shelter, but it was midmorning when someone first noticed smoke wisping out of a shuttered window of the old church. The historic wooden structure had stood on the corner of the avenue near the river for centuries and had once been the pride of the neighborhood, with its intricately patterned boarding, its tall belfry and gilded onion dome. But the revolution had put it out of business. Now it stood forlorn, its gilt faded, its priests impressed into labor battalions, its sacramental treasures looted, its congregation too cowed to disobey the ban on religious observance.

On the day of its final throes the old church once more briefly became the center of attention. By noon the whole neighborhood was massed to watch the fire brigade vainly battling the flames that licked at the corners of the roof. As the shutters burned away one by one and the stained glass windows burst in a kaleidoscope of shards, the interior inferno could be seen — like a sanctified hell of fire and brimstone. All day the church burned, its ancient rock-hard timbers resisting the conflagration while the vulnerable interior fittings generously fed it.

Watching from our stoop, pressed close to Babushka's apron, awed and excited by the flamboyant spectacle, I was thrilled and terrified by turns. I shrieked with the others as long fingers of flame shot up into the sky, shrank back as the shifting breeze carried the acrid smoke our way. As the afternoon wore on, the wind strengthened and blew steadily off the river, spreading panic through the neighborhood. A strong gust might easily send sparks and hot cinders to attack the houses up the hill, and who knew how many might be destroyed before the danger could be contained? This was the fear that kept Babushka out of the kitchen, wasting her time on the stoop.

Already the first house uphill from the church had caught, and the firemen turned their hoses on it, letting the church burn. It was long past saving in any case. The river was at low tide and it was slow and toilsome work for the aging pumper to pull up water. Before dusk, sparks were flying up the hill almost to our corner. Babushka came to a sudden decision. Time to start packing.

What will happen to us? I wondered. Where can we go, in a city full of homeless people and every house crowded to bursting? How will we live with no beds, no chairs or tables, no stove to cook on or keep us warm? Mamma would never be able to stand it. How will we be able to take care of Mamma? And poor sick Zeyde, how will he live without a bed to rest on? As the family rushed to put on their warmest clothes, make bundles of their personal treasures, pack heirlooms, food, silverware and valuables, all to a steady stream of commands from their general, Babushka, my thoughts raced dizzily.

All at once everyone froze in shock as a thunderous crash of sound shook the house, as if ten lightning storms had struck at once. When we could breathe again we all rushed outdoors, where the great booms still reverberated.

The fire in the church had eaten its way up the steeple to the bell tower until, their supporting beams burnt through, the heavy bells came crashing down into the inferno below, clanging a protesting knell for their ancient home. Then, as we all watched, riveted, the belfry and roof collapsed. After that two of the walls caved in. As we stared spellbound at the mass of belching flames that filled the empty space where the tower had always reared its tall spire, a playful swirl of air came down the hill past us, stretching the columns of smoke and flame out over the water.

"Look! The wind!" a dozen voices cried together. "The wind is shifting. We're saved. The fire is turning toward the river."

It was true. As if the bells, sounding for the last time, had commanded the very currents of the air, the wind now blew strong and steady riverward, sending the still-fierce flames to attack empty warehouses and a rickety wharf running out into the water. The homes along the hill were saved.

The old buildings at the river's edge were tinder-dry. They kept the fire fed until long past nightfall, though the church itself had already dwindled to a smoking ruin. Into my memory was burned the gorgeous spectacle of the setting sun, huge and brilliant in the hazy air, sinking into the gilded river and spangling the vermilion plumes of flame that spread along the oil slicks on the water. Dazzling colors of earth and heaven mingling in a rainbow of radiance.

Late that night, after the family had unpacked everything and restored the house to order, the exhausted adults were sitting around the samovar, regaining their composure and rehashing the day's excitements and their providential preservation.

Safe in my bed I felt again the remembered panic of that moment when the family was preparing to be homeless. We were safe now, but . . . What if the wind hadn't shifted? Now I knew for the first time how it might feel to be one of those ragged children I saw every day, trudging behind their mothers with nowhere to go, or curled up in corners out of the wind. They all must have had homes once, I thought, and snug beds like the one I was lying in, hot food to eat, books to read and clean clothes to wear. Now I saw that anything might happen in a moment to change my life into theirs — a famine, an illness, a new regulation — or a fire.

The beast that stalked us had yawned and bared its teeth, and I had glimpsed the mouth of the abyss.

❧ 6 ❧
A Failed Harvest
Samara, 1921

THE FIVE heads ringing the round table were bent at identical angles, all eyes intent on the board over which their ten hands were poised, quivering with the effort not to move, fingertips barely resting on the Ouija in the center. Five minds were focused on the wooden counter on tiny wheels, willing it to move around the printed board. Nothing stirred. In the uncertain light of two homemade "bottle lamps" the motionless group made a tableau that might have served as a charade of "A Seance." Aunt Sonya and her friends had succumbed to the new Ouija fad.

"Shhh," my aunt hissed as fidgety Zinaida, sitting beside her, blew up at her hair to move a stray tendril that was tickling her nose. "Sit still, Zizi! Ouija will never move if you aren't absolutely concentrating all the time."

"I'm sorry," whispered the other contritely, taking advantage of the exchange to move her hand and fix the wayward lock. "But it's so hard to stay still so long," she sighed.

Sonya glared at the culprit hand, and all the

women returned to their determined silence. Mariana, on Sonya's other side, had also used the moment of distraction to flex her tired shoulders and rearrange her heavy hips in the hard chair. Only Nina and Olga stayed unmoving, still in the grip of inertia.

I was watching curiously from a dim corner, where I hoped to escape attention. It was long past my bedtime, but in the bustle of the party, Mamma had providentially been distracted when the other children were sent to bed. I could not help noticing how much easier it was for my mother to sit still than for the others. Nina's hand was trembling with the effort. Zizi, a natural bouncer, could last only a few minutes without moving something. In desperation she contrived to wrinkle her nose without attracting attention.

All of them looked rigid and uneasy with the unnatural effort, except Olga. Her normal state was inaction; it was movement that was an effort. To withdraw into her own inner silence was easy; she did it all the time. She sat relaxed, eyes unseeing, a statue of patience.

Something in the motionless figure frightened me — Mamma seemed to be very far away, lost in some vast nowhere that I could not follow. Afraid to interrupt, I could only yearn silently for the Ouija to begin moving, for something to happen to break off this eerie exercise and bring Mamma back among us.

The Ouija board was the new craze all over Russia: part of a national mania for mysticism, spiritualism, anything outré that might temper the unbearable realities of life. The angry gods, apparently not yet appeased by the agonies let loose by war, revolution and disease, had decreed a famine in the country's most fertile district.

Last year's dire predictions had been borne out

only too well. The family had somehow gotten through the dreaded hungry winter, but that was followed by a hot dry spring and then a disastrous summer drought. Wells dried up. In the parched soil the grain burned and shriveled as it came up in the fields. The river dropped so low that there was no spring flood at all.

It was the final blow for the demoralized country. With farming and industry already in chaos, the traditional reserves against famine were simply not there. The Volga basin, Russia's immemorial breadbasket, itself now became a disaster area. It seemed as if the land's primal fecundity was dying along with its people.

Finding food and fuel — and a way to buy them — formed the sum total of existence for the starving population. As the government failed in its efforts to restore a functioning economy, and kept printing more and more money to meet its needs, a wild inflation devalued the currency. The day came when I went to the bakery and paid a million rubles for a loaf of bread. More and more everyone fell back on barter, since whoever had anything to sell wanted something real in return, not worthless paper.

Having two wage earners in the family — Sonya at her clinic, Pavel Mirkin at his bureau — gave us a slim edge on survival. But without barter, and the periodic arrival of money or a package of precious staples from Papa in Harbin, we would still have come perilously close to starvation. It took all our energies to get through each day, to scrape up the vitality to get up to start the next one.

Gnawing disappointment was among the hardest things to deal with. As the family had stretched hoarded rations during the previous winter, Babushka had buoyed our spirits with constant reminders that if we could just make it through till spring, an upturn was bound to come with the new crop. Now spring had come and gone, and summer too, and winter was closing in again. The cycle of the seasons had brought only more calamity and less food. This year there was no possible way to stock-pile supplies for the hungry months. All the months were hungry now.

How, Babushka fretted, were we going to get through winter this year, without enough nourishment to give us the strength to fight the cold? How could the family protect its weakest members — Zeyde, Olga, Tanya's little Sonyachka — who had no reserves of vitality?

This evening the grandmother was finding chores to keep her busy in the kitchen. She prepared a late supper, largely from the contributions of Sonya's guests, readied the samovar, wiped up obscure corners where lurking crumbs might attract vermin. She had no patience with the goings-on in the dining room, though she sympathized with the young people's need for diversion. About the best they could manage nowadays in the way of socializing were these improvised "*vechera*," evenings around the samovar, when a few friends would gather at one already crowded house, each bringing some small edible toward the refreshments, and spend a few hours together, making believe that a social life was still possible.

Babushka hoped her daughter didn't really believe in this Ouija nonsense. Sonya has always been the levelheaded one, she thought as she busied herself with the samovar. Now she is desperate for some sign of hope. She has to work so hard, and fight so hard, and she still keeps her heart buried with Kolya. The months and years go by, and nothing gets better. Only worse, always worse. Even the grandmother's lifelong optimism had begun to falter. We'll all just die, she thought wearily; one by one we'll all die, even the children — our bright promising little ones who haven't even started to live. Maybe it's better this way. Life in Russia will be terrible for years to come; death would save them so much pain and misery.

But Babushka's heart wasn't quite ready yet to give up the battle. Mechanically moving about the familiar tasks, arranging platters, setting out the tea glasses in their silver holders, banking the miserly fire in the big stove, she let her mind go ranging back over her own hard-lived years. Would she rather have been spared those struggling years, the fears and losses she had endured in those early days? She let herself touch again the memory of the wrenching agony of her first baby daughter's death, choking with diphtheria while she stood by helpless, aching to breathe for her. She cringed with remembered terror at the rumors of a pogrom in a nearby village, of a night when all the Jews of Ula sat grimly behind locked doors, awaiting their turn to bear the madness that somehow passed them by. She recalled the bitter years of poverty, of fears that the little store would not weather the month, of scraping together kopeks for the unexpected doctor bill, the shoes Adya always wore out too fast.

She sat down, staring blindly at the dishrag in her hand, remembering. And smiling. No, she would not wish away those years, with all their pains. Life, she whispered, clutching the damp cloth to her breast. Life is so precious. As long as we have breath we must live it. We have to keep on fighting, keep on trying to stay alive until help comes. Our children, our grandchildren have a right to know their lives too.

This endless labor to survive that we're all enduring, she saw in a flash of illumination — maybe it's like the long hard labor of childbirth. She remembered when her son was being born, her first, and with that big head, how endless the long hours had been, how impossible it had seemed to bear the tearing pain another minute. And how the old midwife had told her, Just hold on, dearie, just hold on one more minute. And another, and another, until the moment of birth came and suddenly it was over, and she held her beautiful son.

Perhaps Russia's suffering now is the pain of birthing a new society, Babushka thought. If we hold on and endure the pain, one day it will be over. One day we'll have a fine new world to be happy in, like me with my new son.

She sighed heavily, shaking her head in dejection. She was too much a realist to believe in such a miracle. A good new world needs good new leaders, she reflected. Our poor country is in the hands of bad ones — the new and the old. They care about their theories and their power, but not about people. They are always preaching 'sacrifice for the revolution' but they repay none of the cost of that sacrifice to the people who make it.

The best ones, the bright and caring ones who might have helped save us are gone, she mourned, lost in longing, thinking of Adya. They're all killed or hounded out of the country. Will they ever be able to come back, to take up their lives again? She missed her son so much, needed his strength so much. And knew in her heart that he was lost to her.

Sunk in her thoughts, she was hardly aware of the sudden staccato of sound in the dining room until I rushed into the kitchen, bubbling with excitement.

"Babushka, come quick, the Ouija is moving, it's answering questions. Come and see." I pulled at my grandmother's hand frantically, not wanting to miss a moment of the wonder.

"What? Ouija? I don't believe it. It's only a toy." Babushka shrugged. But I insisted.

"But it moved. I saw it. It told Nina her brother was coming home. It's spelling out answers. Now Aunt Sonya is asking a question. Hurry!"

Curiosity easily overcame conviction. In the dining room the five bemused young women were spelling out in chorus as the Ouija slowly circled the printed board and stopped at one letter after another.

"J-O-U-R-N-E-Y-B-Y-W-A-T-E-R," they chanted. The counter stopped, and Sonya looked up and saw her mother. Awed, she whispered, "Mamushka, I asked for news of my brother. And it said I'd hear of a journey by water. You saw. What does it mean?"

"Mean? It means you're a silly goose, that's what it means." Babushka's pragmatic mind held no place for spirits and magic. "It's only a trick of some sort. I've no patience with it. It's just another kind of fortune-telling hocus pocus. Come, clear the table." She overrode their clamorous protests. "Supper's ready, girls. It's getting late. Sonyachka, please bring in the samovar."

Overruled, the group reluctantly obeyed her, chattering all the while about the wonderful revelations of Ouija. Nina was thrilled by the promise of her brother's return — he had been gone for years, first at a university, then conscripted into the Red army. For over a year they hadn't known whether he was still alive.

"Be careful, Nina," Babushka cautioned the excited girl. "Don't get your parents too keyed up until there's some confirming news. It would be terrible to get their hopes up for nothing."

Still, it was a gay party that gathered round the meager supper. Mariana had brought a big cu-

cumber which Babushka sliced and marinated to serve with the bread provided by Nina. She was a former teacher who had prudently gone to work in her uncle's bakery "so at least we'll have bread as long as there's any flour for baking." Zizi's mother had sent a bowl of her potato salad, with dill and even a precious onion chopped up in it. Babushka looked around at the chattering young women, laughing and teasing, and marveled at the irrepressible buoyancy of youth, remembering along what harsh paths their lives lay.

Here was pretty Zizi, her giggles and her wayward curls belieing her dingy existence in a cellar with her patient ailing mother and three rowdy young brothers. Only a kind of shadow in her bright blue eyes hinted that she had recently recovered from a vicious rape by two drunken soldiers in an alley.

Blonde Nina's life, though more stable, was darkened by her mother's breakdown. Her only brother had not been heard from since he'd entered the army. The long agony of not knowing whether he was alive or dead had been more than the mother could endure.

Mariana was the widow of a doctor whose medical unit had fallen victim to misdirected shelling at the front. To support her two small daughters, she labored endlessly at anything she could find — sewing, cleaning, laundering, nursing.

Yet here they all were, enjoying an evening's company and a simple meal just as in the old unshadowed world. Perhaps we *can* survive, the grandmother thought, her heavy heart lifting. Perhaps after all some vestige of normal life will be left to remind us of how it could be, to keep us afloat above despair.

Only one voice around the table was unheard, only one face held no animation. Olga sat among the vivacious young women lost in her own sad thoughts, slowly nibbling her bread, miles away from the merry gabble around her.

We're losing her, Babushka worried. She's got no will to live, she won't fight when the crisis comes. And I don't know how to help her. If only Adya . . . Could there be anything in that silly game? Could he be coming? But the way home was not by water. Oh, it's all nonsense, she scolded herself. What an old fool you are. Catching sight of me in the middle of a yawn, she scolded me off to bed.

Mamma, glad of an excuse to leave, went along to tuck me in. Socializing was only an extra effort for her, not really a pleasure. She had joined in the game at Sonya's insistence. She had no heart for the fun, no faith in the Ouija. The strange answer to Sonya's question hardly made an impression on her. She no longer believed her husband would come back. Moving quietly about, getting undressed while I dropped off to sleep in our narrow bed, Olga saw no conclusion to the dark days that crawled by in a narrowing tunnel with no daylight visible at the end.

Slowly brushing her long hair in the dark room, tall and ghostly in her white nightgown, her mind went round and round the cage of loneliness and pain that she lived in, unable to let go, like a tongue probing a sore tooth. I have no life any more, she mourned, no strength to make a new life. It was Adya who made me real, his vigor and enthusiasm, and he is gone. He is living a separate life far away in Harbin, with new friends, new scenes, new challenges. He is meeting new women and probably finding new romances. How could he not? That Madame Vishniak he writes about so often . . . Of course her husband is there too, but there are so many others.

Papa's letters were full of gossip about the large Russian colony in Harbin, where he had found welcome and camaraderie. In the relatively stable Manchurian economy, these émigrés, mostly professional and business families, found a ready market for their talents and had achieved a comfortable life style as they waited for Russia's revolution to fail and for political order to be restored.

With his social talents and his single state her husband would be widely in demand as an extra man, Olga was sure. How could he avoid accepting the consolations undoubtedly offered on every hand? She tormented herself with visions of scintillating creatures throwing themselves at a lonely Adya. His letters told her he loved her, missed her, longed to see her. But she was not there to be loved. How long would his arms stay empty?

How well she knew the ache of empty arms; and how futile the hope for filling her own. Those brief years of marriage had opened the door of her senses, a way through which her body could break out from the soul's lonely prison. She ran her fingers along her flanks, her uncaressed breasts, the hollow of her throat, trying to call up the memory of Adya's touch, which could always awaken her pulses. The lonely flesh stayed cold. It could not remember that sweet excitement, so long denied. She felt dead, too numb even for tears.

We were all becoming numb, succumbing to a kind of emotional anesthesia in the face of the horrors proliferating all about us. There had been refugees around town for years, ragged bands wandering the streets, begging for bones and scraps at kitchen doors, huddled in every sheltered corner. But now that the whole population was so close to starvation and hoarding every crumb, their share had dropped to zero, and the last remnants of human inhibition began to fall away. Ugly rumors were whispered about. While the weak ones patiently died, the will to survive drove many others to acts of brutality that sent shock waves through the city.

The animals provided the first signs that the rumors might be true. The strays of course had been disposed of long since. You could walk all over town without seeing a mangy dog or scarred tomcat. Occasionally one of the remaining horses was reported stolen. Now as the winter began to close in, household pets began to disappear.

One day the family missed the early-morning yip of the frisky puppy that lived in the basement flat, whose shrill barking used to be such a nuisance. Gradually people became aware that for quite a while there'd been no barking to be heard anywhere. The old-timers recognized it for an unerring signal of famine. They shook their heads, muttering darkly.

Babushka had always kept a kitchen cat to keep down the mice who lived in the warm walls around the stove. Even during hard times, a kitchen cat is no problem. She can keep herself fed by hunting and licking platters. But in the spring old Kochka had the bad luck to produce a late litter of three kittens, the result of one of her infrequent forays from her corner. I was entranced by the three cunning babies, especially the all-white one, delicate as a snowflake with blue eyes. I had never had a pet of my own, and Babushka found herself unable to resist my passionate pleadings.

As the kittens grew into frisky young cats, the common doom of Samara's animals loomed just the other side of the front door. No matter how hard I tried to keep them safe, I couldn't be on the watch every minute. They *would* dart out when the door opened, eager to explore the enticing world outdoors. And one by one they failed to come home. First Mopsy, the bold black one, was lost. Then Flopsy, a fat ball of gray and white.

I was determined I would at least save my darling Cottontail. I hardly let her out of my sight. But all in vain. One sad day when I had gone to the library, first carefully shutting the kitten into the pantry, she vanished too. In a house full of people, no door stayed unopened very long.

I was inconsolable for weeks, but at least I learned a vital lesson about the dangers beyond the door. For now, as the days grew short and often dark, a new terror stalked Samara's streets. Children began to disappear.

More than one whispered tale of small bones turning up in dustbins ran around the shaken town. Frightened mothers hardly dared let their little ones go farther than they could see them. No one with any good sense, young or old, stayed out after dark except in the direst emergency, and then only in large groups.

My terrified mother tried to keep me from going out at all. But I put up a stubborn battle.

"But Mamma, I *have* to go to the library," I insisted. "I have to get books to read."

Mamma's "I'm sorry, Niurochka, but I can't let you go out" fell on deaf ears.

I just kept saying, "I have to have books to read" over and over until the war was won.

"Very well," she agreed at last. "You can go twice a week, but only at midday, and only with Mara and Ara, and *only* for an hour." Once on a bright sunny day we thoughtlessly stayed out playing for twenty minutes past the curfew hour. Mamma became so frantic that I was overwhelmed with guilt for days.

In any case, nobody was healthy enough to do much more than they had to. Poor diet naturally produced a bumper crop of infections. Tanya's migraine became a chronic threat. Her little Sonya developed a stubborn rash. Toothache plagued both young and old. We counted ourselves blessed by having a dentist in the family. Sonya always managed to fit a relative into her crowded work schedule.

My first trip to the dental clinic came on a bright winter day crackling with cold. Well bundled up by Mamma, I sat on my sled like a small fat Buddha while Sonya pulled me along the snowpaved streets, generously sacrificing a rare day off to repair a badly decayed molar. I shrank in terror at my first sight of the big drill and the threatening array of picks and probes. But even at six, I forced myself to sit still through the ordeal. It was worth anything to be rid of the nagging ache that had rattled my head for a week. Besides, I knew all too well my aunt's small patience with fussy children. I admired Aunt Sonya deeply and was resolved to make my aunt proud of my fortitude.

The years of fear and famine bred stoicism in youngsters as well as grownups, teaching many hard lessons in endurance. Few children were still allowed the luxury of caprice or willfulness. No one had energy or patience enough to put up with tantrums in these harsh days, nor the means to indulge a fretful little one with treats or toys. Many parents hardly had vitality enough even to love their young. A child like me, who still had a family and a home, felt overwhelmed with gifts when she saw the starving scrofulous beggar children everywhere.

In a world without safeguards, short on medicine, cleanliness, nutrition and warmth, epidemics were spreading unchecked. These enemies — typhus, diphtheria, whooping cough, even the dreaded cholera, that killed with such agony — could not be kept out by bolting the front door. That summer the whole family was inoculated against cholera, for this plague posed an even greater risk than the deficiencies of local clinics. It was marching up the Volga from the south, providing a grim solution to starvation for four out of every five people who came down with it. Because this disease seemed to be associated with eating harmful food substitutes, it inevitably surfaced in a time of famine. Twenty thousand died of it that summer in Samara province alone.

Waiting our turn at the clinic, I shrank in fear against Mamma as I listened to the wails of children, the sudden moans of women, the stifled groans of men. Could a needle hurt so much? I wondered. Then found out, as the serum went home between my shoulder blades into a muscle that knotted in agony. It was a week or more before I could sleep on my back again, and Mamma was sore even longer. Writing about it after three-quarters of a century, I still remember the shock of that vicious stab along my spine.

When nature struggles to restore the balance between population and resources, both death and birth are its weapons. As the weakest and least determined people died, so also did less sturdy embryos fail to come to birth. Lowered vitality, poor nutrition and unremitting tension were doing their work among the mothers, according to Darwin's relentless law, by selecting the strongest of the next generation to face a harsh world. Not only did the conception rate drop sharply — luckily, since it was not a time to favor the special needs and strains of pregnancy — but many women miscarried or delivered stillborn children.

Sofia's mother upstairs became another such statistic. I heard about the coming baby from my two chums, who talked unendingly about the little brother they were going to have. They were full of plans. They were going to bathe him and dress him and teach him to walk. In the drudging sameness of their lives it was a major excitement. I felt my importance eclipsed. Used to being the leader, I had no way to compete with a new baby. Even Sofia's interest in our French studies was waning.

"Sofia is going to have a baby brother," I told my mother peevishly. "I want one too. Why can't I have a baby brother too?"

Even now I can smile inwardly at the memory of Mamma's uneasy laugh. Ever since she had heard the news from upstairs, Olga had known the time had come to explain about babies. She knew her child's sharp mind too well to hope the event would pass by unchallenged.

"Darling, it's not so easy to have a baby. First of all, you need a Mamma *and* a Papa to make a baby. So we can't have one till Papa comes back."

"Oh." I stood still thinking about this problem. "But you write to Papa all the time. Just tell him that we want a baby. He could write — "

Mamma's infrequent laugh exploded. Not for worlds would she make fun of her earnest child, but *a baby by mail.* The idea was too delicious. "Oh, my darling, you can't make babies by mail. It's . . . " she dissolved in giggles again, unable to go on. But I was too offended to appreciate the rare treat of a merry Mamma.

"What's so funny?" I demanded crossly. " *Why* can't you? How do you make babies anyway?" Ignorance was an enemy I had to battle at every turn. "Mamma, why are you laughing at me? How can I know about babies if you won't tell me?"

This frontal attack sobered Mamma at once. She knew she could not sidestep the issue with "You're too young to understand." I never believed there was anything I couldn't at least try to understand.

"I beg your pardon, Niurochka," she said. "You're quite right. It's time for me to tell you about babies. You see . . . a man and a woman must . . .

there's a seed . . . but it's rather complicated . . . "
she floundered on.

How well I now realize her quandary! How could she make clear to a six-year-old the complex chemistry of conception? She who had never been able to speak frankly about sex even to her own husband. She tried, and tried again, but each time her vocabulary failed her. Her inbred modesty refused to allow the explicit terms and graphic descriptions to pass her lips. I stared at her amazed, awed by a subject that turned my circumspect mother red-faced and tongue-tied with embarrassment.

Finally she took refuge in the impersonal. "It's really too difficult for me to describe, darling, but I'm sure one of Papa's medical books has a good explanation. Why don't we just find one, and you can read all about it," she concluded, relieved.

Among Papa's youthful dreams was that of becoming a doctor. His circumstances made it totally unattainable, but for years he had indulged a hobby of collecting medical texts. Thrilled that his sister Sonya planned to bring a doctor into the family, he had passed many of his books on to Kolya. But several basic ones were kept for family reference.

I spent many hours in my corner struggling with the technical delineations of insemination and gestation, and came away with only the vaguest idea of the birth process, and no inkling at all of the passion that initiated it. But the smattering I gleaned served my purpose. My lofty explanations to the fascinated Sofia and Irina fully restored my status and my out-of-joint nose. Now I could enjoy a share in the girls' plans for the baby brother to come.

These expectations were rudely frustrated late one stormy afternoon. The two sisters came running down into Babushka's kitchen where she was showing me how to peel the boiled beets carefully, without wasting any of the flesh. "Please come, Gospoja Lurye," Sofia begged. "Mama is bleeding. She thinks the baby is coming. Please hurry. Papa's gone for the doctor."

Babushka, stopping only to cover the pot and command brusquely, "You two stay here with Niura," grabbed up an armload of towels and disappeared. The three of us sat obediently at the kitchen table, too shaken even to talk about the mysterious drama taking place upstairs. We were already schooled enough in vicissitudes to realize that the baby brother was somehow in jeopardy. Even when Aunt Tanya came in and, hearing the news, took over the dinner preparations, clucking in sympathy and shaking her head as she worked, we sat in silent misery until she shooed us out of her way.

Retiring to our usual refuge on the stairs, we kept our vigil, our halfhearted efforts to talk of other things dwindling into uneasy silence at any noise from above. At last Babushka came down wearily, her disappointed shoulders eloquent. "What in the world are you girls doing here? Come, let's get something to eat. Irina and Sofia, you'd better stay down with us this evening. Your Mama is sleeping now. I think she'll be all right; she just needs to rest. Come."

"But the baby . . . " ventured Sofia anxiously.

Babushka sighed. "The baby was too little. We couldn't save him."

"It was a boy?" Irina asked. "We knew it was going to be a boy."

"Yes, a nice little boy, but too tiny. He came too soon to live." In her dejection Babushka had no heart to be cheery for us children. She went heavily down the stairs, followed by the three little mothers in mourning for our baby-tending plans, in awe of the perils of motherhood glimpsed for the first time.

Our family too had a special grief to face.

Zeyde's health was steadily deteriorating. On the surface he seemed much as always, a gentle presence in the harried household. Physically unable to do much, but always there to pet a fretful child, listen to me read, hush Mara's exuberance with a quiet word. But his vitality was perceptibly ebbing.

One night in the fall, I woke to hear Babushka's voice sending Pavel for the doctor. "Zeyde's burning with fever. Tell him to please hurry."

Our friend Dr. Abramovitch came quickly but reminded my grandmother that he had few resources to deal with the fever. He pronounced the trouble to be a massive inflammation. Since drugs were almost unobtainable now, all he could do was prescribe cool compresses and warm fluids, home remedies Babushka had been using all her life.

She left the household to Tanya's care and concentrated on nursing her husband through the shattering crisis, relying on patience and prayer either to pull him through or mercifully to end his suffering forever. He rallied at last, but the attack left him more debilitated and vulnerable than before.

For once we found Pavel Mirkin to be the hero of the day. In the family, his job at the bureau had privately been considered rather déclassé. There was a feeling that working for this inhuman government was futile at best; perhaps even exploitative in some hard-to-pinpoint way, like making a bargain with the devil.

But Pavel had gone after the post deliberately because he felt it would be important to have a foot in the ruling camp if a crisis should arise. In the end he was proven right.

During Zeyde's long convalescence he was the one who found means to get special sedatives and milk for the invalid. No mean feat when the drought had affected cows to the point where even the children's milk ration was seldom obtainable.

Soon after, Pavel's official connection became even more precious. As the catastrophic year was drawing to a close, he came home one day with stupendous news. "Help is on the way." he exulted. "They say at the bureau that food is coming from the west. Even from America."

"Food!" Babushka breathed the magic word like a prayer. "You think it's true, Pavel? Not just another rumor?"

"I'm sure it's true," Pavel reassured her. "We've been told officially that we are to work with the relief groups when they arrive. They're going to appoint two liaison committees, one for the European group, the International Russian Relief Commission, the other to work with the Americans, under the American Relief Administration." The official titles rolled importantly off his tongue.

Tanya and Olga looked at each other in bliss, each reading her own thought in the other's face. Their children would survive.

Sonya wanted to know the practical details. Who were these people, she asked Pavel, who were leaving their own comfortable lives in a prosperous world to come to this poor dying country to help its famished people?

Pavel was full of information. Both groups were made up from different committees that were organized during the war. They helped feed suffering people in places like Belgium, where there was so much damage. Now these same people were banding together to fight the Russian famine. "Nobody knows yet when they'll arrive, but we were told to be prepared for them."

Sixty years later, while visiting a daughter in California, I spent a day at the Hoover Library at

Stanford, reading the records of this extraordinary humanitarian rescue halfway around the world from our own fortunate land. The outpouring of aid came none too soon. I learned that a second disastrous harvest had doomed the Volga basin to a winter of starvation. Seventy percent of the grain fields had failed completely, and the rest produced less than ten percent of a normal yield. By the beginning of winter two and a half million people in the region needed outside help just to stay alive, and many times that number were barely subsisting.

Though the initiatives from abroad were only grudgingly acknowledged — and often hamstrung — by the embarrassed government that had failed to feed its own population, the foreign relief made all the difference between life and death. During the first year the IRRC fed nearly two million people, while the ARA, under the energetic leadership of Herbert Hoover (an organizing genius, it was said, and who had greater resources at his disposal), fed more than ten million. Part of this effort was in the form of direct relief, especially to children, and part came through packages paid for by relatives and friends in America.

The ARA especially was a boon for our family. Ever since Pavel brought home the wonderful news, "Samara is going to be a distribution center for the American relief," we waited eagerly for his daily report. The best one was on the day he came in grinning from ear to ear.

"I got a new work assignment today. Guess what it is." He tried to hold out against our wild guesses, but was too excited himself to keep us long in the dark. "I'm going to be on the liaison squad at the relief center. What luck! We're going to work with the Americans to run the warehouse. So I'll know right away whenever supplies come in, what we have to do to apply for them, everything."

For once, Pavel got his full measure of glory. Questions rained from all sides. Of course he couldn't answer most of them, since nothing had really happened yet. But the hope of better rations was a tonic for the family's flagging spirits, especially when the Americans soon began to arrive.

"The warehouse is starting to really take shape," Pavel announced as he came home from work, throwing open the front door and bouncing into the dark hallway. "The first relief trains will be leaving Moscow next week."

Working with the dedicated young Americans was helping to restore Pavel's faith in humanity, which had never been too great and had been battered by the opportunism of fellow bureaucrats.

"The Americanski are so eager, so full of energy," he reported wonderingly. "They don't seem to understand about going through channels, or waiting for weeks for somebody's signature. If a program doesn't move fast enough, they go right to the top and find out why." He sighed happily at the miracle of it all. "They really make things happen. And they really care."

Sonya was another family member whose life brightened in this dark time. She had a new friend whose first act of kindness had been to rescue her from the attentions of Commissar Abrashin. In her heart, Sonya took this escape as a sign that Kolya's enduring love was reaching out to protect her. An irrational idea, but it was melting some of the ice around her heart.

When Leonid first saw Sonya, he was newly appointed to head the Children's Clinic of which Sonya's dental department was a part. It was simply her beauty that attracted him when he first noticed her in the small staff lounge. "Who's that pretty brunette in the staff coat?" he asked a colleague. "Is she a doctor?"

"No. A dentist, Sonya Lurye," was the reply.

"Ah, Lurye . . . Hmmm . . . " His companion eyed him curiously, then, shrugging, turned back to his tea. The less one got involved in the affairs of others, these days, the better.

Leonid had known Kolya at medical school in Kazan, had often listened to him rhapsodize about his adored fiancée, and in fact had been there, in the hospital, the day Kolya was picked up wounded in the street outside. Such a waste, he thought now, not for the first time. Kolya had been a good man, and would have made a fine doctor. Quick-witted, he recalled. Quick to laughter as well. A man to remember, indeed.

He was on the point of going over to introduce himself when he saw Commissar Abrashin accost Sonya with his usual air of mingled menace and bravado. Even from across the room, Leonid could see quite clearly the abrupt change in her manner, the shrinking of her shoulders, her obvious distaste and the heroic effort she made to conceal it, trying to reply coolly without overt rudeness. A trained observer and a skilled diagnostician, he read at once the whole shabby story, and his chivalry as well as his sympathy was aroused. He set his attractive jaw firmly and turned away.

Within a day or two, Leonid found an opportunity to make himself known to Sonya without attracting notice. Because he had been Kolya's friend, and was sympathetic, Sonya soon found it quite natural to confide her dilemma to him. It was not difficult, given his status as clinic head and his contacts in the political community, to have some pressure brought to bear on the unpopular Abrashin. The disgruntled commissar became excessively correct in his behavior toward Sonya, having been given to understand that her welfare was of interest to certain persons at a rather high level of authority, and that it behooved him to refrain from even the most token sort of petty reprisal.

With a lighter heart than she had known in many months, Sonya was aware only that Abrashin had inexplicably retreated even as Leonid was becoming a regular presence in her life. Whether or not she suspected any connection between the two circumstances, she found Leonid's friendship very welcome. Predisposed to like the man who had been a friend to Kolya, she soon warmed to him for his own sympathetic self. Her recent helpless outrage at her vulnerability surely made her even more ready to respond to a man of character with whom she could feel safe and respected.

Soon Leonid was a regular visitor. The family found him charming as a friend, and the new sunshine in Sonya's smile made the prospect of more very welcome. He usually walked her home and often stayed for a glass of tea. So he was there when a letter from Adya arrived with Pavel, who'd picked it up at the post office. We all gathered around the table while Mamma read the letter aloud.

"By the time this reaches you," Papa wrote, "I will be at sea, on my way across the Pacific. It has been three years now, and I still see no hope of any improvement in the situation at home. Not for a long time, I'm afraid. I want my family. I want to settle down. I know I can't come back safely, and I can't stand this separation much longer.

"So I am sailing to Vancouver in Canada. From there I'll take a train across the continent to New York, where I can get a ship for Europe. When I get settled, probably in Germany or Switzerland, or maybe France, you can apply for an exit visa. I am longing for the day when you and Niura can join me, and we can be a family again. I'm sure I can establish myself in business somewhere, or find a job, and then I'll be better able to help the rest of the family. And at least we'll be together again."

What a bombshell! The room buzzed with surprise. But after the first shock had faded and the torrent of comments dwindled, Sonya became aware that Babushka wasn't there. She found her mother sitting in the kitchen, lost in thought, her eyes fixed on empty air.

"See, Mama, the Ouija was right." Sonya was triumphant. "Now do you believe it's more than a toy? Imagine, Adya will be in Europe."

Babushka shook her head sadly. "Adya will never get to Europe. He'll stay in America, you'll see."

"America? What do you mean? He says he's thinking of Germany or Switzerland. He'll be much closer."

"Mark my words." Babushka prophesied. "Since he was a child your brother has dreamed of going to America. Once he gets there . . . " Her faded blue eyes darkened with grief to come. "I'll never see my son again."

❧ 7 ❧
Spring of New Hope

Samara, 1921–1922

HOW WELL I remember that re-markable spring of my eighth year, the last Russian spring of my life. Vibrant with new hope that life could be sustained, might even one day become comfortable again, even (dared one hope?) on some distant day, secure. Yet poignant with premonition for our family. Above all for Mamma and me. Pictures bloom in my head of those days filled with activity, when we all tried to act as if the dreaded farewells were not lying in wait just ahead.

Sound bounced off the walls of Babushka's dining room, where eight noisy children were crowded around the table. We were chattering and giggling our way through an early supper, enjoying the sense of holiday, as our mothers were busy in the kitchen preparing for the Passover. Three Jewish families in the neighborhood had combined their scanty resources to create a Seder. How else could we make *Pesach*? There was no way to buy any of the special foods the holiday required.

Before the revolution each community had its arrangements for kosher foods, but it had now been a long time since such luxuries were possible. It was all anyone could do just to get food that was edible. Public religious rituals were, of course, strongly discouraged by a government whose official policy was atheism, though there was no actual prohibition of private observances. But the Seder ritual feast required foods that were just not to be had.

It was April again. At the center of the house we children could barely hear the steady patter of the rain that was sluicing channels in the old rotting snow along the street. Somehow, the family had managed to survive another relentless winter, though there had been many days when we did not believe we would live to see the spring. But the seasons turned as they did every year. Indifferent to whether people lived or died on it, the earth renewed itself and put forth its small new shoots of hope.

For three days now warm wet weather had been washing away the dingy crust of winter, thawing the numbed inhabitants of the city as well as its blighted streets. This spring the rain was doubly welcome, as a sign that the drought might be over, as well as a herald of the benign season. Then at least there would be one less foe to battle — the inexorable cold.

It was cozy in the crowded dining room. The heat of many small active bodies tempered the usual damp chill of the underheated house, helped by the warmth radiating from the kitchen, where the matzos were baking in the big brick stove fed by three fuel rations. We children were eager to finish our potluck meal and get back to the exciting holiday bustle. In the meantime we were engaged in an odd ritual of our own at the supper table.

The bowls of kasha and turnips, the platters of cabbage salad and bread, the condiments, even the teaspoons in their cut-glass holder, nearly everything except our plates and forks, were ranged around Ara, to be dispensed by him on request with a Lord Bountiful air. Ever since the American Relief Administration, known by everyone as ARA, had come to town the previous fall, the children in our household had been playing the ARA game at meals. Since we were lucky enough to have our own Ara, the honor of doling out food naturally fell to him.

No one ever said "Please pass the potatoes" any more — it had to be "Ara, I wish to apply for some potatoes."

Ara would shout "Request approved," in official tones, and graciously spoon out some potatoes onto the tendered plate.

Though the rest of us grew tired of the game and of Ara's airs — for he had easily fallen prey to the bureaucrat's native pomposity — he would not let us stop playing it. As soon as he sat down to each meal he gathered everything in front of him and prepared to grant food as favor to all who petitioned for it.

This preoccupation with ARA food distribution was hardly surprising. It had been the region's main lifeline during the dreadful starving months just past. Much of the talk around Samara tables all winter was of ARA and its tribulations — or failings, depending on a family's pro- or anti-American leanings. Our family, with Pavel working in the ARA warehouse, coming home every day with admiring tales of the heroic "Amerikanski," was of course strongly partisan.

In the late months of 1921, ARA's energetic staff had set up their offices and warehouses in Samara, and had begun coordinating the work of the liaison committee and recruiting local employees. The ARA people were eager to send food supplies out to the perishing villages and to feed the mushrooming hordes of refugees in the city.

They soon discovered that this was not a simple

task. A hostile Red bureaucracy and a transportation system barely worthy of the name presented formidable obstacles. Yet the situation was desperate. As early as September the daily *Samara Novosti* had reported, "The population [in the province] is feeding mainly on substitutes. All the grass is eaten, and acorns and field rats are considered a luxury."

On their first field trips, before the winter closed down, the Americans were appalled by what they found in the villages. Pavel heard about it from Charlie White, the friendly young field worker who had taken to practicing Russian with him as they struggled through the paperwork together.

"Charlie White's field group is back from the villages," Pavel reported at home. "He says they couldn't believe what they saw. Do you know how they're making bread? They dry birch and lime leaves and pound them to powder. Then they mix that with ground acorns, dirt and water. This is what they bake into bread. Charlie says it looks and smells like baked manure."

"Ugh." Babushka's soul revolted at the thought of giving such a mess the holy name of bread. "We'd better stop complaining about our sawdust flour. But I suppose it does give people something solid to put in their hollow bellies."

"Yes, but it's almost indigestible. Most of the children have already died from it, and the others, Charlie says, all have that unmistakable stamp of famine, the bloated stomachs, large heads, rickety arms and legs like sticks. There are practically no babies left. Even those who manage to get born can't be fed, because the mothers have no milk."

The women listened to him with stricken eyes, holding their heads in horror. As mothers they all felt the pain of those unknown women who could only pray for a quick death for their little ones, to spare them a slow agonizing end by starvation.

"My God." Babushka wailed. "We're losing a whole generation."

"That's right," Pavel said. "Charlie says that before 1921 is over they expect that at least nine tenths of the children under four will be dead."

In the city that winter there was still some food, with ARA on the spot and local distribution comparatively simple. But as news of the relief program spread, desperate refugees kept pouring in, bringing dreadful epidemics and swamping relief facilities. Then, when the winter took hold in earnest, the bitter cold killed many, refugees and townsfolk alike, of those who had managed to survive hunger and disease. Once more corpses lay unburied in the streets. The living learned to walk around them unmoved, numbed by the familiarity of the daily sight.

The exhausted relief workers, many of the local ones already weakened by starvation, tried vainly to cope. Even to receive their own shipments, sent through from the points of entry, they had to fight a constant battle with the authorities. And when the stocks of food finally arrived, there remained the enormous problems of regional distribution, a challenge that even the determined Charlie White found daunting. Pavel got many an earful on the subject.

"How are we going to get this stuff to the villages?" Charlie would demand rhetorically. "We can't find enough wagons or horses. The trains hardly ever run. The rivers are freezing. Half the roads are cut off by huge snow drifts." He flung out both arms in a gesture of total frustration. "If we wait till spring, everyone out there will be dead."

"You can't wait for spring." Pavel explained. "When the snow melts, the roads will be too muddy to carry heavy freight. And when the rivers thaw,

they'll be in flood for weeks. Winter is when shipping is easiest. You can drive right across the river
on the ice. You have to push through all the shipments you can before the warm weather comes."

"What a country!" Charlie howled, full of outrage and disgust, which the passing of each week
did nothing to diminish. Disgust fed by too many
horror stories of the people's war with the bureaucracy, and the government's futile programs to nationalize agriculture, even at the expense of people's
lives. The dreadful fate of the Volga Germans, down
the river around Saratov, was a case in point.

This ancient city, also a traffic hub for the lower
Volga region, was ringed by a number of farming
communes of German immigrants. When the stran-
gling confiscations and taxation persisted despite a
meager harvest, these thrifty farmers finally rebelled.
Many of them joined a mutinous regiment led by
Valukin, which captured grain stores and distributed
food to the hungry. But the rebellion was put down
with great cruelty by troops from the Saratov garri-
son. Hundreds of villagers were shot in reprisal.

Yet in this harsh climate the dedicated young
humanists of ARA were still valiantly struggling to
stem the tide of suffering washing over the Volga
delta. They were determined to salvage at least the
children from the maw of starvation, and they were
not in a mood to be thwarted. Pavel constantly
brought home new stories of the "Amerikanski" who
refused to give up, despite the infuriating obstruc-
tionism of the top brass in the Russian liaison group.
In the safety of home Pavel could vent his own frustration over their tribulations.

"Again they diverted our freight cars in Moscow," he sputtered. "The crates are sitting at the central warehouse nearly three weeks now, and they
promised we'd have them last week at the very latest.

It's that Eiduk and his gang again. I know it. They just don't want the Amerikanski to do a good job when they couldn't do it themselves. They don't care that people die while they save face."

Alexander Eiduk was the plenipotentiary appointed by the Soviet Central Committee to be the liaison with all the foreign relief organizations working in Russia. Suspicious of ARA on general principles, he was also offended that the distribution had not been placed in Russian hands. His regional commissars understood that the more problems they created for the foreigners the better would be their standing with their boss.

"Can you imagine?" Pavel burst out one November evening as soon as he'd shut the door behind him. "They've arrested Ivanchuk and one of his inspectors, a woman, yet."

"Arrested?" the family chorused. "But why?"

"Ivanchuk?"

"How come?"

"What did they do?"

"Do?" Pavel spat the word in disgust. "Nothing, of course. They worked hard to help the Amerikanski, that's all. No reason was given. You think they need a reason? Ivanchuk is a good target, that's all. He's the top-ranking Russian on our distribution staff. He's a good boss, he gets things done. They don't want us to cooperate so well with the Amerikanski. That's the real reason they arrested him."

Tanya, always ready to see calamity lurking, clung to her husband. "Pavel, you must resign. They might take you next. If you went to prison — "

"Don't get upset, Tanyachka." As his wife's level of anxiety rose, Pavel's sank. "They won't take me. I'm not important enough. They've made their point now. They'll probably let those two go in a few days. The Americanski won't take this lying down. They'll fight back But it's hard." He sighed. "You want to do your best. So many people are desperate for this food. Yet our own government does nothing but put roadblocks . . . "

The same sort of thing was happening in a number of distribution centers, but Pavel's shrewd guess had been accurate. It wasn't long before the arrests were curbed. Pavel came home triumphant.

"I told you the Amerikanski would call their bluff. I was right. ARA announced publicly that all food distribution would be suspended until their workers were released. The authorities can't face the hullabaloo this would create. There'd be another revolution. Now Ivanchuk will be freed."

As Pavel predicted, it was soon determined that the "charges" were unfounded, and the prisoners were reinstated.

Obstructions created growing strains on the relief program until ARA Director Haskell finally confronted Kamenev himself — the all-powerful chairman of the Moscow Soviet and of the All-Russian Relief Committee — and pressured him into improving cooperation. Without it, Haskell promised, he would halt the entire ARA program, withdraw his workers, and publish the reasons for his action in damning detail throughout Europe.

Though it was many years later that I had the chance to read the reports of those relief workers in the Hoover Library at Stanford, the outraged comments of the idealistic young Americans who had been so frustrated in their life-saving work served to flesh out my own memories of those days of hope mixed with disappointment — and often despair. As a child I heard much and understood little of the political games that controlled our lives then, but at the Hoover Library much of my own history was clarified for me.

The Central Committee was having enough troubles dealing with a starving population and a bankrupt economy. It did not need American charges that it was denying relief. There had already been food strikes in Moscow protesting the drastic short-ages. Now the "Iron Broom" collectors were no longer able to feed the cities by requisitioning food. Farmers had nothing left to give — or even to eat. When even the sailors on the battleship Kronstadt mutinied, Lenin realized that he would have to loosen the reins in order to keep the Bolsheviks in power.

His solution was the New Economic Policy, NEP, which granted concessions and encouraged private enterprise. It even legalized free trade, and a tax in kind replaced the hated confiscation. When these re-forms were published, our family like thousands of others began to feel that hope might still be possible, that life might finally become a shade more livable, move a step away from despair.

Pavel carried each morsel of good news home like a present, announcing it at the supper table for dessert.

"Now maybe these terrible searches will stop," he reported happily one day, "because confiscation has been outlawed."

Of course he was over-optimistic. Night searches and spying went on as before. They were the heart of the Soviet system of control. Keeping people frightened and off balance made them easier to govern.

Still, little by little, things began to ease. The relief program now began to make some headway against the famine. Millions who had been barely surviving on inedible scraps began to revive, restored by rations of real flour, rice, beans, oatmeal and fat, even the forgotten luxuries of sugar and cocoa. Rickety children were given canned milk and cod liver oil. And the seasons turned, and with the rainy spring came the prospect of a new crop.

Our diet that winter had been as coarse and unpalatable as most people's, but we did not starve. Both Sonya and Pavel, like most salaried workers, were paid partly in food and fuel coupons, and Pavel's work with ARA entitled him to a staff ration. Best of all, in September Papa had reached New York. Frantic with worry at the reports of famine, he began sending a steady stream of packages, a number of which were actually delivered.

Pavel's assignment gave him a direct connection to the Food Remittance program. This inspired plan enlisted relatives and friends in the United States to help feed Russia's hungry people. Since Famine Relief was earmarked for the destitute, the new program was providential for families like ours, who still had some resources of their own and could not qualify for the original program.

"It's a miracle." Pavel exulted as he burst the door one November evening. "Those Amerikanski are so smart. Do you know what they've thought up now? They're distributing millions of postcards all over Russia, for people to mail to their relatives in America and Europe, appealing for help. A person in the U.S.A. can buy a monthly Food Draft for ten American dollars, they say, and ARA will deliver a big food package to his relatives in Russia. And such food — "

"You mean Adya can — " Sonya's sharp wits were the first to make the connection.

"Exactly." Pavel would not be sidetracked. "Listen. A package is going to have 49 pounds of flour, 25 pounds of rice, three pounds of tea — real tea — and ten pounds of sugar, too. Can you imagine? Oh, yes, and ten pounds of fat and 20 cans of preserved milk. A full diet, they call it. We haven't seen such a full diet in at least three years. And delivery will be much safer, not dependent on the postal service and its stealing. Now we're going to eat like people again, not like animals."

Babushka clasped her hands as if in prayer. "Milk. And rice. What kind of flour?" she asked anxiously.

Pavel grinned triumphantly. "White."

Tanya and Sonya hugged their mother in silent ecstasy, their minds all on one track. Zeyde would have food he could eat.

"When do you think the packages will start coming?" was the next question. Pavel was sure it wouldn't be long. "The cards are out already. I brought some home and we'll mail one today."

He was a bit optimistic. The hostility of the authorities and the dislocated transport system still created delays, and the Reds were busily spreading rumors blaming ARA for them. As people waited months to receive the packages they'd been alerted to expect, they felt sure they'd been cheated by the relief workers. Once again ARA threatened to cut off the Food Draft program entirely and publicly announce why it had failed. Only then did the authorities move to expedite transport. Finally, in February of 1922, regular deliveries began and quickly gained momentum. By September over a hundred thousand packages a month were being delivered.

Naturally Pavel saw to it that packages for our family were processed promptly. What a thrill it was when we gathered around the first big carton, opening each separate package, rhapsodizing over the fine white flour, the clean shiny rice. We children stuck surreptitious fingers into the sugar. We had forgotten the luscious sensation of its sweetness. Everybody inhaled the rich pungent smell of the cocoa delivered in place of the missing tea.

"They're trying to find out what happened to the tea," Pavel shrugged. "It was listed in the shipment that left the border, but it never arrived in Samara." He grinned at the innocence of the Amerikanski. "Of course someone important in Moscow wanted it and arranged to get it off the train. It's just a waste of time to try to track it down. At least, I'm glad they didn't hold up distribution till they found it. How many years is it since we had good cocoa like this? Doesn't it smell delicious?"

Babushka didn't give them too much time to gloat. "Come on, Tanya, let's get everything into the pantry. I want to make Papa some rice pudding right away. How he'll enjoy it, with milk and sugar. I wish I had some raisins to put in. Tomorrow we'll bake some white bread for him. What beautiful flour." She sighed sadly. "I feel a little guilty, having all this wonderful food when all around us people have nothing. Maybe we could — "

"Now, Mama," Sonya warned her. "You know this has to last us a whole month. We could use some of it for barter too, for vegetables and other things we need."

"I know, I know." Babushka sighed. This was her personal cross to bear during the famine. Never before in her long life had she been forced to choose between charity and her family's survival.

By April, when it was time to begin preparing for the Passover, the family had pretty well recovered its health and vitality. Zeyde's abused digestion, coddled on rice puddings and white bread and milk, was performing reasonably well. He was putting on a little weight and sleeping more comfortably. We children began to throw off our sniffles and coughs and rashes. Babushka was all smiles at the thought of being able to prepare something like a proper Seder. The early thaw even gave her hopes of being able to trade some oatmeal or sugar for a nice fish from the river and a couple of eggs.

Papa was sending packages in Olga's name as well as Babushka's, and with ample supplies of the precious white flour there was enough to invite two Jewish neighbor families, the Popkins and the Abramovitches, to participate in the holiday meal. Now on this rainy evening all the women were absorbed in the tricky job of baking matzos for the communal Seder.

Something like a semblance of normal life seeped into the warm kitchen where the huge white-washed stove, its fire banked for even baking, sat like a benign idol. Two of its priestesses alternately fed the thin cakes into its red maw on long-handled wooden paddles and withdrew the crisp browned matzos, while the others rolled and shaped the dough. As we children came rushing in from our supper, we too were given small chores. I was awarded the coveted task of rolling the little perforator along in parallel lines.

"Be sure to keep the rows straight, darling." Babushka warned me, concerned for my first public baking success as well as for the precious matzos. "We want to be able to break the pieces evenly."

Carefully guiding the wayward wheel, my tongue tucked in the corner of my mouth in concentration, I was happily anticipating the Seder. I still dimly remembered the ritual meals of former times, with candles in Babushka's heirloom candlesticks and the best damask tablecloth, and the delicious fragrances of holiday food. Zeyde, son of a rabbi, chanted the traditional Haggadah. It had been a long time since it was possible to have a real Seder.

Now it would be like old times. The children

were even going to be allowed a sip of the precious sacramental wine that was Leonid's contribution to the feast. The only thing lacking would be Papa.

Yet by the time the Passover arrived, I sat at the long table — opened with all its leaves to accommodate all the families, crowding the dining room nearly to the walls — with my mind filled with a new idea. This was to be my last Seder at Babushka's table.

In place of Papa, we had a letter with his holiday wishes, and an astounding piece of news. His mother's instinct had been sound. Her son loved America, especially New York. He wanted to settle there instead of going on to Europe. He wanted Mamma and me to come to America.

"You'd better go to Moscow as soon as you can and apply for an exit visa," he wrote, "because it may take a while. I hear the central Cheka Bureau is the only one that issues them. Couldn't you stay with Luba's family? I don't see any hope of having a decent life in Russia for a long time, if ever. And here in America there are so many more opportunities than in Europe.

"I've gone into business with my cousin Barney. We are importing toys and novelties from Germany, and we're doing pretty well already. Tell Niurochka I have a beautiful new doll waiting to meet her.

"I'm going to night school to learn English. They have free classes for everything. It's a wonderful country, America. You'll love it here, Olenka. Hurry and come.

"You'll probably have to go to Latvia to get a decent ship, so I'll send your ticket or money for your passage to your cousin Amelia in Riga, to hold for you until you get there. Let me know how you progress. And hurry, hurry! I miss you both."

Though Babushka was not really surprised,

Mamma was overwhelmed and terrified. Such a journey, across a whole ocean! She had prepared herself for the ordeal of taking a train to France, or Switzerland or Germany, all familiar from her student days. She was at home anywhere in Europe. But to cross the Atlantic, alone with her child, to a strange country far from any place she had ever known. Could she really do it? And the idea of facing the dreaded Cheka, where so many people had disappeared without a trace.

Even the Soviets were trying to counter its sinister image by renaming it. Now it was known as GPU, but not much else had changed. The internal police organization had a number of departments for ordinary bureaucratic functions. One of these was the Department of Foreign Passports, the one Mamma would leave to deal with. But the idea of entering Cheka headquarters was enough to strike dread into stauncher hearts than hers.

Yet after the Passover celebration, made poignant for us all by the sense of finale, Mamma's solitary thoughts and long discussions with Sonya could lead to only one conclusion. She had to go if she and I were to have any hope of a real family life again. Without a husband she could only hang on as an extra burden in the crowded household. She longed to be with Adya again, and to reunite her child with its father. Yet her heart shrank, and not only in fear of the unknown dangers of the long trip.

"So much has happened to us both," she worried to Sonya. "I'm sure Adya and I are both very different people now. How will we find each other?"

Sonya of course had little patience with such subtleties. "Olya, you're just borrowing trouble. Adya loves you. And you love him too, you know you do. You are husband and wife. And you've waited so long to be together again and have your family life. Of course you must go."

Suddenly aware that she was pushing, Sonya took a deep breath and began again, more gently. "Life in America will be so much easier for you, Olya dear. It won't exhaust you as the awful pressures of our life here do. You really ought to take advantage of this chance to get out of Russia while you can. Because until things get straightened out," she added loyally, still trying to believe in the future, "life here will be very hard, probably for some years yet. Why should you and Niurochka have to endure it when you have a chance to leave? If it were me, I'd go in a minute."

"I know." Olga admitted. "I've really made up my mind to go, if I can get a visa. But I can't help thinking . . . "

In spite of the black thoughts, she applied for a travel permit to go to Moscow and wrote to Luba's mother. Aunt Zoya's husband was a career government functionary, one of the breed of bureaucrats who know how to make themselves indispensable to the authorities. He had been transferred from Samara early in the war and Olga had not seen them since then. But Aunt Zoya was happy to help a niece who had always been a favorite, whose marriage she had promoted and could now help restore. She wrote that she and Uncle Maxim, still in possession of their apartment in Moscow, had a small maid's room now used for storage, and kindly put it at our disposal for as long as needed.

While awaiting her travel permit, Mamma concentrated on the gargantuan task of preparing to leave. Her mind buzzed with the endless details that must be arranged.

She must sort out all our belongings, and make the inevitable decisions. What to take, what to leave behind. How to make the right choices, to di-

vide a life's accoutrements, to overlook none of the
necessities, to discard all the precious fripperies? Trying hard to be practical, Olga sold the bigger valuables and devised ways of stowing small treasures to
comfort her in her alien new world. She mended the
clothes we would take and gave away all she thought
she could spare to the family. They might have to
wait years before they could buy new things. She
could replenish our wardrobe in New York.

All through the solitary hours of planning and
sorting and packing, her confused feelings ran rampant. So many black fears dueled with the timid
hopes that happiness might still be possible for her.
The thought of Adya's tenderness reassured her. But
when she looked in her mirror, she was afraid. I would
see her sitting at her dressing table staring at her
frowning face for long minutes.

Even now I can imagine the fears she struggled
with. How would this thin dejected woman with the
deep-shadowed eyes, the lips pressed tight from years
of tension, be able to hold the exuberant man she
remembered, who loved a girl's slender grace and
dark elegance? He will be disappointed, but he won't
admit it, she tormented herself. He'll live with me
out of pity, not love. But my child has a right to be
with her father, and to an easy life in America. Olga's
mind touched the word, kept exploring the idea of
America tentatively, like a tongue probing a sensi-
tive cavity, afraid it will hurt, but unable to leave it
alone.

All she had ever read about life in the new
world was alarming. Its crude energy, its pushy
progress, the passion of its people to build and make
fortunes, to be the biggest, the strongest, the rich-
est. It was all too formidable for her. She felt she
could never be at home in the raw "city of the future," as Adya had called New York. She would have

preferred the age-mellowed charm of a Vienna, a Budapest, a Zurich. But she knew her husband must love it. Its character surely suited his own vitality and drive.

Living in New York might be like living with Adya, she imagined. It might be that he and the city would stir her sluggish pulses to life once more, as he had in their early days. Perhaps we'll have another honeymoon, she tried to hope. Perhaps there will be joy and laughter and excitement again. We're still young, I'm not 35 yet, we can still have years.

She made herself think of walking new streets with Adya, laughing and looking at store windows. I will be hopeful, she told herself. I won't worry. Energetically she attacked another box. We'll get the trip over with, and then . . .

The trip. Her heart sank again as she remembered the pitfalls that lay in her way, and the black thoughts rose to plague her again. That stormy sea — I'm such a bad sailor. I was even seasick on our wedding trip up the Volga, that windy day when the steamer pitched and tilted. What will it be like on the Atlantic in a storm? What will happen to my child if I get really sick? And just to get our visa . . . She could imagine the endless days of waiting to see officials, of arguing and pleading, of filling out endless forms.

Thus she worried and worked through the weeks of waiting, nervous and uneasy, wishing she could get it all over with, yet shrinking from the prospect. But with the help of the entire household she managed it all at last. The packing, the selling, the travel permit, arranging for the train trip, writing letters and sending wires.

Meanwhile I also spent the long days of waiting in a confusion of feelings. I was torn between the anticipation of seeing Papa and the adventure of travel on the one hand, and on the other the sad thought that I was leaving my whole life behind — everything and almost everybody that made up my world.

Now that the dangerous dark days of winter had given way to the safer sunshine of spring, and relief efforts had made the hungry less desperate, now that Mamma was too preoccupied to worry about me every minute, I could wander about the town with Mara, saying my goodbyes to all the familiar places I knew I would not see again, ever. I'd heard of many people who had gone to America, but never of one who had come back.

The two of us, determined to spend our last days alone together, became adept at slipping away from Ara and disappearing before he missed us. Leaving Mara was going to be very hard, I was coming to realize. My favorite playmate all my life, by now he had become chief confidant and fellow explorer of an enlarging world. His ranging mind and adventurous heart matched my own. It became important to share all my new thoughts and dreams with him while I still could.

Hand in hand we wandered the streets uptown and down, talking, talking . . . Mara envied me my coming adventure. "What do you think Moscow will be like?" He slung a stone at a rusting park sign. "I wish I could see it."

"I wish you could too. But you will. I know you will." I wanted him to believe in his own adventures to come. "I bet you'll go there to university."

"I want to. I want to be an engineer, to build bridges and roads. I want to cover all the muddy roads with concrete, to build big buildings so people can have good places to live." Mara always dreamt big. "I want them to be warm, with lots of windows. What do you want to be when you grow up, Niurok?"

This was a big decision. I pondered it as we swung on the branches of the lime trees in the park. "What do I want to be? I want something to do with books. I love books so much. Maybe in New York I could work in a library. Do you think . . . ?"

"I wish I could see New York. You must write me about New York, and about Moscow, and specially about the ocean. About everything!" He skipped ahead along the path, turning to face me. "Maybe you could write books?"

"Oh, what a wonderful idea! I would love to write books." I hugged Mara in delight. "You must learn English, so you can read them. I'll send them to you. And you must send me pictures of your bridges and buildings." I stopped short. "Oh, Mara, we won't see each other. Will you forget me? I'll never forget you."

"I'll never forget you, Niurok. Do you think we'll ever see each other again?"

"We must. Mara, don't marry anybody else. I won't."

"I won't either. I'll wait for you. Will you come back when you're grown up?"

"If I can." I had a happier thought. "Maybe you can come to New York. Try to come, Mara." I patted his arm. "What will you do when I'm gone?"

"Oh, I guess I'll play with Ara now. He'll like that. But I hope they let me go to school next winter. Then I'll make new friends there." He put an awkward arm around my shoulder. "But you'll always be my best friend, Niurok." Embarrassed by his own emotion, he ran ahead. "Let's go see my old house across the park. Come on."

I followed sadly through the avenue of limes, dressed in tender new green among the dismal flowerbeds filled with last year's dead weeds. I knew in my heart that there was no way to weld the bond that (the fear lay unspoken in both our hearts) would be broken by distance.

"All right, and then let's go see my old house too, and go down by the river."

The yellow house was turning a dingy gray. A broken window was boarded up and the ornamental ironwork was rusting. It did not seem at all like my dear home. But across the street, the lilacs were swelling once more, bringing memories of those happy springs lost long ago.

We cheered up when we got to the river and skipped along the esplanade. "Look, Mara, see the Volga."

"Hurrah! It's in full flood. See it splashing up against the hills." Mara pointed across the river.

"And it's splashing so hard against the stone walls down here." I looked over the wall to the abutments below. "There must be so much water coming down." I was thrilled. The overflowing river promised a renewed fertility, an end to famine. "I know this will be a better year. I know it will."

The sinking sun was spreading its red and gold across the Volga.

Mara took my hand and sighed. "I guess we'd better go back."

We climbed our hill, back to the home I was leaving. Mara gave me his treasured colored postcard of Ivan Tsarevich as a memento. I gave him my pink marble egg that looked like dawn.

How hard it was for me to imagine never walking these streets again, to think that another, very different, place was to be my hometown. How much harder still to imagine life without Mara. Without dear Aunt Sonya, my role model. Without Babushka's lap to climb into. Without the tight family circle that was my citadel. There will be Papa, I thought, and there will be Mamma and me, of course. But around us three there will be only strangers. How will it be when it's just us?

Inexorably the day arrived when we had to leave. Everything was ready. The huge straw trunk packed and roped, the suitcases filled, the tickets bought. Babushka had cooked and packed the food for the journey. The wagon arrived to take us to the station. Nothing remained but the goodbyes.

Now I began to feel the real pain of parting, effacing the excitement of adventure ahead. Tightly clutching Mishka, I stared hard at the family gathered around the wagon, trying to stamp their faces on my mind forever. Even old Nyanya had come that day to give "her child" a last fierce hug and a whispered plea. "Don't forget me, my little one."

Everyone had to have a last hug and kiss, while the wagon driver sat grumbling that we would miss the train. By the time the wagon was finally in motion, both Mamma and I were too blinded by tears to catch the last glimpse of the sad faces, the waving hands, the familiar street, and the worn stoop of the house that had sheltered us through the hard years.

At the station we sat guard on the pile of luggage until the Moscow express, remarkably only an hour late today, came puffing in. Days before, Olga had a long conference with the station master about getting the heavy luggage to Moscow, and had been assured, in return for one of Papa's good suits, that he would see it and us safely aboard.

Olga's nerves were twanging like a harp long before the train arrived. I stroked her trembling hands, whispering over and over, "It's all right, Mamushka, don't cry. The train will be here soon. Then we'll be in Moscow, and Luba's Mamma will take care of you. You'll see. We'll go to America, and Papa will be there, and everything will be all right.

You'll see. Don't cry. The train will be here soon." Like a litany to reassure us both and keep the tears at bay, "Everything will be all right. You'll see. Don't cry, Mamma."

The years since Papa's departure had reinforced my resilience. I knew things would go well sooner or later, for I had told Mamma so many times that they would.

When the express pulled in at last, the stationmaster, true to his word, found us an empty space in what had once been a compartment. The seats and door had long ago been ripped out by rampaging troops. Even the overhead luggage racks were sagging and useless. But there was enough room for everything but the big straw trunk, and we arranged ourselves in reasonable comfort by sitting on the leather suitcases. We might even manage a nap on our bundle of bedding tied up in a sheet. The trunk was safely stowed by the crew in their own compartment, with directions not to unload it until we arrived in Moscow. The tracks followed the river on its westward leg before crossing the narrows at Syzran.

When the bustle of boarding and getting settled was over, when the train finally pulled out and picked up speed, Mamma's resolve finally collapsed. Leaning her head on the dusty windowsill beside her, she let the tears come. I'm sure she mourned the loss of the life she knew, hard to bear as it had been, and surrendered to the dread of all the unknown trials to come. The letdown after the long busy weeks when she'd driven herself to prepare for this trip, to remember everything, to gather her courage and beat down terror, had exhausted her. She was wrung out. I soon persuaded her to lie down on the bedding and try to sleep.

Luckily traveling conditions had improved somewhat since Mamma had gone looking for vegetables at the Karsavins. The rolling stock was still deteriorating and the schedules were hardly more dependable, but the horrendous crowds of refugees that once filled every corner of a train were gone now.

The end of the civil war and the famine in the Volga delta had served to put an end to the desperate movement of people. The few remnants of starving refugees now clung to their corners in the cities where relief was filtering through to them. The long hunger had drained vitality to the point where to stay put was easier than to move. Besides, no one was allowed to travel any more without an official permit.

In any case, the train now had more space than passengers. Though the "express" often halted for hours, occasionally at stations, mostly in open country, and three days would pass before it covered the 700 miles to Moscow, at least we had the compartment to ourselves for the most part. A large family got on at Kovulkino and tried to squeeze in, grumbling about the space taken by our luggage. Luckily the oldest son soon came running back to say he had found an empty compartment in the next car.

It was only at Ryazan that a countrywoman with a baby and a bundle came in and, half apologetically, half defiantly, made herself comfortable in a corner. Since by this time both Mamma and I were in a fog of fatigue after two days on the rails, this invasion was hardly noticed, even by Mamma, whose intense need for privacy was often an irritant.

She spent her waking hours sitting on her suitcase, leaning against the wall in a dejected lethargy, hardly rousing herself to reply to a direct question, lost in painful thoughts and worries. She held a book in her lap, but only rarely thought to turn a page. At intervals she would remember that I must be tired, hungry, bored or impatient, and would exert herself to perform a mother's tasks. We would eat some of the cold snacks Babushka had provided, or take a nap on our bedding sack – me with my head on Mishka's familiar stomach — or look at one of my books together. Babushka's foresight in packing a chamber pot in our carryall relieved us of the need to visit the filthy washroom at the end of the car more than once or twice a day.

Whenever the train stopped at a station, village women in shawls and bark shoes would be selling tea or *kumyss* or hot blini or pirogi. We'd drink the scalding tea thirstily, eat the warm food gratefully. It might be many hours before another chance came to vary our cold fare.

As my mother sank deeper into apathy, I worked harder to rouse her interest. "Tell me about Moscow." I pleaded. "Is it very *very* big? Bigger than Samara?"

She would smile at the provincial limit of my experience. The effort to paint the wonders of the metropolis would animate her, but only briefly. Soon she would grow tired and still again, leaving me to my window gazing and imaginings of the city I'd heard about all my life as the hub of our world.

Always avid for new sights, I spent most of the time with my nose pressed to the window, pointing out to Mishka villages or farms or rivers or forests — any variation in the vista of rolling plain sliding endlessly past. As we went west the flat steppe became more hilly, and there were more forests. Out of the forests ran streams whose dark waters were stained brown with peat from the bogs and marshes. Small streams joined bigger ones until at last the waters poured into a broad river sparkling in the sun as it ran toward a distant sea.

In the vast earth and immense sky, occasional changes in the redundant landscape were a gift to the benumbed eye: the blue bubble dome of a church rising above the trees, a small lake shining in dark woods, an outbreak of red sandstone or granite in a sudden brief uprearing, a woodcutters' village with huge piles of split wood around the low gray *izbas* with their painted shutters and potted geraniums. Each was a boon to be treasured as long as it remained in sight. Even a meadow bright with the vivid flowers of spring — cowslips and celandine, the bright trailing bird cherry and the yellow globeflower — made a gay exclamation point in the soft colors of the countryside.

A wagon full of wood, a rowboat on a lake, a boy waving at a crossing. I stared in fascination at every sign of life, my imagination sparked. "Look, Mishka. That boy might be running away from a cruel stepmother . . . Maybe that boat is carrying a doctor on a lifesaving mission . . . Do you think that cart is bringing wood to town to trade for a chest for the driver's bride?"

Eager to share my impressions, I was constantly turning to my mother. "Look, Mamma, how pretty those trees look in the sunshine. They remind me of the lime trees in the park at home, don't you think?"

And a few minutes later, "We went over a long bridge, Mamma. The water looked so muddy. There must have been lots of rain here. Isn't that good?"

Anything that might create a diversion from the unending clickety-clack of the train wheels, the monotone of the early flies droning about the ceiling, the droop of Mamma's head bent over the same page mile after mile.

After a second wearisome night spent in restless snatches of sleep, punctuated by long hours of wakeful tossing on our lumpy bundle, both of us were nearly at the end of our strength. But the sight of pretty dachas and villages nestling in pine and birch woods sparked a little of my normal enthusiasm. Finally, beyond the villages, the golden domes of Moscow gleamed in the sun, like a mammoth jeweled cluster ringed by small pearls.

"We're here, Mamma! Look at Moscow. See." I shook my mother's thin shoulder urgently. "Mamushka, look. Our trip is almost over already. Soon we'll be in New York. Soon we'll see Papa."

⪉ *8* ⪊

A City Summer

Moscow, 1922

MOSCOW! When Mamma and I arrived on a sunny May morning, the teeming metropolis was a revelation to me, whose idea of a city was provincial Samara. I had never seen such wide boulevards, such imposing public buildings, such elegant mansions. My untutored eye found it all beautiful. I didn't notice the dirty streets, the shabbiness of the fine old houses. The air of bustle and business stirred me, and even energized Mamma.

Aunt Zoya, with many apologies, showed us to the little room behind the kitchen. It was a welcome haven to my exhausted mother. Clean, quiet and private, it was more than she had dared hope for. She hardly knew how to express her gratitude without dissolving in tears.

Kind Aunt Zoya, realizing that her niece was perilously close to exhaustion, soon persuaded her into the white iron bed to recuperate from her journey. Cousin Luba, whom I remembered unfondly from her visit to Samara, was delegated to take me for a walk. She showed me the nearby park and the Moskva River which ran through the city.

Though the park was to become our second home, it didn't make much of an impression at first. It was large and beautiful, with avenues of trees and flowers in bloom, but it lacked the homey untidiness of the park at home where Mara and I used to play. It was just a park. But the river was just the opposite, a nice small river with the Kremlin on one side and streets and houses on the other. It was nothing like the broad Volga I knew so well, but it wound through the city so that it was sure to turn up unexpectedly now and then on our walks. It seemed a friendly little river.

As soon as Mamma was rested, and had made her application for a passport and exit visa, she eagerly set out to show me the city she remembered fondly from her student days. At first it was a sad reunion. The broad Bulvar, which she remembered as a gay concourse of elegant carriages and fashionable people, was dingy and littered. The sunshine spotlighted the peeling paint on the pastel house fronts, the spreading cracks in the pavements. Broken windows were nailed over, or stuffed with rags. Here and there water oozed from cellar windows, a sign of broken pipes within. Just as in Samara, there was an inescapable air of neglect and disrepair of places, of things and of people. Mamma's spirits sank visibly again.

Still we spent many of the bright spring days wandering about the city. The rows of apartment houses along the boulevards were classic and lovely in their fading yellows, greens, pinks and blues. The ornate mansions along the sun-dappled river drowsed behind their crumbling garden walls. I was entranced by the gorgeous palaces and churches inside the thick red brick walls of the Kremlin, the fantastic fairytale cupolas of St. Basil's Cathedral in the huge square outside it. This Red Square, an ancient marketplace always known as *"krasnoye,"* was now the regime's main parade ground and gathering place. And it was aptly named, since the word means "beautiful" as well as "red."

In my imagination, long steeped in folk tales and romances, every ancient courtyard and crenellated battlement of the citadel evoked a vision. I could see Ivan Tsarevich riding his wolf triumphantly through the high gateway in its massive wall, a swan boat gliding beneath the willows on the sparkling river, dragons lurking in the shadows of imagined dungeons beneath the towers.

Now that the Kremlin belonged to the people, it had become the greatest attraction in Moscow. In Olga's student days its palaces and cathedrals had been the domain of the nobles, the tsar and his administrators, even though the capital was then in Petrograd. Lenin had moved the seat of government to Moscow, and the Kremlin was now the heart of the new regime.

The first time we walked through the tunnel formed by a vaulted aperture in the twelve-foot-thick wall of the fortress, I gripped Mamma's hand nervously and shrank closer to her side. The dim light threw long shadows on the worn cobblestones. The brick around us had been blackened by the smoke of countless fires lit by the homeless who sheltered in the tunnel. Along the walls stood haggard people hopefully holding out bits of old embroidery or worn clothing, baskets of beads, combs, bric-a-brac. Whatever might be of value to someone and would buy them bread. Under the protecting arch they were out of the wind and rain, but within reach of visitors to the Kremlin's glories.

How much they reminded us of the poor refugees who huddled in the alleys of Samara. Mamma's eyes softened in pity. She could see by their once-elegant outdated dress, the haunting delicacy of their timid manners, that these had once been gentry. Shuddering, as she thought how easily one of these wretches could be herself, she bought me some colored pencils from a woman with a child at her side, a girl almost my age.

I smiled at her, but she just stared. I wondered what it would be like to be her, to have to stand by my mother for hours, hoping someone would buy something so we could eat. How pleasant our life seemed by comparison. I squeezed Mamma's hand in gratitude that I was not the girl in the tunnel. She smiled at me, not understanding, but pleased to know that I was happy.

One day we took a tram up into the hills, where we could look down on the panorama of the vast city. The Sparrow Hills, once an imperial forest that sheltered the palaces of nobles, were now a picturesque desolation of overgrown gardens fast reverting to woods, ruined orchards, a cluster of once-gilded domes high on a wooded slope. Lilacs and wild crabapples were in bloom. In the woods nightingales trilled their liquid notes.

We wandered through the arcades of GUM, the enormous department store that faced the Kremlin across the expanse of Red Square. Though many of the stalls were shuttered and bare, a number of merchants, encouraged by the NEP, were trying to stay in business with pathetic displays of the few things they could still find to sell. But since we weren't really shopping, this hardly mattered.

Once Mamma took me to visit the university where she had studied, and told me stories of her own student life. And we loved to stroll along the sunlit river, where we watched the busy traffic just as we once used to do along the Volga.

The treat I remember most was our visit to the

Moscow Art Theatre. The play was a children's matinee of "The Blue Bird," Maeterlinck's sentimental fairy tale, the first live theatre I had ever seen. The allegory of two children's quest for the bluebird of happiness moved me deeply. Wasn't my own long journey to find Papa just such a quest?

I was enchanted by the brilliant costumes and sets, charmed by the rollicking antics of the metaphoric characters: ominous Night and adorable Milk, Sugar breaking off his long fingers for the hungry pilgrims to suck. The entire spectacle captivated me. Like the first time I had read a real book, a new door into the world opened to me. My only complaint was that I could not enjoy a play over and over, as I went back repeatedly to reread favorite stories.

As the weeks added together to make months, as summer came on and the days turned hot, the fine edge of our enjoyment frayed. Though Uncle Maxim's sage advice had guided her past a number of bottlenecks and dead ends, Mamma's applications were still grinding their slow way through the ill-meshing gears of the bureaucratic machine, with no hint of when they might be approved. She went regularly to the passport bureau, waited for hours to get a five-minute interview with a brusque clerk who shuffled endlessly through piles of papers. Just as regularly, he would dismiss her with a laconic "Nothing new to report."

Once he varied his routine with a slight effort to explain. "The commissar is away, but we expect him back next week. Come back in ten days. We might have some news then." But when she returned there was still no progress.

Still clear in my memory is the droop of her mouth as she returned home from these visits. Occasionally she was required to fill out an additional form that had been overlooked or added to the regulations, or to explain an entry, or correct a minute "inaccuracy." Each time she would begin to hope that now the last obstacle to progress had been removed. Yet each time there was only a return to the old routines, waiting for the approval that never came, more futile inquiries at the bureau, like pebbles dropped down a bottomless well to sink silently into a void.

After three months the passport was finally issued. But the relief was short-lived. We still needed an exit visa, so the waiting routine began all over again. Olga's precarious patience was frayed to tatters. The visit that had started so happily now became more and more trying. The generous offer of houseroom, presumably for a few weeks, perhaps a month at most, was becoming, at least to her acute sensibilities, the endurance of an intrusion that might continue indefinitely. How much longer would Uncle Maxim be tolerant of the extra mouths at his table, especially of the presence in his orderly adult household of an exuberant child who skipped about, talked loud, and bumped into things? The ARA packages that came regularly from Papa seemed a small recompense. Yet there was nowhere else we could go.

The household that we had innocently invaded was socially and politically allied to the new ruling powers. Uncle Maxim was that rare bird, a bureaucratic genius. He knew how to run with the hare and hunt with the hounds so well that he had managed to enhance his official status while others were losing jobs, homes, and sometimes lives. He was indispensable to the work of the export bureau, which brought in the foreign currency that was lifeblood to the bankrupt economy.

He had even artfully managed to convince the housing authorities that his drawing room was essential for the entertainment of foreign capitalists who came to Moscow to buy or invest. Olga was amazed to see that the spacious apartment, in a handsome building on the Bulvar near Serebryany, was as elegant as those she had visited in her student days, and had no additional tenants.

In these last years, when everything had broken down, been confiscated or was worn out, when homes were only precarious shelters from the weather, stuffed with humanity and hoarded possessions, it seemed incredible to find these spacious rooms intact in the very heart of upheaval. On her arrival, Mamma stood speechless in the doorway, staring in delight at the ordered luxury she had once known. She had no idea such a home could still exist anywhere in her benighted country. But Aunt Zoya explained smugly that her husband's work with buyers from abroad required a "showcase" of the stability of life in the new Union of Soviet Socialist Republics.

"Enjoy it." She waved expansively at the brocade sofas and needlepoint chairs, at the heavy velvet portieres and delicate Sevres ornaments on the mantel. "I know how much you always loved beautiful things, and I was sorry to hear that you lost your own home. Luba wrote me when she visited you how lovely it was."

The roomy flat easily held the family of four. Their son Mark was a junior deputy in his father's bureau and spent most of his time traveling in search of exportable goods. Luba's engagement two years before had ended badly when her fiancé's parents were arrested for counterrevolutionary activity. She stayed on at home, bitterly resentful of her father's arbitrary decision to break off the match for political expediency, yet with nowhere else to go. Her always capricious temper grew shorter and surlier as the years went by and eligible men became ever scarcer.

Looking back now on that haphazard waiting

life, without the structured everydayness of Babushka's house, with nothing to use up my abundant energies and no firm hand to keep them in control, I can see why I was growing restless and capricious as well. Too young to discipline myself and too strong-willed to be restrained by my unhappy mother's sporadic efforts, a once-biddable child was turning into a moody, thoughtless daydreamer. I bickered over small matters and seemed to take a particular delight in irritating Luba, whom I had disliked ever since her visit to Samara.

That frustrated young woman was nursing a growing resentment over the frequent child-care chores delegated to her by necessity. Her mother, between daily shopping forays to feed her family, and the social demands on a bureaucrat's wife, was seldom at home during the day. So whenever Mamma had to go out on passport business, it was Luba who was commandeered to take care of me; an infuriating fact in itself, pointing out as it did the unimportance of her status.

On one such day, when Olga was trying to see the first deputy commissioner, I was again left in the unenthusiastic care of Luba. While we were eating a cold pick-up lunch in the parlor, Luba, not feeling obliged to entertain as well as feed me, was leafing through an old illustrated journal. Bored and fidgety, I wandered listlessly around the room, humming one of Nyanya's old folk songs and munching on a cold cutlet, my mind miles away in Samara. On a hot summer day like this, Mara and I would be down by the river, our sandals hidden under the porch steps, running barefoot along the esplanade or hanging over the parapet to watch the fishermen land their catch on the shore below.

"Niura, stop that." Luba's petulant tone broke into my reverie. "Stop throwing meat on the floor."

"Oh, sorry, Cousin Luba." Coming back to reality, I became aware that as I found stringy tendons that could not be chewed up, I was spitting them out. "I wasn't thinking." I apologized. But in a few minutes I again unconsciously cleared a meat string from between my teeth and dropped it. Twice more Luba scolded me, with growing irritation. The second time she did not merely scold.

"If you do that again, Niura, I'll . . . " Looking around, she saw Mishka propped in the corner of the sofa. "I'll throw that bear out the window," she threatened in a temper.

"Oh, no, Luba. Please. I won't do it again." I shuddered at the terrible idea. I took up a book and sat down by Mishka to be good. But in ten minutes, I again began to fidget. Still reading, I got up and took another cutlet from the plate. Again the dry stringy tendons stubbornly resisted my teeth, and unthinkingly I removed one from my mouth and let it fall.

In an instant, Luba rose in a fury from her seat and grabbing Mishka rushed to the open window and hurled him out.

"I warned you." she screamed, venting how many angers and disappointments on one handy scapegoat.

Frozen in shock, I gasped, then shrieked "No, no." But it was too late. I rushed to the tall casement, hung out over the narrow balcony, seeking a glimpse of my darling on the busy boulevard. All I could see was a kaleidoscope of moving people and vehicles, with not a bit of caramel yellow plush.

"Mishka," I wailed. "Mishka."

I imagine the heartbreak in my voice broke through the red haze in Luba's brain. Too late she realized the cataclysmic result of her rage, even as her body began to relax. She had not really meant to deprive me totally of my favorite toy, only to teach a lesson, she told herself. Now she was ready to relent.

"I told you what would happen . . . " she began sententiously. But I was already gone — down the hall, scrabbling to open the heavy front door, dashing down the long flight of stairs to the foyer. Luba hurried after me.

Perhaps three minutes had passed since Mishka's fall. But there was no sign of him. He could only have fallen on the wide sidewalk directly below our window, or possibly out into the roadway beyond.

But he was not there. Not along the curb, not in the small recess around the cellar window, not squashed by passing wheels in the road. It seemed impossible for a shabby toy, of no value to anyone else but priceless to me, to disappear so completely, so rapidly.

Luba stood out in the street, turning around and around in puzzlement. The bear must be somewhere. I, on the other hand, having run into every corner and searched every crevice, had already realized that Mishka was really gone. I knew I would never see him again.

With a lead weight where my heart should be, I turned and went back into the house without a word. In the finality of my loss I could not cry. Woodenly I went back up the stairs and into the apartment. In the little room at the back I sat down on the bed, shut up alone with a sadness I could not deal with, but could not turn away from, filled with a pain of loss too big for my body.

Finally giving up the search, Luba ran panting back upstairs, anxious to console me. Now that her temper had vented and her mind had cleared, she knew how much my punishment had exceeded the crime. Seeing the parlor empty, she came to look for me in the back room.

"I can't imagine what could have happened to the bear," she began contritely. "There was really no time for anyone to steal it. Unless it landed on top of a wagon or taxi going by . . . I only wanted to teach you a lesson." Even to her the words sounded inadequate. "I didn't mean to," she tried again, only to fall silent before the wall of stony silence. "I'm sorry, Niurochka," was all that seemed worth saying. Helplessly she went away.

It seemed to me as if a part of me had been torn away. I could find no way to adjust to Mishka's absence. I couldn't even understand why the loss was so overwhelming. I only knew that I hurt, that my arms felt an emptiness no doll, no pillow, not even Mamma, could fill. It was too big a pain to be dealt with by anger, by petulance, even by tears. I could only shut it up inside myself and mourn my friend alone. I moved silently about the house, speaking only when spoken to, and to Luba not at all. Nobody understood that Mishka was not a toy but a brother as real to me as one of flesh and blood. When I looked at Luba I saw a murderer.

Then, just as time was beginning its healing work, I came down with whooping cough, the first serious illness I could remember. In the first bad days of raging fever and tearing spasms of coughing, I had no thought for anything but survival. The doctor came but there was little he could do. No drugs existed that could conquer the bacterial infection, and even soothing nostrums were in desperately short supply in the depleted city.

"Keep her quiet and as cool as possible," was all he could prescribe. "Cool wet cloths on her head and sponge baths will make her more comfortable. And give her warm drinks to soothe her throat. If her system can just tolerate the fever until the crisis is past, she'll come out of it pretty well," was all the dubious comfort he offered Mamma. In those days of raging epidemics and low resistance, doctors made no rash promises.

The misery of those days has faded, but I still remember how awful it was. Hour after hour my mother sat by the white iron bed in the stuffy little room, changing cloths, offering sips, holding my hot hand, while in a semiconscious stupor, I tossed uneasily or muttered snatches about Papa or Mishka or Little Eva. For three days she could hardly be persuaded to take a short rest on the sofa while Zoya or Luba took her place.

Later she admitted, "Your illness seemed the final calamity. Deep in my heart lay the fear that I would have to go to Papa alone."

At last, late on the third day, my hot dry skin turned clammy and the heavy sweats began. Slowly the crisis passed and, drained yet undamaged, I emerged from the soggy sheets and lay exhausted in Mamma's arms. Now I could sleep and begin to rebuild my strength.

During my convalescence, restless and fretful, too weak to play yet too fidgety to rest, I felt all over again the loss of my lifelong companion. Mishka would have shared and comforted the hours that went by so slowly. I would have told him stories out of my favorite books, planned how we would meet Papa, imagined what the ocean would be like. Everything was so much harder, so much less fun, without him — my other self, with whom I could communicate in absolute freedom, who understood and approved totally, never criticizing and demanding nothing.

Mamma, sensing my need, worked hard to distract and amuse her listless child. In her relief at my recovery, she ignored her own fatigue and frailty. She spent long hours playing dominoes and Old

Maid, retelling the old beloved fairy tales, or talking softly of the wonderful days to come when we would at last be allowed to go to America and Papa. At such times, her eyes sometimes darkened with anxiety and her voice faltered. I know that vagrant fears of what the future would really be buzzed in her weary brain. But she would never voice them, and she would resolutely turn her mind to a happier subject.

During the times when Mamma had to be away, she was careful to leave a pitcher of fresh water, books to look at, paper and colored pencils, anything to help me pass the lonely hours without requiring attention from the rest of the family. I remember I took special comfort in drawing. I covered sheet after sheet with blue cornflowers, the harsh angles of their jagged petals somehow satisfying my fractured psyche more than the smug round shapes of lusher flowers.

Gradually health began to pulse again in my lanky body, which seemed to have stretched as it thinned during my illness. Only the racking whoop hung on for weeks. As soon as I was strong enough, Mamma took me back to the park, where the leafy shade invited every errant breeze. There we could spend the humid dog days more comfortably.

The bench under our favorite linden became a second home. Around it I played with my ball or hoop, skipped rope or lay stretched on the grass to cool off, while Mamma sat with her book or her mending, or wrote letters. Each morning she stocked a roomy carryall with as much food, drink and diversion as her limited strength could carry. After we ate our cold lunch I'd curl up for a rest with my head in Mamma's lap, drowsing while she softly sang old nursery songs and lullabies.

One August afternoon I was halfheartedly rolling my hoop along the walk, back and forth near the bench where Mamma sat writing a letter to Papa. Instinctively I veered to the shadier side to escape the relentless sun. The heat and the racking cough that still shook me at intervals left little energy for running after the wayward hoop that kept twisting sideways or trying to fall over. It had to be constantly guided by the short stick clutched in my sweaty hand.

Soon I gave up the game and sat down by Mamma on the shady bench. "I'm too tired to run," I complained peevishly. "How much longer will this cough last, Mamma?" I opened my mouth wide and stuck out my tongue, trying to cool my irritated throat. "Is there any water left in the bottle? I'm so dry."

Mamma poured a scant dollop of water into a tin cup. "We have to make this last all day, dushenka. But here's a little to wet your throat. You know I don't want you to drink the park water. Who knows what terrible germs can be in it."

She cradled me close as I sat drooping and rubbed my bony back tenderly. "I know it's hard to keep coughing; but you must be patient, darling. You are getting better. Your cough doesn't come nearly as often now. Little by little . . . "

I sighed. Little by little was too slow for me. I'd been whooping for weeks, and there was nothing to be done but wait for the spasms to dwindle away. I found it hard to keep at anything for very long, and Mamma had to keep thinking up new amusements.

So it was a welcome diversion when a tall thin man with sad eyes took the empty end of our bench, while I was skipping rope down the walk. It had been our own so long that Mamma was surprised.

He sat down with an apologetic bow. With his long legs stretched out and his chin propped on the tarnished silver head of his cane, he was a poignant figure of dejection as he sat drooping in the linden shade.

How much of my recollection is memory and how much conjecture is impossible to know. Obviously, I could only imagine their feelings. But now that I'm old enough and experienced enough to put myself in my mother's place, I have recreated the story of those Moscow days by instinct.

From then on the tall man appeared each day. Even when he shyly began to remark on the pleasant spot, the charming child, the warm weather, his manner was so gentle and courteous that even Olga's reserve was soon disarmed. She found herself easily drawn into conversation; his dispirited air aroused her sympathy and even her curiosity. His look so nearly matched her own frequent mood of discouragement that she felt an instant rapport, most unusual for her.

Perhaps being able to speak freely to a stranger was a spark that released each shut-in spirit. Whatever the catalyst, their casual talk quickly burgeoned into friendship. Instinctively sensing the other's kindness, each felt secure in the other's integrity. Some strange chemistry counteracted their natural shyness and reserve.

Away from him, Olga wondered at herself. How could she, to whom even ordinary social pleasantries were difficult, find herself talking animatedly of her family, her music, the home she had left behind in Samara? With this quiet man whose gray eyes held a twin melancholy to her own, she felt free to be open, at ease as with a friend of many years, so naturally that it was hard even to wonder at it.

As Olga set free her hoarded memories of old joys, the dead days of ease and grace flowered again, and a like catharsis was going on in Andrei Kurakin. Andrei Petrovich, as she was soon calling him. As they discovered matching tastes and experiences, their eagerness grew to explore each other's personality and history.

In his turn Andrei opened wide the doors on the shambles of his own life. The revolution had destroyed his career as a banker. His years of loyal and honest guardianship of his depositors' funds meant nothing in a nationalized economy, where banks were run by commissars, appointed by the party to reward the faithful. Andrei had lost his post, his wealth, even his liberty. His wife was an invalid, her mind broken by the loss of their younger son in the war and her husband's arrest. Months in the dungeons of the Lubyanka prison had ruined his health. Andrei gazed about him at his native city knowing that for him it held no future hope or present comfort.

"Our life depends entirely on the influence of my remaining son Petya," he confided one day. "It hurts me so much, this dependence. Petya joined the Reds and fought against his own brother. Against everything his family has always stood for: decency, loyalty, concern for people's rights, respect for people's souls. He broke his mother's heart. He was a traitor to our class.

"Yet it's only because he is a commissar that I was released from prison, that I could be treated for my heart ailment, that I can get some part-time work as a clerk in my old bank. You can imagine my feelings. And it was Petya who got his mother into a sanitarium, too."

"But he sounds like a good loyal son, Andrei Petrovich," comforted Olga, her heart aching for the humiliation she sensed in the words. "Though he disagreed with you, he did all he could to help you. He must love you." By now the confidants had progressed beyond mere listening to offering encouragement and consolation. Imperceptibly they were

growing indispensable to each other. To both, the
luxury of an understanding heart, after their long
fast of feeling, was becoming a necessity.

Again and again one would begin a reminiscence only to be interrupted by the other: "So you
know Lausanne too? When were you there? My wife
and I spent our honeymoon nearby in — "

"You also heard Paderewski in 1912? In Moscow? That was probably the same concert I heard. In
the fall, wasn't it?"

"How marvelous it was. He played the
Appassionata . . . "

When I tired of my games and sat down between the two to rest, I could not help noticing the
new roses glowing in Mamma's sallow cheeks, the
new animation in her voice. At first I could only sense
her new pleasure in life, and be grateful for it.
Mamma feels so much better now that I'm getting
well, I would think happily, setting adrift my own
worries about Mamma's uncertain health.

So many old delights, long tucked away in the
back corners of minds intent only on surviving one
more crisis, came welling up offering new joy, even
— hope. The two discouraged souls remembered that
there were other worlds besides this barely endur-
able one of theirs. Somewhere people still lived gracious lives in spacious homes, traveled for pleasure,
wore elegant clothes, gave delightful dinner parties,
listened to music, let their feelings flow.

"I miss my music so much," Olga confessed.
"My piano was my voice. I've been mute for so long."

"Once you are in America," Andrei consoled
her, "I'm sure your husband will provide one for you.
You'll be able to play again, you'll see."

"Yes, in America," she replied uncertainly, her
eyes deep with doubt. "What will it be like in
America?" She looked up into the kind face that

showed such concern. "Sometimes I am afraid. After four years apart, how can we take up our life together again? I am so changed, so old and weary . . . " Her voice trailed off mournfully.

Her friend smiled at the absurdity of "old," ventured to pat the hands that lay clasped in her lap. "My dear Olga Nicolaevna, you are not old. You are only worn out by the hardships of life. Once you are in a kind land, with your family complete, with good food and no worries, you'll see. You will bloom again, I know." A sigh escaped him at the thought that he would not see that bloom, miss the color of health returning to that lovely face.

From worlds so different that in their former lives they could scarcely have spoken, let alone become friends, in this new topsy-turvy one they sat entranced by the current that flowed between them, irresistibly drawing them closer.

After a while, I began to wonder. Maybe it was not the thought of America that was chasing the shadows from Mamma's eyes.

Jealous for Papa, I would talk about him whenever I was resting on the bench, tired of playing. "Don't you think we should have our papers soon, Andrei Petrovich?" or "Papa must be getting impatient, waiting for us to get to America." But I consoled myself that they were only friends, and that it was good for Mamma to have someone to talk to besides me, and that we were leaving soon, and going to Papa.

Soon August heat cooled into the crisp days of September. As the yellowing leaves began to drift to earth one by one, Olga and Andrei were sharing all their small defeats and triumphs over the iron system that ruled their days. When a spell of chilly rain interrupted their meetings, Olga waited impatiently to report that her cousin in Riga had written that Adya had sent their tickets.

Andrei came to lament the latest indignity at the hands of the new bank manager, a loyal party hack but a fiscal ignoramus, knowing that Olga's indignation would salve his hurt. They rejoiced together when my whooping ended and the roses returned to my cheeks with the fresh fall weather.

Who can say when amity crossed the line to amour, when the urge to confide, to seek balm for a wounded ego, imperceptibly became a need to sit close, to touch hands timidly, when dulled senses came alive? Long before the falling leaves foretold the end of their idyll, their eyes admitted what their words carefully ignored. Both so long deprived of a sensual love, both so tender and needful, how could they commune closely in their minds and keep their hearts untouched?

During the bright windy days of *babuye lieto*, the "grandmother summer" that comes before the cold, they tried to believe that winter was still far away. And then October arrived and with it notification that Olga would have her visa before the month ended.

As she and I walked to the park, full of the important news, chilly gusts swirled dry leaves along the paths. With a divided heart Olga admitted to herself that the success of her long effort to leave Russia also meant the ending of a communion that had become precious to her. As she told her news she could see all too clearly by the pain in Andrei's eyes that in his mind the same mournful bell was tolling. They looked at each other in silent longing as I danced about chanting "We're going to see Papa. We're going to America and we're going to see Papa."

"But won't you be sorry to leave Moscow?" Andrei ventured. "Won't you be sorry not to see me any more? Won't you miss me?" he asked me as his eyes spoke to Olga.

"Oh, yes," I agreed politely, "we'll miss you, Andrei Petrovich. But you know we're going to see *Papa!*" In my mind nothing else mattered half as much.

"Of course, child, I understand." The man nodded. But as I skipped off down the path, bouncing my ball in time with my refrain of "We're going to see Papa," he turned to Olga desperately. "My dear, you must know how I feel. I think you must feel the same way. You are such a light in my darkness. How can I stand to lose you?"

Olga shook her head despairingly. "I know, my dear." The endearment slipped out so naturally she was unaware of it. "I know how we both feel. These weeks in the park have been such a tonic to my spirit, too. But there's nothing we can do. Our lives lie so far apart, there's no way — "

"I know, I know. But there must be *something* . . . there must be somewhere. At least let's try to find a way to be together, alone together. I've ached so long just to hold you, to kiss you, to feel you close."

The stress to control herself was too much for Olga's frail nerves. Shaking her head violently, she was horrified to feel the tears running down her cheeks. Hiding her face in her hands to shield her breakdown from public view, she could only whisper brokenly, "There is no way, there is no place, I have no right."

Instantly retreating, Andrei gently patted the quivering shoulder, making his touch butterfly-soft and undemanding. "Shhh, my love, don't cry. It's all right. I could never ask anything that would hurt you. I understand. Please don't cry," he crooned over and over, as her sobs subsided and control returned. "I know you must go to America. I know we have only this bench, our only home . . . " His own impotence overcame him, as he admitted to himself that indeed there was nothing they could do, and he knew it.

A more aggressive man, one with a stronger sense of self, might have been more determined to find a way to relate their love to reality, might have tried to convince Olga that "the world's well lost for love." But Andrei Petrovich had bowed years ago to his own helplessness to rule events, had submitted to fate in quiet despair. Even as he clutched at this final bittersweet gift, a last flash of fire in the dreary black of his days, he knew it would slip through his fingers just as had all the early sweetness of his life.

And Olga too, before she even came to believe in the power of her own feelings and Andrei's, knew that this nascent douceur would vanish like a dream, that the warmth stirring in her breast was doomed to cool even as the sun of summer chilled into the gray autumn weather.

Oh, they must have tried. When looming winter made the days too cold for the park, perhaps they managed short meetings in hotel lobbies, in small cafes, in museums. The Museum of Fine Arts, though sadly neglected, was still a haven of marble and soft light. I can see the two strolling slowly among the antique artifacts and plaster reproductions of Greek statuary, shyly arm in arm, their eyes seeking, savoring the small contact.

I imagine they permitted themselves one last day alone. I know I was left at home on a pretense of last-minute business at the passport bureau. But it was probably a sham rendezvous. Sadly Olga and Andrei must have faced the fact that they would never have a place to be private in, that they were not adventurous enough to risk exposure. They could only press hands in final farewell, gaze despairingly into each other's eyes, and part.

⁂ 9 ⁂
Out of the Bear's Paws
Moscow/Riga/At Sea, 1922

IT WAS near midnight when I woke from a restless sleep. In a confused dream I was rolling my hoop along the tilting decks of a great white ship that pitched and yawed in an angry sea. I was frantic to avoid the outside rail as it dipped low to the enormous waves. Expecting every moment to be tossed overboard, I tried to hug the inner wall, ready to grab the safety rail, yet at the same time I stubbornly kept guiding the twisting hoop. Once more the deck tilted precariously close to the water, and this time I felt my feet slip out from under me, sending me skidding down into the yawning mouth of a waiting wave!

Helplessly I felt my bottom leave the slippery wood, my legs slide between the protecting rails. I opened my mouth to scream in dread at the watery grave rushing up to snatch me — and awoke trembling and sweating in the safe narrow bed at Aunt Zoya's. Turning to Mamma for comfort, I discovered I was alone in the bed. Where was Mamma? I came wide awake and sat up. A candle was burning dimly in the far corner, where my mother sat sewing, her head bent low to see in the flickering light.

These last memories of our months in Moscow have remained vivid in my mind both because the time was so dramatic and because I later created memory pictures of what Mamma's life must have been like at that moment when she left every vestige of her past for a wholly unfamiliar world. How much did I actually know at the time? Probably very little. Only what I observed and what I instinctively felt. How much did I acquire afterwards from my parents and my sympathetic imagination, trying to recreate a lost mother whom I really knew so little?

Quite a lot, I'm sure. I'll never know how much. But I *have* created a mother who has remained a part of my grownup life.

"Oh, Mamma," I sobbed as I untangled myself from the twisted bedclothes and ran to throw myself on her. "Oh, Mamma, what a terrible dream I had! I fell overboard from a ship. I was just going to be drowned in the sea when I woke up." I shuddered at the horrifying memory. In my landlocked existence I had never seen the sea. The idea of it both fascinated and terrified me. "Does it mean there'll be a storm and we'll be drowned? Do you think dreams tell the future, like Luba said? I'm afraid of the sea, Mamma, aren't you?"

"Of course not, darling." My mother hurried to reassure me, blaming herself because her own growing nervousness about the coming voyage must have injected itself into her usually intrepid child. She held my quivering body tight. "Whatever gave you such a silly idea?" She made her voice deliberately bright. "Luba talks a lot of nonsense. Dreams don't mean anything except an upset stomach, or a runaway imagination. The ocean is beautiful. And ships have been sailing on it for hundreds of years.

You know we have to cross the ocean to get to Papa. He crossed an even bigger one, twice as big, and he didn't have any trouble." How often she must have recited this litany to herself, to steel her own sinking heart for the ordeal ahead.

The nightmare retreated. I leaned against her, listening to the heavy rain beating against the building, like the waves pounding the ship's side in my nightmare. "Listen to the rain, Mamma. It sounded just like that in my dream. That must be what I heard, what made me think of big waves." I sighed in relief. "The rain sounds like a sea. Is that how a storm sounds?" Then I noticed the sewing in Mamma's lap.

"Why are you sewing so late at night, Mamma? That's my new blue dress. It wasn't torn, was it? Why don't you go to sleep, Mamushka?"

Glad that the nightmare was forgotten, but sorry to have her secret work noticed, Mamma bundled up the navy serge that used to be her own skirt, agreeing that it was time for bed. As the cool fall days came on, she had cut up a couple of her things into warm dresses for me. I had shot up during the summer and outgrown most of last winter's old clothes. Just last week I had had my eighth birthday, though we had long ago decided that we would not celebrate it until Papa could share it.

Though her dressmaking talents were rudimentary, she had already learned how to produce plain but adequate garments for me out of her lavish pre-war wardrobe. The serge dress in her lap, a simple belted shift, had two cloth-covered ball buttons on the belt, saved from the original skirt trim. It was these buttons that she had been industriously reattaching with many stitches.

"Why were you sewing my buttons on again, Mamma? They weren't coming off," I again demanded. I noticed everything, often more than I was meant to.

"I was just making sure that one of them wouldn't come off during the trip. We could never match it. I made this dress for you to travel in. I want you to wear it whenever we are en route. It's nice and warm, and dark so it won't get grimy looking."

"But it's scratchy, Mamma. It makes me itch. Why do I have to wear it all the time?"

"Don't always argue, child." She folded the dress into a drawer. "Just do as I tell you. We won't be able to wash clothes while we're traveling. I'll have too many other things on my mind to worry about your clothes. Just wear the blue dress."

The rising note of hysteria in Mamma's voice warned me to drop the argument. Keeping her nerves from fraying mattered much more than an itchy dress. And in this last week of our Moscow sojourn she was clearly getting close to nervous collapse. Bedeviled by last-minute afterthoughts in preparing for so major and irreversible a move, nagged by her dread of the sea voyage, and anxious about possible eleventh-hour bureaucratic caprice, Olga also had to deny her need to see Andrei Petrovich once more, to share her worries and fears with him. The knowledge that she was still in *his* city, yet already parted from him by social restraints as she would soon be by geography, must have pushed her already ragged nerves closer to breaking point.

Hearing her voice rise shrilly, Mamma forced herself to calm. "You're right, darling, it's late. Get back in bed. I'll be right there." She gathered up her needle and thread, tidied up the bits of cotton stuffing on the table. Struggling to hang on to a precarious composure, afraid of dangerous questions, she quickly prepared for bed and blew out the light before a sleepy child could start wondering again. "Sleep well, my child," were the last words I heard as I drifted off, cozy and safe in the circle of Mamma's arms.

But I know that, tired as she was, Mamma must have lain awake, helpless to stop her mind from ranging around the familiar prison yard of anxieties. Would they really get out of Russia at last? Would the old straw trunk survive the battering of travel? Would her secret ruse be discovered and doom them both? Would she weather the rough November ocean crossing without breaking down, she who had always been such a bad sailor?

Would Adya still love her — four years older, forty years more worn, with no energy or optimism to match his verve, his lust for life? Would he still want her? With a gentle Andrei in her heart, would she still want him? What if they had become strangers, with no ground left to meet on? Uneasily the exhausted spirit let fall its weight of what-ifs, at last allowed oblivion in.

Pushing herself to complete her preparations, Olga began to feel at last that she was cutting her ties to the city. It now seemed as if Moscow was casting her out, as if she was a traitor abandoning this despairing world for an easier, more comfortable one. As the fading days of October dribbled away, even the weather seemed to deny her; it brought vagrant early snows, then endless drenching rains that stripped the last leaves from the despondent trees. They left no opportunity for farewell walks about the city, for a final visit to the park, for the chance of a last glimpse of Andrei Petrovich. The pitiless sodden autumn finally loosened Moscow's last hold on Olga's heart.

By the time we were launched on our travels again, her relief was almost as great as my anticipation. It helped smooth the rigors of the train trip, which was, in any case, much more bearable than the last one. So few people were getting permission to leave the country that the westbound train to the border was not crowded. Though almost as dilapidated as the last one, it was relatively comfortable. At least we had seats to sit on. I think Olga's inner turmoil must have dulled in the long sleepy hours while the train rattled and jolted its way along the neglected roadbed. Her overburdened mind gradually set adrift its worries. She could doze and gather her forces for the next assault.

At last the train slowed down for the bridge that spanned the Velikaya River. The conductor went along the corridor calling, "Prepare for customs inspection at the border."

I can imagine how Mamma's heart came up into her throat, how her nerves knotted again and sang with tension. This was the last fearful hurdle before we reached the rational realms of Europe where authority was not a deadly adversary. Would we be allowed to clear it?

At the Latvian border there was an interminable wait while everybody's belongings were taken off the train. Officious customs inspectors searched the baggage for contraband. As our turn came we were taken into a building where an official rooted in our carefully packed belongings and examined our papers with a suspicious eye. The inspector kept twitching his small brush mustache as he turned every document over to check each point, and finally laid it aside reluctantly, unable to find a flaw. Holding our breaths, we silently blessed Uncle Maxim for his meticulous care in making sure we had the special documents permitting us to take out what we had brought from Samara.

The final trial was a personal inspection. A hard-faced matron, looking military in her stiff uniform, briskly ordered my mother to undress. She checked all the seams of Olga's coat and skirt, the heels of her shoes, even the lining of her fur hat. Her expert hands then ran along Olga's body to probe for hidden treasures.

White with shame and fear, my mother was finally told to dress, and the matron turned to me. But this search was more perfunctory, and consisted mostly of patting me all over while I giggled. "I'm so ticklish," I squealed.

A human smile briefly creased the surly mask of the matron's face. "Passed," she snapped. "Return to the inspector for approval."

Mamma's shaken control nearly gave way when she saw two older women from the next compartment, shabby-genteel and obviously terrified, being led away by border guards, their luggage trundled after them.

"They must have been smuggling valuables," Mamma whispered fearfully while I stared wide-eyed. "I wonder what will happen to them." But she held herself sternly in check while our papers were stamped "Approved for exit," and waited with outward calm until our luggage was taken across the border to the Latvian train.

Because of Russia's historic dread of invasion, her railroads had been built with tracks in a gauge incompatible with the rest of Europe. Everything and everybody that entered or left the country by rail had to cross the border on foot or by hand truck and enter a different train.

As the bulky straw trunk and three leather suitcases were wheeled across into Latvia and put into the Riga express, Olga silently followed them, my hand held tight in hers. Instinctively, we both tried to call as little attention to ourselves as possible. Only when we were seated in an empty compartment and the train began to move, did the full realization dawn that we were really safely out of Russia. Only then did Mamma's long-leashed panic finally erupt in an agony of sobbing, shocking me by its abandon.

"Don't, Mamushka, don't cry. It's all right now. We're out of Russia. We're on our way to Papa. Please, please don't cry. You'll get sick. Please, oh, please, Mamma . . . "

The rising fear in my voice was the most effective rein on Olga's hysteria. She could not bear to frighten her child. Hugging me close, she forced herself to breathe deeply and bring her tears under control. Finally she dried her eyes and managed a watery smile.

"It's all right, dushenka. I'll be all right now. I'm just so relieved. You don't know . . . "

I kept patting her arm automatically. I wasn't sure yet that the storm was over. "But why were you so worried, Mamma? We had all the papers. Why?"

At last Olga could rid herself of the terrible weight she'd been carrying. In the sudden letdown from anxiety she could no longer keep the secret prudently bottled up. "It was my diamonds, dushenka. They only let you take household goods and clothes out of the country. Only what is necessary, no luxuries, no jewelry. But I knew that in America we'd need *something.* I wanted to take something that — after all, they were *mine.* But I was so afraid."

"Diamonds, Mamma?" I jumped up, astonished. "I never saw any — "

"Hush, not so loud." But Mamma was laughing as she shushed me. Still on the verge of hysteria, her spirits now soared at her own success at subterfuge. "I couldn't tell you, dushenka. I didn't want you to know anything so you wouldn't be worried, so you wouldn't have to lie. But now we're safe. Still you must *never* say a word about it, not till we get to America and give the diamonds to Papa. Promise?"

I nodded solemnly, eyes like saucers at the thrill

of my first intrigue. "Oh, Mamma! I promise, Mamma. But where are the diamonds? Why didn't the soldiers find them when they searched you? How did you bring them?"

A triumphant smile lit my mother's pale face into radiance. "No, dushenka, *you* brought them. That's why I was so afraid. If they had found out that we . . . " But she shook off the shadow of fear. "There are two diamonds inside your ball buttons, my darling, one in each button. I took the two big diamonds out of my brooch and stuffed them inside. That's what I was sewing that night when you woke up with a nightmare, remember? Now do you see why you have to wear your blue dress whenever we travel, Niurochka? It's the safest place. And you must never tell *anyone*."

She glanced fearfully around the empty compartment, as if the walls had ears. "It's dangerous to carry anything valuable. If people knew, they might . . . " Again the shadow fell across the fearful eyes. There were so many pitfalls, so many burdens on her frail shoulders.

But I had long practice in battling these shadows. "Oh, Mamma, how wonderful. What a clever idea. Won't Papa be proud of you, getting two diamonds out of Russia for us?. We won't talk about it any more, and no one will ever know until we get to America. Don't worry, they'll be safe. I'll wear this dress *all* the time. Just rest now and forget all about it. We're safe. We're out of Russia and on our way to Papa, and safe."

Proud of Mamma's ingenuity and encouraged by her rare initiative, and proud too to have a part in the stratagem, I happily hugged my mother. If only Mishka were here to share this thrill with me. How I missed him! I settled down to be quiet, to stroke Mamma's thin hands and aching brow, to relax the tension and induce repose.

Once my mother, drained by her long effort, sank into an exhausted sleep, I sat by the window watching the gray wintry landscape slide by. I listened to the train wheels clacking on the track. Safe and on our way. Safe and on our way. In my mind's eye rose the image of Papa, waiting for us on the other side of the angry sea, smiling a welcome to his recovered family. Like my favorite fairy tales, I felt sure life would now be a "happily ever after."

And so it seemed at first. Arriving at Riga, we found ourselves in a different world. This was a city where order and comfort was the norm. We had lived so long where everything was a struggle against want and decay, against an inflexible bureaucracy, against the hostility of a disheartened population. It seemed miraculous and almost unreal to find polite porters, cabs waiting with cheerful drivers, stylishly dressed people strolling at ease along well-lit boulevards, fresh paint on trim houses.

Our ten days in Riga were a happy interlude. Mamma's cousin Amelia, married to a prosperous merchant, was a sunny tonic to her bruised spirit. Amelia was delighted at the rare opportunity to gossip with her old schoolfellow, to show off her rosy babies, to catch up on family news, to coddle her pale cousin with cream and eggs and delicate desserts. After the ravaging war years, when the area was bounced like a ball between German and Russian occupation, Latvia was savoring its long-dreamed-of independence. The people of Riga were working hard at settling back into a pleasant middle-class city life. Signs of war were still evident, but they were being steadily effaced by an optimistic population.

I was turned over to the care of the buxom nursemaid who had charge of Amelia's brood, leaving Mamma free to rest and relax from maternal cares.

How strange it must have seemed to her to be back in the life she had once lived, a life of pleasant strolls and drives, past shop windows displaying fashions from Prague and Berlin, and markets where oranges from Italy were piled side by side with local vegetables, fresh and plentiful. A life where long-forgotten small comforts were once again taken for granted. It was hard to remember that she could accept all this abundance without guilt or fear.

Feeling shabby but exhilarated, Olga allowed herself to be carried off to concerts and the opera. As rest and nourishment restored her depleted body and music her starved spirit, she even sat down at Amelia's piano and indulged herself with her favorite Chopin and Debussy, wincing as she stumbled through familiar pieces with fingers clumsy from lack of practice, something she had seldom had the heart to do in Moscow.

In the meantime I was sharing the children's happy pastimes. Pola, their pleasant nursemaid, took us on a daily outing to the park or the zoo — a new delight to a provincial visitor — or to the amusement park with its giant carousel and scary Ferris wheel. Though I was older than Amelia's little ones, after the deprived years when no one had means or energy to devise entertainments for children, I delighted in everything. No matter how babyish the ride or how simple the game, it was new to me, and the sense of fun was a tonic, a proof that life could be normal again.

All too soon the time came to leave our happy haven. With exit from Russia so difficult, its American quota was not filled. The required entrance visa was soon obtained from the American consulate. Before mid-November we were ready to cross the peninsula to the port at Libau, where we would enter the immigration mill and the final stage of our peregrination, the long sea voyage to the new world and our new life with Papa.

As soon as we reported to the steamship company in Libau we were sucked into the ponderous cogwheels that chewed up each anxious immigrant, spewing out another faceless bit of flotsam to be set adrift on the broad sea of misery and hope that flowed steadily, and so deliberately, toward the promised land.

This time the inevitable paperwork was relatively routine. Our papers, carefully checked and rechecked by expert Uncle Maxim, were all in order. Thus we escaped the fate of many frantic people who found they had come so far, given up so much, only to find themselves halted by a last stumbling block of omission or error by a careless clerk or their own ignorance.

Heartsick for the woebegone people who sat rejected to one side while the successful ones were waved through, Olga, with me tightly in tow, passed into the "health examination," a euphemism for what turned out to be a degrading disinfecting process. Herded in lines into barnlike barracks called "dressing rooms," we were told to leave all our clothes behind. Mamma carefully hung my blue dress with its precious buttons under all her own things, trembling for its vulnerability. We moved through to a long row of unscreened communal showers, where bodies and hair had to be scrubbed with strong disinfectant soap.

Poor Olga, whose extreme modesty had made even an evening décolletage or short sleeved summer dress seem an impropriety, who since she'd shared a room with me had undressed nightly under her nightgown, now found herself stark naked in a crowd of equally denuded women and children. All were busily scrubbing their intimate parts with total unconcern. Unable to rest her eyes anywhere without shock, Olga could only force herself to concentrate on getting herself and me soaped and rinsed as rapidly as possible.

Her haste resulted only in our having to stand idle and dripping until the rest of our group were done. Only then were we allowed to return to the dressing room. As we passed through the door, each of us received a rough towel.

To those responsible for the sanitation of the ships and the arrival of the immigrants at American ports in acceptable condition, it made no difference whether a candidate for entry was a steerage passenger who'd been on the road for weeks, sleeping in haystacks, or a second-class traveler with refined middle-class habits. Officials were charged with preventing infestations that would have quickly spread through a crowded ship. A lapse could result in large numbers of infected persons having to be returned to Europe at the expense of the steamship companies. Their orders were to see that all immigrant baggage, clothing and bodies were fumigated or disinfected before boarding. Everything else was irrelevant.

At last, dried and dressed and in possession of our belongings, we submitted to the real health inspection, a brusque and humiliating examination of our heads, as well as a check of eyes, ears, and skin for any overt sign of disease or infection. Only then were we allowed to file aboard the Lithuania, which would take us across the long miles of ocean to the final inspection in New York harbor.

The battered old liner, a poor relation to the large French and British steamers that crossed the Atlantic in five days or less, looked too small and vulnerable to face its heavy seas and autumn gales. I'm sure my mother's apprehension doubled as she tried to settle into the tiny cabin with its double bunk and stale air. As she thought of being trapped in this small musty space, unable to retreat to firm ground for the next two weeks, Olga must have been fighting a rising panic that thwarted her efforts to show a calm and cheerful face to her child.

Too thrilled at the prospect of sailing to notice my mother's desperate mood, all I wanted was to run all over the decks, find out where everything was, and watch the shore recede. Mamma could hardly restrain me until our things were safely stowed and we could go up on deck together. At least the tussle with me turned my mother's attention from her own nerves.

We had time for a leisurely tour of the public decks, a rest in the lounge and another turn around the second-class deck, and still there was no sign of casting off. More hours of waiting passed before all the cargo, both material and human, was properly disposed and the tide was right. Reluctantly I agreed to return to the cabin for a rest. I fidgeted in my upper bunk with a book until three blasts of the ship's whistle made me scramble down.

"That must be the signal, Mamma. Hurry up, they must be getting ready to sail. Please, Mamma, let's go up now. I want to see us sail."

"All right, darling." Reluctantly Mamma came out of the lower bunk. "I suppose we should go and watch the sailing. You've never been on a big ship before. You have a right to be excited."

On deck the railings were crowded with passengers, most of whom were immigrants. They stood staring at their native shore, knowing they were probably seeing it for the last time in their lives. Though most were leaving want and deprivation, there were tears in many eyes.

In Mamma's heart, too, the relief of finally achieving her goal was surely mixed with the same anxiety she saw written on the faces around her. She was leaving all she had ever known and going to a strange world where nothing would be familiar.

Everyone stood waiting for the lines to be cast off, lost in their confused emotions, until the last hawser fell free. In silence we all watched the water widening between us and the pier. Then a sudden "Hurrah" galvanized the passengers, as if all their sorrows were being left behind on the shore. A spontaneous burst of applause rippled along the deck.

"Here we come, America!" yelled a tall thin youth, his eyes wildly excited behind thick lenses, his long arms waving farewells to unknown Latvians watching from the shore.

"Here we come, America!" a hundred exultant voices, took up the cry in a dozen languages. After all their struggles and disappointments and delays and anxieties, incredibly the goal of all their longings lay over the horizon.

Once out of the harbor, however, the thrill of departure soon dwindled into the monotony of idle waiting. The choppy gray waters of the Baltic were matched by the sullen November sky, as gray and nearly as dark as the sea. A raw wind sprang up that sent many of the landlubbers below.

Poor Mamma! Certain that she would be seasick, she created a self-fulfilling prophecy. As soon as the ship breasted the heaving waters outside the harbor, her shaky equilibrium was shattered. She would not even try to move about. Queasy and dizzy, she retreated to her narrow bunk. It was to be her haven and her prison for the entire voyage.

All my urgings to see how much better it was on deck in the fresh air were met with a sad look and a deaf ear. It was unthinkable to Mamma to risk throwing up in public. As the ship reached open water it began to plunge down into and up over the long waves stirred up by the winter gales. Flat in her bed, holding on for dear life, all she could manage was to survive each racking spasm that shook and drained her. For the first time since our journey began, my mother was totally unfit to supervise her daughter.

Periodically I appeared to check on her, but she could never do more than lift her head feebly from the pillow, manage a wan smile and a "How are you feeling, darling? Are you eating? Wonderful. Are you being careful up on deck?"

Assured of her child's well being, she would turn her head to the wall again and try to find the oblivion of sleep. A kindly stewardess came every few hours and coaxed her to take a little weak tea, a cup of bouillon, a cracker to settle her heaving stomach, a little fluid to replenish the wrung-out tissues. The ship's doctor paid a daily visit, bringing a sedative. But nothing helped much. All she could do now was hang on and try to survive until the ordeal was over. She had used all the strength she had in fighting Russia. She had none left to battle the sea.

Slanting through the porthole, the watery sun rising over Europe stole into the stuffy cabin, fetid with yesterday's nausea, and pierced the gloom of the upper bunk where I lay. The vagrant light tickled my eyelids, floated me up out of the deep well of exhausted sleep. Slowly I opened my eyes, carefully moved my head, happily discovered that I didn't hurt. Gingerly I leaned over the edge of the bunk to peer down into the lower. Mamma was still asleep.

I lay quiet, stretching cautiously, savoring the absence of pain and thinking back over the terrible day just past. I'd started out happily exploring the ship, fascinated by everything in this strange float-ing hotel and everybody in it. But when the wind came lashing around the corners and along the deck, and waves came roaring up the ship's sides, I found myself lurching and grabbing at anything to keep from failing, just like in my dream, and swallowing hard to keep my churning stomach quiet. This was an onslaught against which I had no defense. Soon I too was down in the cabin with Mamma, disgorging my last meal and collapsing on my bunk in a companion misery.

Now with morning came the sun, and a calmer sea. The long sleep had steadied me. I was ready to leave the smelly cabin for the cold fresh air above. I climbed down to dress, happy to see Mamma's eyes open.

"Good morning, Mamushka! Look what a nice day it is. The sun is out. I feel so much better, don't you? And I'm *hungry*. Let's go have some breakfast."

"Uh, don't mention it." Olga turned her head away. "I couldn't eat a thing. I'm glad you feel better, dushenka, but I'm not going to get up while this terrible motion goes on."

Unable to interest Mamma in food or locomotion, I sighed and went up to breakfast.

At first, the uneasy memory of my ominous dream in Moscow made me timid on deck. I cautiously avoided its outer edge, and kept my hand poised to grab a safety rail wherever rows of deck chairs did not get in the way. But as my body caught the rhythm of the swaying deck and my refilled innards steadied, I found my sea legs.

The ocean drew me again and again to the ship's side. Gray and mysterious, threatening yet mesmerizing, rolling endlessly away to an endless horizon, always the same yet always changing as cloud shadows darkened it or the peek-a-boo sun lit up a line of sparkles on the wavecrests. The sea constantly called me from my explorations. I took possession of a nook by a lifeboat, where I could be alone with this restless new element, never before a part of my landlocked life. I would stare at it and dream of romantic sea adventures I'd read about but never really visualized before.

Nothing could keep my curiosity at bay for long. A ship at sea is a world in space. Completely on my own for the first time in my life, I was free to follow every impulse. Too busy to notice the unsettling motion, I roamed the decks, popping in and out of salons, investigating out-of-the-way corners and staircases, learning my way around my new domain. Full of questions and not at all shy, I rapidly made friends with the stewards and officers whom I buttonholed whenever they passed by.

Soon enough this small realm began to unlock its mysteries to me. I learned that the fur-swathed ladies and tweedy gentlemen strolling on the top deck above ours, who looked the way Papa and Mamma used to, in the old days, were the first-class passengers. Not many of them were immigrants; most were Latvians or Estonians headed for the gaieties of Berlin or Prague, and enjoying a pleasant sea voyage en route.

The crowded lower parts of the ship were the domain of the immigrants. The stuffy third-class cabins below the water line and, even more, the semi-sheltered space out on the lowest deck, where people slept on their bundles, were not conducive to a "pleasant sea voyage." But the cost was low. Here energetic young men played cards, wrestled playfully and ogled pretty girls. Young women whispered and nudged each other, gossiped while mending their threadbare clothes. Children ran about, devising little games to fill up the long hours. The careworn older folks, bundled up in shabby sweaters and shawls, sat guarding their meager possessions, their minds on the coming ordeal of entry into America. What if they were found wanting? Where would they go? How live?

The desultory talk that ran around the deck was about quotas, health examinations, literacy tests, the comparative difficulties of various ports. Everyone had some rumor of calamity to contribute. An ailing child separated from parents. A ship held up by storms that had to take back many of its passengers because their national quotas had been filled by faster vessels. An unsuspected infection that had doomed whole shiploads to the terrors of quarantine on Ellis Island. Ellis Island — the name was pronounced with dread. It was the gateway to Elysium, and as strictly kept.

Between these upper and lower ranks, poised between heaven and hell, as it were, was the second class, where we belonged. Here the range of passengers ran the gamut from plush to threadbare, from worn but stylish fur hats to faded wool shawls. Here the amenities were nearly as evident as on the deck above. But here the talk in the salon or along the deck chairs was also of the hazards of the confusing immigration process. These people had managed the higher passage fares in order to avoid Ellis Island, but they knew they were still subject to the same stern regulations.

Many newspapers reported the trials of those who had made it all the way to America only to be detained or deported. Letters home from successful immigrants also told of their tribulations en route and at the entry ports. Especially since the new quotas had gone into effect in July, the race to be among the limited number that gained admission created chaos on both sides of the Atlantic.

A prime topic of anxious comment, already widely reported, was the horrendous crush at Ellis Island on the eve of the first of July, when a dozen liners lay at anchor outside the three-mile limit waiting to land more than four thousand steerage passengers right after midnight. Compounded by a heavy

*fog that delayed several ships, and the upcoming In-
dependence Day holiday for the staff, the confusion
in the harbor and on the island was indescribable.
The Cunarder Aquitania from Southampton almost
collided with the Argentina, after dodging several small
craft. It had actually plowed into a couple of dories
earlier, near the fishing grounds off the Grand Banks.*

I would sit spellbound in the salon, listening to
these accounts as to tales of dragons and monsters.
Did grownups really conduct their affairs with such
irrational confusion? And could such a terrible mix-
up happen to Mamma and me? Was it possible that
we'd be sent back to Europe after this long grueling
journey? Mamma could never stand it, I knew. Sending my mother back to sea would certainly kill her.

I wished I had someone to talk to about this
new worry, someone who knew what would really
happen, who could reassure me that the stories were
exaggerated. It took all my dogged optimism to fight
off the nightmare vision of being kept aboard as the
ship left the dock in New York, with Papa watching
helplessly from shore and Mamma in collapse. I certainly couldn't talk to Mamma about this. Just repeating the stories I was hearing would be enough
to frighten her into hysterics.

Since I was a friendly child, I did not remain
solitary for long. Roaming about the ship, my smile
found a ready response among my fellow passengers. In fact, I soon had to curb my natural sociability. Too often it saddled me with unwanted mothering from women to whom a child unattended was a
child in need of attention.

It was definitely not mothers that I wanted. I
was enjoying my first liberty too much, and had long
lost the habit of depending on a mother. In my life it
was the other way round. My mother depended on
me for support and strength. Part of my present plea-

sure was the respite from that responsibility. Mamma was safe in the cabin and I had only myself to be concerned about.

The biggest nuisance I longed to escape was the family whose table I shared at meals. The first evening, when I walked alone into the dining salon, a kindly waiter seated me with a large noisy family of Russian Poles to "give me company." Hearing of my mother's illness, Madame Warszawski immediately appointed herself my custodian, while her three rowdy boys at once adopted me. Jan, Lech and Boris found me much more fun to tease than their older sister Jadwiga, who considered herself too grownup for "little brats." Their boisterous rudeness spoiled my pleasure in the ample meals, especially the rich desserts that, to a child of famine, were delectable beyond words. I was still awed by the sight of so many foods to choose from, and was rapidly developing an incurable sweet tooth.

It was through the Warszawski boys that I made friends with Jacob. They were teasing me unmercifully, pulling my hair, pushing me from one brother to another, even grabbing me by my precious belt, and I was frozen in fury, the unbidden tears streaming from my eyes adding to my anger at my impotence. Suddenly a sharp high voice demanded, "Leave that girl alone, you bullies!"

The brothers turned in amazement at the intruder's daring. A chunky boy with russet curls and a cherub's face was scowling at them ferociously. Jan, who stood nearest, promptly knocked him down.

Happily for both us victims, the second mate came along. "What's going on here?" he demanded, seizing Jan by the scruff. "Can't you boys find anything better to do than fight?"

"We were just playing with our friend," Jan whined, "and he came along and bothered us."

I could stand no more. "They are *not* my

friends," I declared indignantly. "They were teasing me and making me cry, and *this* boy," turning a grateful smile on Jacob, "tried to make them stop. And then Jan knocked him down."

The bullies were dispersed in short order, surreptitiously shaking their fists at me, vowing revenge, leaving us to improve our acquaintance. Jacob was nine, an orphan from Warsaw who was going to live with a pair of American relief workers. He was a character in a real romance, I decided, as he told his story.

His American friends had fallen in love during their work at the orphanage, not only with each other but also with Jacob's bright curls and endearing ways. "After they went back to America and got married, they decided to adopt me," he reported ecstatically. "The orphanage people found Dr. and Mrs. Henkin, who are going to America to live with their son, and they agreed to bring me with them."

He hugged himself, still trying to believe in his good luck. "So I will live in America too. And study, and have a wonderful life, with a real family again, at last." The gray eyes clouded over at the memory of the desolate past, but Jacob refused to be sad.

Then I had to tell my story, and then we were friends. Jacob was as buoyant and ready for adventure as I was, and a perfect companion.

Frieda became the third musketeer. She was twelve and was also traveling alone. She and her mother were on their way to an uncle in Chicago who had paid their fare, when the mother died of pneumonia the week before they were to sail. Jacob and I ran into Frieda, literally, in a corridor. We saw with surprise, as we picked her up and apologized, that she had been crying. By common impulse, we at once took her under our wing. Less optimistic and more fearful than her new friends, Frieda faced the future with trepidation. Her shaky confidence conjured up every possible calamity. Her uncle wouldn't meet her. He would be disappointed when she arrived alone. She wouldn't be able to work hard enough to repay him. He wouldn't like her. She wouldn't be able to learn English.

It took constant effort to encourage the fainthearted girl to keep up her spirits, but we two young optimists felt ourselves equal to the task. We made short work of her apprehensions, knocking them down like tenpins, one by one. As our enthusiasm began to rub off on her, Frieda too began to look forward to America with more hope than dread.

"You'll learn English in no time," I assured her. "Papa wrote that there are special classes to teach foreigners. He's going to one himself, in the evenings. And it's free!"

"All the schools are free," Jacob added, eager to paint the glories of the country he'd heard so much about, "and every child has to go. My friends said there are even free colleges. I'm going to college and become a doctor."

"I've never been to school yet," I admitted. "I'm dying to go. We're lucky, all of us, to be going to America."

Running down the southward leg of the Baltic, the Lithuania entered the broad mouth of the Vistula to pick up its last dozen passengers at Danzig. After the monotony of the open sea, with only distant glimpses of piney shores, the medieval city presented an exciting change of scene. Once an outpost of the Hanseatic League, Danzig had long been a busy international port and shipbuilding center. Now liberated from Prussia by the Treaty of Versailles, under the supervision of the newly formed League of Nations, Danzig was working hard to build a prosperous future.

Passengers crowded the ship's rail to stare at the new arrivals coming aboard. In the busy harbor, filled with ships flying an array of foreign flags, freight was being hauled up on huge cranes into ships' holds or onto the bustling docks. In the shipyards beyond, we children glimpsed tall keels being built or restored.

The clamor and clang of an industrial water-side made a startling change from our remote world on the Lithuania. Stevedores shouted, wagons rattled by, crates were dumped with a bang. The immigrants were reminded how fleeting their quiet shipboard days were, before they too would be swept into the clanging world of a humming American city.

As the Danzig passengers came aboard I noticed a slim dark lady whose grace and understated elegance reminded me of Mamma. It seemed a gift of providence when the lady chose a deck chair right opposite my favorite nook. Whenever I turned from looking at the sea, I would find soft brown eyes fixed on me. It was not long before I ventured a smile, to be rewarded by a delighted one in return.

"Are you traveling alone, my child?" the lady asked shyly.

Shyness was not my problem. Soon I was chattering away about Papa in America and Mamma sick in our cabin, and asking dozens of questions in rapid fire. We both became aware of the flowering of one of those spontaneous rapports that happen so rarely and are so precious. By dinnertime we were old friends.

Madame Marina Karlova was going to America to live with her brothers. The revolution had robbed her of her husband. Her two children, one a little daughter just about my age, had been lost to typhus and cholera. She was delighted to have an eager child to talk with once more, and was happy to clarify many of the problems that had been worrying me.

It wasn't long before I admitted my tribulations

with the young Warszawskis. Twice that afternoon the boys had boldly interrupted our conversation with demands that I come and play. Since they were only running around the decks bumping into people, I was glad to have a good reason for refusing. When the dinner gong sounded, I heaved a deep sigh.

"Now I've got to go and sit with those terrible boys again," I mourned. "They spoil every meal for me, and we have such good meals. If only they'd leave me alone to enjoy them."

Mme. Marina was happy to find so simple a way to help me and please herself into the bargain. We entered the dining room together. "My little friend will sit with me until her mother recovers," she told the waiter at her small corner table. "Please set another place for her."

As I sat down I noted Mme. Warszawski's flush of disapproval. The boys thumbed their noses at me, but I turned my back on them with a triumphant toss of my head, and grinned gratefully at my rescuer. So much for Boris, Lech and Jan.

The clear weather held as we sailed along the busy southern rim of "the Mediterranean of the North." Jacob and I were constantly rushing to the rail to watch passing steamers, until the smaller coastal vessels became too numerous for novelty. And Mme. Marina was on hand to satisfy my passion for names and labels. She had done much traveling with her husband before the war, and northern Europe was familiar ground.

After the long coast of Pomerania lay behind us, we rounded the ragged point of Rugen and entered the Kadet Channel. Verdant Danish islands loomed distantly to starboard, and the German coast was often visible on our port side. Proud of my expanding sea lore, I loved to use the nautical terms, and tried to be the first to point out fresh sightings to my new friend, who was now playing mentor to all three of the "Musketeers."

"Wait till we get into Fehmarn Strait," laughed Mme. Marina. "We'll be sailing between islands only a few miles apart. You'll get dizzy running from side to side to see everything."

But it was getting dark when we sailed past the island of Lolland and through Fehmarn to enter Kiel Bay. When I came up on deck early next morning, I was astonished to find that we were moving slowly through a long narrow waterway among a swarm of craft of every size and nationality. Mme. Marina had not yet breakfasted, but Eric the steward passed by in time to save me from bursting with curiosity.

"What is it? Where are we? Where are all those boats going? Are we — "

Eric laughed at my excitement. "It is the Kiel Canal, Fraülein. It is the short route to the North Sea. Without it we would have to go all around Denmark. This cut will save us many hours of sailing. All these ships are going west, to Holland or the British Isles, perhaps to America, like us. And the others, over near the opposite bank, are coming from those places, going east. It is a busy water here, you see."

The Kiel Canal. I was awed by the thought that this long river, filled with the traffic of Europe, was made by men. I remembered when I first saw the Kremlin, filled with its many gorgeous palaces, shining domes and vast encircling wall. What wonders people could create. When so much could be done to make life easier and more beautiful for their fellow men, what made men waste their genius in producing chaos and desolation instead? All the sad immigrants on our ship, their lives broken by war and revolution, were the victims of men who wanted to make the world over their way, no matter how much trouble it brought to others, who had no say at all in the matter. I shook my head and turned my mind away from the hard question. It was a mystery I could not fathom.

The quiet transit through the canal, when even Mamma felt well enough to sit up and brush her hair, was literally the calm before the storm. All too soon the Lithuania emerged into the mouth of the Elbe and the cantankerous North Sea. Even in the lee of the Frisian Islands, the ship felt the buffeting of the frigid winds that swept down unchecked from the Arctic. And when it turned south into open water, the waves rose deck high as they rolled in to beat on the low coasts of Holland and the sandy beaches of Belgium.

By the time we approached the narrowing entrance into the English Channel, the vessel was a toy in the grip of a mad giant who shook and batted it about unmercifully. Even I, who thought I had become immune to it, succumbed to the mass *mal de mer* that swept through the passengers. I was once more lying limply in my berth, as miserable as Mamma below me.

Even in relatively mild weather, turbulent cross winds from the Atlantic and the North Sea often collided in the narrow sleeve of the Channel and kept its waters and its coasts in turmoil. Now, the November gales roaring in from the grim gray ocean were a wall the ship must breach to win through to the open sea and the new world it sought. As the Lithuania battled her way west under a sullen sky, only a few of the hardiest aboard her ventured up on deck. The last sightings of Europe went by almost unnoticed by the sufferers. Turning wretchedly on my pillow, I barely glimpsed the green Isle of Guernsey drift by the porthole. Then the fog closed in, and the ship passed like a ghost between the unseen portals of Brest and Land's End, its foghorn wailing, into the dark waters beyond.

How completely everything else falls away when

the body is in crisis. I neither saw nor cared when our shipload of emigrants left the continent of our birth. While the ship wallowed in deep troughs or was flung crazily up huge wave crests only to shoot down again, my mind and will were fully occupied in keeping my wrung-out vitals out of my lacerated chest. As the endless hours crept by, all I could do was seek a way to ease muscles aching from repeated bouts of retching, look for a cooler spot on the sweaty pillow, long for the oblivion of sleep.

I'd been sick before, but nothing in my life prepared me for this grinding agony. Now at last I could understand my mother's misery. If Mamma felt like this even in calmer weather, no wonder she wouldn't try to leave her bed and move about.

Mercifully sea and ship calmed down during the night. When I awoke from my exhausted sleep, a reluctant sun had sprayed fitful gilding on the diminishing waves and the battered vessel was proceeding steadily on her way. Letting myself down shakily from my tumbled bunk, I found that my stomach was much more stable, my head throbbing only faintly, and, unbelievably, I was hungry. Glad to discard my sour and crumpled nightgown, I washed at the little corner sink and got into fresh clothes as quietly as I could. But before I was done, Mamma too opened her eyes and wearily raised her head from the pillow.

"You are feeling better, dushenka? I'm glad. Isn't it terrible to be seasick?"

"Oh, yes, Mamenka," I said fervently. "It was awful! But now . . . " I put extra brightness in my voice, hoping to rouse my mother to activity. "Now the storm is over, and the sun is coming out. It feels so much quieter. Why don't you get dressed and come to breakfast with me? I feel much steadier when my stomach isn't empty. Come up on deck for awhile. It's so much nicer in the fresh air, it makes you feel better right away. Please try, Mamma."

Olga only shook her head sadly, and gingerly eased herself out of the low bunk to attempt washing and a trip to the lavatory down the corridor. "You don't understand, darling. You only get sick when the sea is very rough, but my stomach heaves with every wave. If I can manage to get cleaned up and into a fresh nightgown and back into bed without a spasm, I'll be happy. I just have to stay still till we land, that's all. But I'm glad you're all right again. Go and eat your breakfast."

Sighing, I did what I could. I fluffed up my mother's pillows and tried to brush some of the tangles out of the long dark hair. "I'll send you some tea and toast," I promised. How could Mamma get used to the ship's motion if she wouldn't try? I mused as I went upstairs. I knew already that when my mother decided she wasn't up to something, nothing would convince her otherwise.

As a second slow week went by, one long uneventful day followed another. Even the energetic ones on board were running out of momentum. The wintry wind that swept the decks even under the occasionally sunny skies made the walkers shorten their circuits. There was nothing to vary the watery vistas and the empty horizon except an occasional faint smokestack in the distance. Only the unending card games and the non-stop talk in the salon went on and on, punctuated by meals and bedtimes.

During these cold days, when even company palled, I reverted to my old passion for reading. I spent hours curled up in a corner near the "library" of the ornate Victorian salon. The shelves provided an ample selection of popular classics in several languages, including Russian. There were also some fairly recent magazines from Berlin, Paris, and even New York.

These American periodicals interested me the

most. I pored over pictures of strollers on Fifth Avenue, of the tall new skyscrapers around Madison Square, of elevated trains that seemed to run right above the streets. This was going to be my city. I wanted to learn all I could about it. I tried to make some sense of the unfamiliar words. Often one would remind me of a word I knew in French or German, but only enough to tantalize me.

Whether it was a magazine full of pictures or even a favorite book, I found it impossible to stay absorbed for long. A snatch of conversation would drift in, and I'd find myself listening and storing away bits of new information about our destination.

"We are all so worried about the strict rules at the port," I heard a fat untidy woman confiding to her thin but equally shabby companion. "If there's any sign of vermin on the ship, they say, *nobody* will be allowed to land. Have you seen some of those people down in third class? They look like they've been sleeping in haystacks."

"They probably have," was the retort. "In America they seem to have such strange ideas of health. I hear people there take a full bath every week, or even oftener."

"We ought to try to clean up the children. I'm going to trim their hair before we land."

"Good idea. We should also shine their shoes and brush their clothes. Do you have a needle and thread? There are a couple of loose buttons — "

"You really think such things will make a difference?"

"You never know. I'm going to make sure my family looks as good as possible. Even if our second class doesn't go to Ellis Island, we still have to pass a health inspection on board."

Another health inspection. I wondered anxiously what we could do to make Mamma look less emaciated and ill. The shadows under her eyes were so dark, her cheeks so sallow.

"I just hope we don't run into fog," worried a man playing cards at a round table nearby. "If we don't get into New York by the first, the December quotas might be filled. Imagine, if we had to go back to Europe after all this."

"My God. My wife would die." His partner slapped his cheek as he looked fearfully out of the window at the sullen sky. "We must pray that God will not send fog."

Amen. I sighed, shuddering at the thought of Mamma having to go back to sea. Each day her strength was ebbing. Our only hope was to get her on dry land where she could build up her health again. I was counting the days until I could turn my mother over to Papa's care.

Today there was no one to share my troubles with. Mme. Marina was keeping to her cabin, nursing a new cold in the hope that it would be gone before the dreaded health inspection. Jacob and Frieda didn't seem to be around either. My only distraction was this constant hum of anxious talk that filled every corner of the salon. I was not usually a worrier. In all the fairy tales Nyanya told, in all the Victorian tales that had been my companions, at the end "they lived happily ever after." But it was hard to keep believing that promise amidst the apprehensions all around me.

⊰ *10* ⊱

No Snow in December!

New York, 1922-23

AT LAST, the final day at sea! Word
went around that the next day we would be in
America. Hardly anybody ever called it New York. It
was always "America" — the magic word. The pall of
anxiety on board lifted, giving way to an almost hysterical gaiety. The perilous ocean was nearly crossed,
the shoals of Ellis Island and its judgments not yet
reached. Now was the time to enjoy what might be
our last secure hours.

Even the ship's officers got into the spirit. A
gala dinner was announced. A call went out for vol-
unteer talent to perform at an impromptu concert. I
breathed in the general excitement and was wild with
expectation.

If I could just get Mamma to get out of bed and
come share in the fun. I tried hard. "The concert is
going to be wonderful, Mamma. Famous singers from
the Imperial Opera, a . . . a baritone and his wife,
and a lady who plays the violin, and . . . and . . . "

But it was no use. Mamma felt safe only on her
back in bed. A calmer sea the last two days had almost put an end to the attacks of retching, but she
was terrified of starting them up again. In spite of all

my urging, she was determined to stay still until she could get off the ship onto dry land. For the reunion with Papa and all the new experiences to come she would need all her strength, and she had so little left.

But for me it was a magical evening. Mme. Marina and my other friends were there to share my pleasure. The music was irresistible, the dancing delightful. My first public entertainment was a great success.

The next morning sure signs of land began to appear.

The seagulls came first, flying out of the west as if to welcome the new arrivals. Then drifting seaweed floated by. Soon we spotted small vessels, apparently sailing along the still unseen coast.

As the day wore on, we children haunted the rail. Suddenly the horizon bloomed into misty shapes. Were these really low hills, or a mirage thrown up by the desert sea?

"Look, look!" I shrieked, jumping up and down, "Look over there. New York."

"We are hours away from New York yet, Fraülein," a passing steward said. "That is probably Rhode Island or Massachusetts, or perhaps only one of the outlying islands. We have to sail the length of Long Island, before we get near the harbor."

Whatever it was called, that low dark line was America. The wide ocean lay behind us. Ahead was my new world, and Papa.

Night was falling by the time we were outside New York Harbor. The passengers watched as distant lights came on, a magic show punctuated by the revolving beam of Ambrose Light. The ship, its engines slowed to a faint hum, turned broadside to the shore and drifted.

"Why are we stopping?"

"There is New York!"

"We're nearly there!"

"What's wrong?"

The growing commotion brought the captain out of the wheelhouse. "Nothing to worry about, ladies and gentlemen. We're just going to wait here overnight. Today is November 30th. We want to dock early on the first, when the new quotas open. Tomorrow you'll be dining in New York."

Even Mamma perked up at the news. Still queasy with the soft rocking of the anchored ship, she would not go to dinner, but did manage to eat a light meal the steward brought her. When we awoke next morning, the ship was moving again.Through the porthole I saw the docks and slips of the outer harbor, and beyond them a giant woman rising from the water.

"Look, Mamma, look! There, that big statue. Isn't that — "

"Yes, my darling," Mamma said, her eyes misting. "Yes, that is the Statue of Liberty. We are in America."

Barely stopping to dress, I rushed upstairs to see America. Passengers crowded the rail, staring at the fairytale towers of the approaching city, at the harbor filled with barges, tugboats and ferries, as well as liners heading for their piers like homing pigeons. In their midst the august presence, alone on an island, lifted her torch to welcome the refugees from Europe's agonies with the promise of a new life. The golden door no longer swung wide, the multitudes thronging in were blunting the welcome, but the door was still ajar. Every anxious passenger gazed prayerfully at the guardian of the gate, hoping to be among the favored ones who slipped through.

So many different feelings filled my heart as the ship passed by the statue to anchor off a nearby island. Mostly glad ones. The end of the tedious voyage, the end of Mamma's seasickness, and the beginning of — so many beginnings. Above all, Papa.

Once more we would all be together. Papa would help Mamma get better, he would take care of her now. But there were anxieties too: Would Papa be there? Would he find us? Would Mamma be well enough to pass the health examination?

My own worries were put aside when I saw the third-class passengers begin to go down the steep steps lowered at the side of the ship. The steps led to a small platform floating on the water, where a number of barges and small boats were coming alongside one by one. Terrified old women and little children all had to submit to the precarious descent. I held my breath as I watched a small stout woman, heavy with child, stumble and nearly fall into the sea. Two sailors grabbed her at the bottom and guided her into a barge, where she collapsed in frightened sobs.

"Why are they getting off the ship here?" I asked a man standing next to me. "Why don't they land on the dock? Do we have to do that too?" Mamma would faint if she had to go down that swaying stair, I knew.

"No, little one," the man said, "only the third class has to get off here. They're going to Ellis Island for their examinations, and the ship can't dock there. It's too big."

I turned away. I couldn't bear to look any longer. From the opposite rail I watched instead the docks and piers on the mainland, the piled towers of the city behind them. Everything seemed so tall, so large, so crowded and busy. This was my new home. I tried to imagine living in it, but it did not yet have a human dimension for me. I hung on to the thought of Papa, waiting there on one of those piers.

All through the waiting hours while the Ellis Island group debarked, while the final stretch of water was crossed, while the second-class passengers lined up in the salon for what turned out to be a fairly cursory health check, that name rang in my head. Papa, Papa, soon we're going to see Papa!

I passed the endless time in chatting with my friends and was able at last to introduce Mme. Marina to my mother, who was glad finally to be able to thank her for her kindness.

And now it was time for the last goodbyes, time to gather our belongings and get ready to land. Time for me and Mamma, a pale but fairly steady Mamma whose explanation of severe seasickness was readily accepted by the health inspector as the reason for her emaciated state, to walk down the gangplank to America, looking around anxiously for the first sight of Papa.

We paused uncertainly at the landing, searching the sea of faces behind a wire fence as we were being pushed forward by eager passengers behind us. Where was Papa? As we reached the dock I worried. What will we do if Papa is not here?

But before either of us could voice our anxiety, there was a tap on Mamma's shoulder. She turned to see her Adya, his face alight, his blue eyes sparkling as his arms went around her.

"Papa!" I shrieked, and was swept up in an enormous hug.

In the moment before he embraced her, Mamma stood looking at her husband. How real the word suddenly sounded. Was she thinking how much he too had aged? I still remember so clearly what I felt, and can imagine what was in her mind too.

Adya's romantic matinee-idol mustache was gone. The chestnut curls had thinned, and faded to a pepper-and-salt brown. The bright blue eyes were the same, but the face they were set in was almost as worn and shadowed as her own. With a pang she remembered that in a couple of months he would be forty. But the thought that his youth, too, had fled was strangely a comfort.

Papa hugged me tight and smiled at his wife, whose ravaged face wore the story of the four years that had passed since their last meeting. With a guilty pang he realized just how terrible her life must have been while he was comfortable in Harbin.

Of course I was his big surprise. Papa left a chubby child of four, and a thin leggy eight-year-old returned to him. "How big she is," he kept saying. "How much she's grown."

While Papa bustled about arranging transport for our luggage, Mamma, almost in a daze, was trying to absorb the new impressions that flooded her senses. I was noticing with pleasure that Frieda's uncle had found her and was hugging her tight. I saw only Jacob's back as he walked off between his new parents, but I noted with delight how cozy he looked with both their arms around his shoulders.

At last we were settled in a taxi, threading our way through the traffic, following the wagon with our belongings uptown. My parents sat stealing glances at each other, getting used to the new Adya, the new Olya. Every so often, shaking his head, Papa looked at me and said wistfully, "How much she has grown," or "Where did my baby go?" and I realized how much of my childhood he had lost.

I was so busy learning Papa's face again that it was many blocks before I remembered to look at New York and be awed by the tall buildings around us that shut out the sunlight, the cars and buses crowding the horse carts, the people flooding across the busy intersections.

Suddenly I uttered a cry of surprise.

"What is it, Niurochka?" Papa asked. "What do you see? It's a wonderful city, isn't it?"

"Yes, but Papa, it's the first of December."

"Of course, dushenka. So?"

"But Papa, look at the street. There's no snow."

For the first time in my life I was seeing bare pavements in winter.

As we continued uptown and my parents became absorbed in their talk, I began to look at the city. New impressions came so fast that my head was soon spinning. Everything I saw was strange. We reached midtown and the glitter of Broadway sparkled around us.

"So many lights — and they flash. What is it, Papa? What is it?"

Papa grinned at my excitement. "They are theatres, dushenka. They show movies." He saw my puzzled face. "Moving picture shows. I'll bring you and Mamma down here to see one. You'll love it."

Moving pictures. Absorbed in trying to imagine this wonder, I screamed and clutched Papa tightly as a sudden terrible roar passed over us. We were riding under an elevated road and I was sure it was going to fall down on us. But Papa's merry laugh soothed my fear, even as the roar dwindled away in the distance.

"What was it?" I whispered in awe. "It was like thunder."

Papa patted me reassuringly. "It's only a train going by, darling. We're riding under the tracks of an elevated train." He explained the marvels of his new city. "It's called the El. We also have trains that run under the ground, the subway. We'll ride on it when we go downtown to the theatre."

As we left behind the wonders of downtown and entered the broad tree-lined avenues of Harlem, I tried to absorb these new impressions. "Oh, Mamma, isn't New York wonderful?" I sighed. "Even better than Moscow."

"Yes, darling, wonderful," Mamma agreed absently. To her the city was only a haze going by. Between exhaustion and the emotion of seeing Papa and the surprise of what he was saying, she was dazed and close to collapse.

Papa and I looked at each other. Then he smiled. "Mamma is too tired now to be excited," he reassured me. "Give her time to rest and recover from her seasickness, and she'll love New York too."

"Oh, yes, Adya." Mamma tried to brighten up. "How wonderful it will be to get home and rest in our own apartment. Is it much farther?"

"Olya, you must be prepared." He pressed her hand. "As I was saying, I've had business reverses while you were en route, and just now we have very little money. It's not a very nice apartment, but it's all I can afford now. It's only for a little while." He turned pleading eyes to his wife. "Please don't be too disappointed."

Mamma rallied her waning strength to respond. "Of course I understand, Adya. I know you'll do your best." She turned her head to see that we were crossing a bridge. "Look, Niurocha, there's a river, just like at home. How nice."

"It's the East River," Papa said. "It runs through the city, like the Moskva. But we don't live near it, I'm afraid."

As we entered the shabby streets of the east Bronx, I could see the loss of hope in Mamma's face as she began to realize that her dream of recapturing her former life with Papa was not going to come true. How often in her narrow bed in Moscow did we talk in the night of "how it would be" when we were all together again, just like in the old days in the yellow house.

But nothing prepared her for the reality of walking through the squalid tenement hallway into a dingy flat at the rear, with long-unpainted walls, worn furniture and a view of clotheslines across an alley.

"Oh, Adya," was all she can say. In that moment her hopes died and despair took possession.

America was only another betrayal.

In his Manchurian exile Adya had long pictured the reunion of his family. Now that it had come, where was the joy, the love, the pride in his elegant wife and his adorable daughter, that he had imagined? He knew that the four hard years of separation were bound to have marked them all, that it would take time to knit them into a family again. Still, his heart turned to the dead life he had so loved, that he now knew could never be revived. A whole new family pattern would have to be built, but he didn't know whether he had the patience or the strength for it.

Of course he tried. His first effort was to make Olya understand the business fiasco that made everything so much harder. So often he had replayed in his tired mind the collapse of his plans, searching for some way he might have staved off disaster. When he talked to me about it, years later, I finally came to understand how he had been caught in the bizarre turns of history once again.

In the thin-walled flat I could hear them talking night after night, Mamma trying patiently to understand, but still unable to believe that her Adya, who had made so much out of such slim beginnings, had been unable to save himself this time.

"But you must understand, Olechka, how helpless I was. When I arrived in America last year, my prospects were so good. I wasn't one of those destitute immigrants who come crawling into America hoping just to survive. I didn't come without money. I made money trading in Manchuria with the funds I brought out of Russia, and I was ready to do it again in New York.

"You know about my cousins the Saldins, she's my mother's cousin. They came here long ago. She raised her six children in Brooklyn. Her husband is in the dress business, and they've all done well.

"When I got here I looked them up. They were very friendly and happy to help me get started. They were the ones who encouraged me to settle in New York. I specially liked Barney, the only son who wasn't working in his father's dress company. We got along so well, I thought we could go into business together. My offer of a business partnership appealed to him. He was between jobs. So he got a loan from his father for his share of the investment.

"My plan was to import toys and novelties from Germany for the retail market. It seemed to be a sure bet to succeed. I had my old business contacts in Germany and I knew how to sell. That's what I've always done. And Barney, with his local merchandising connections, and the English that I didn't have. It was a perfect combination."

"It sounds wonderful, Adya," Olga said. "Just what you needed. So what could go wrong?"

"For the first six months, everything went right," he said. "Our firm was doing well, and the future looked even better. I was busy learning English in night school." I heard a deep sigh from Papa. "Only we hadn't counted on the terrible inflation that hit Germany this year. If we'd had better connections on the scene in Europe, somebody who had some financial know-how, we might have turned things to our advantage. But our German agent bungled it all, and instead of manipulating our funds to make a killing, he managed to lose everything."

"My poor Adya." Mamma must have kissed him. Nobody said anything for a while. But then Papa began again. "Just when you cabled me that your visa came through and you were on your way, we found ourselves out of business, with no capital and a pile of debts. So we had to liquidate. Well, I felt I had to give Barney the little that was left. After all, the business was my idea. Barney only went into it to help me, and it wasn't his own money. I couldn't load him down with more debts. He's got children, house payments. You understand, Olechka . . . " His voice trailed off helplessly.

Papa was now aware that the noble gesture had actually been made at the expense of his own family. He was forced to bring us into a neighborhood such as his wife had never known. He was at the low point of his life, enduring his first failure just when he desperately needed success for our welfare. With his limited English, the only work he had been able to find was as a jobber selling sweaters from store to store on the East Side. For the first time in his life, living from day to day like his slum neighbors, I could feel that Papa was afraid.

My memory summons up an evening in December when our reunited family was sitting at supper around the rickety kitchen table. Two gas jets in tarnished brass wall brackets threw their unsteady light over the soiled walls, bumpy with old paint, the scuffed floorboards and dilapidated furniture.

The exchange of news and reminiscence that brightened our evenings at first had given way to discouraged silence. It was hard to reweave the threads of our family fabric while survival remained a nagging anxiety.

As I toyed idly with my mealy potatoes, the underdone beets, the pale overboiled beef, I looked around the table. Papa's face bore the shadow of weariness from a long disappointing day on his feet. Around Mamma's mouth the drooping lines of blighted hope were etched deeper every day. My own normal chatter was squelched by the pall of gloom that hung over the shabby room, where the three of us sat enclosed in our separate miseries.

Sadly I wondered what had happened to the glow of reunion that lit up our lives like a brief candle. Sighing, I squirmed in my chair and turning, saw, drifting across the uncurtained window, fat flakes of snow. What joy! I jumped up and ran to stare out into the alley, where the sprawling garbage cans and ranged clotheslines were slowly being shrouded in fairy white.

"Oh, look, it's snowing at last. How pretty it is! Look, Papa, see. Look, Mamma. Now it will be like home." Lifted out of my gloom by the gift of snow, I expected Papa to share my joy.

"Niura! Come back to the table at once. Don't you know better than to jump up like that in the middle of supper? What manners!"

"I'm sorry, Papa." My buoyant mood sank like a stone at Papa's anger. "But it's snowing. Come see."

"Now. At once! Olga, this child has no sense of discipline at all. She acts like a little hoyden. She must learn to obey. I know . . . " He struggled to control himself and speak more gently, as I returned meekly to my chair while Mamma stammered excuses. How could he admit that he was really raging at a profitless day, that the snow would make his rounds harder tomorrow?

"I know it has been hard for you to train her, the way things were, but now . . . " He turned to me and smiled forgivingly. "You must learn to act like a lady, Niurochka, not a tomboy."

"Yes, Papa," was all I could trust myself to say. I would *not* cry. "I'm sorry, Papa."

My father and I were having a hard time. Finishing my meal in silence, I cleared the table for Mamma, then went back to the window to stare unseeingly at the heavy snowfall that whitened it, my mind deep in troubles.

All my dreams of happiness in a new land with Papa — were they all just rosy dreams, would they never come true? I could sense that each of us held our own vision of what we expected, all different from the reality. I could see that Papa had no idea of who I really was, or even who Mamma was. He has only four-year-old memories of a lost life. But he must have known how much those years changed us. Of course we didn't really know how they had changed him either, a flash of insight tells me. He'd been living a whole life we didn't know about. But how would we ever find out about each other, the real each other, if nobody talked about it? And how could we be happy together if we didn't?

No matter how hard I tried, I knew I couldn't be the sunny plump little four-year-old who used to bounce on Papa's knee and twist his mustache, the mustache that had been such a vivid memory and that I missed. I'd spent four years learning to be strong and self-reliant, taking care of Mamma, sharing hunger and fear, carrying diamonds in my belt buttons, being responsible and brave. How could I go back to being a carefree baby? I knew that Papa had a lot on his mind. His business had failed, he had no real job, his money was gone. I heard my parents talking at night in the bedroom, worrying about money and debts. Still, I wanted Papa to love me unconditionally, as in the old days, no matter what.

And Mamma. Once more I had to worry about her and try to protect her. Papa was discouraged because Mamma didn't know how to keep house, how to cook or how to manage. But she never had. Babushka and the aunts ran the household. After that we stayed in other people's houses. Mamma would never be able to learn now. She's so disappointed in America, she won't even try. She wouldn't go to English classes with Papa, even though she studied English at school, and even started to teach me in Moscow. Now she refused to learn it. How could she live in America without trying to be an American?

I'm sure that in each mind within the small household, isolated in our sad separate shells, thoughts were unknowingly running in the same channels. Papa, lying on the lumpy bed, curling his toes to ease the cramping in his tired feet, must have felt more helpless than when he first left his village for the forests and wolves of Siberia. At first he tried hard to give his wife a sense of hope in the future, to lift her sagging spirits as he'd always been able to do in the old days. But this time he couldn't make her believe that "things will get better soon."

Was it because he couldn't really believe it himself? Where was that vitality and confidence that had once carried him through every trial undaunted? Why had it drained away now, when he needed it as never before, needed it to sustain the family he loved and who depended on him for everything? He'd always been proud to be the strong one, the prop of his family. Now here he lay, balding and seedy and spent, saddled with a despondent wife who hated America, an unruly child whom he didn't seem able to handle, a ramshackle excuse for a home that he might not even be able to pay the next rent on.

Now he himself needed support and comfort, but there was no one to turn to. He was alone in a strange land far from kith and kin. "Alone." The word pounded in his brain, constricted his chest. In the end, he had to face his panic frightened and alone. Ashamed to be heard weeping, he buried his aching head in the pillow. In this hovel with its thin walls, he could not afford even the luxury of letting go.

In the kitchen at the other end of the apartment, the rattle of dishes and the splash of water masked Mamma's matching despair. Up to her elbows in sudsy dishwater (reluctantly admitting to herself that in this kitchen where hot water ran unstintingly she really enjoyed washing dishes), she worried about the growing clashes between father and daughter, mourned her shattered hopes of once more finding grace and joy in life.

A swarm of miseries buzzed around her weary head like bees. No money to live on, her health failing, the struggle to be an adequate housewife, aching homesickness, the ugliness of this world she was trapped in. She knew it would overwhelm her in the end. Most devastating of all was the crashing of her hopes. Once we reach Adya, she had told herself during the long journey, I'll be able to let go, be taken care of, be loved and comforted once again. Adya will be in charge. He'll make life easy and wonderful as it had once been. Out of the bleeding Russia of the Bolsheviks, the world will be a livable place again. Adya will push back the enveloping sadness I live in every day. He will help me take some pleasure in life once more.

But none of it had happened. The shock of walking into this horrible flat, with its peeling walls and scarred clumsy table and creaky old bed, with its view of a littered alley. There was so much to say on the way uptown from the pier, she admitted to herself, so much to look at. I hardly heard what Adya was trying to tell me, to prepare me for his poverty. I pushed it all to the back of my mind, and blindly walked into it. But how can I live with it?

As always during the long hard time, her mind must have reached for the anodyne of memories, to their first magical years of marriage. She shut out the dreary kitchen and its dismal view with visions of her elegant drawing room in the yellow house, with all the things she loved around her. Wherever she turned, her eyes had fed on familiar beauty and order. And how she had starved for it ever since, with a longing that nothing in this ugly world could slake.

In all those years at Babushka's house, she'd thought of herself as useless baggage, carried by the others out of kindness and love for her husband. But the months in Moscow and en route had given her some small measure of self-confidence. With all her uncertainties and insecurities, she had brought herself and her child safely across the sea. Left on her own, she did not sink, she did swim to safety. She remembered too, with a small complacent thrill, how she had managed to take out the forbidden jewels, which were now helping to feed the family, while Adya tried to get back on his feet.

Yet in this new life with Adya, she was back in the old slough of failure. She couldn't seem to do anything right. Each grim day drained away more of her strength, and she was even less able to perform her tasks.

Her husband was grumpy and dissatisfied, her child pulling away from her. She felt at odds with them both, divided from them by a widening gulf.

Only yesterday, bored with the rainy weather, I was rummaging in the dresser drawer for something interesting to do. Delighted to find a pile of picture postcards, I was sitting on the floor spreading them out when Papa arrived, wet and cross. As he went into the bedroom to put his coat away he nearly stepped on me and the collection.

"What is this?" he demanded, barely missing a card with his wet feet. "What are you doing with my postcards?"

"Oh, are they yours, Papa? They're so pretty. I thought they belonged to Mamma."

"Get them up off the floor before they're ruined." He carefully went around them to get out of his wet shoes and into his slippers. "I've carried these cards all through Manchuria and America. What were you doing in my drawer?"

"Oh, I'm sorry, Papa. I thought it was Mamma's.

247

She always lets me — "

"Unbelievable. Have you no sense of respect for people's privacy? Don't you — "

Hearing his angry voice, Mamma hurried in from the kitchen. "What is it, Adya? Are you looking for something? You're home early today."

"It's too wet to work. Do you see, Olya, how the child has all my precious postcards on the floor, getting muddy?"

"But darling, she didn't know how special they are to you. She was just looking for something to amuse her, and . . . and there's so little space. Put them on the bed, Niurochka, and be careful with them."

"That's not the point, Olya. Niura has to learn to respect other people's things and places."

Mamma and I spoke together:

"I didn't mean to disturb your things, Papa. Mamma always — "

"But Adya, I've always let her — "

"Be quiet, Niura. You have no sense of propriety, you're like a little savage. You never think, you just do anything that pops into your head."

Mamma, taking the guilt on herself, just bowed her head and wept. I stood up in a rage.

"Papa, that's not fair! Mamma has always taught me to be careful of other people's things, and I was very careful with your cards. I only wanted to look at them. I had nothing to do, and they are so pretty. I was going to put them back right away. Please, it's not Mamma's fault."

Startled by my spunk, Papa stopped. He took a deep breath, looked at me, then said to Mamma, "I'm sorry, Olya. It's not your fault. I know how hard it's been for you, and I'm so sorry I wasn't there to help." He put his arm around his wife's shaking shoulders and held her. "But the child has to learn to think about other people and respect their property, and not do things without thinking. But now I can deal with it. You must just rest and get well."

I drew a deep breath. The axe had not fallen. "I'm so sorry about your cards being on the floor. They were so pretty, I just wanted to stop and look at them right away. Could you tell me about them, Papa? Why are they so special?"

Papa smiled and took the cards I had just picked up. "I'm sorry I was so sharp with you, dushenka. I do want you to learn to control yourself and think about what you do. But I know you can't learn it overnight. Let's both try to be a little patient."

He looked at the cards in his hand, then sat down on the bed and pulled me between his knees. "These are the cards that Mamma and I wrote to each other the year we were engaged. When I had to leave you and Mamma behind, I took them with me to be a little closer to you both. Now that we're together, I don't need them for comfort." He tucked them carefully back into the drawer. "But of course I'll always keep them because they meant so much to me."

He sighed wearily, and lay down on the bed. "Go play with your things, Niurochka. I'm so tired. I need to take a rest."

Mamma managed a wet smile and went back to the kitchen to finish the dishes, but still listening to the conversation in the bedroom.

I wasn't willing to lose Papa's attention so easily. "But there's nothing to do here, Papa. I get so bored. Why can't I go to school now?"

"What do you mean, bored?" Papa wearily sat up and pressed his fingers to his temples. "I gave you a beautiful doll and a new bear, and you're still complaining. You can go to school after New Year's. Why do you always have to argue with me and question everything I say?"

"But Papa — "

"No more! You're so eager to learn. Here. Take my English book and let me rest." He closed his eyes to shut me out.

Mamma sighed at our eagerness to become Americans. She wanted only to leave this alien country for the Europe she knew and loved, for a place where she could feel at home. Would she ever get there? Or would she slowly die of loneliness here with her family around her?

She saw that I wanted to play in the street, to talk English, to launch myself into this community which she saw only as a slum — a place which sickened and terrified her. I'd been her closest companion for four years, and now I was always straining to get out of the house. She had not one friend to talk to or turn to for sympathy.

And poor Adya, so beaten down by his first failure, too discouraged to see what she needed, to see how like him his daughter was. He needed her strength now. They had so little to give each other, it seemed. The fires that Adya could always kindle in her seemed dead, and his own vitality was banked by discouragement. The passion that always drew them close in the past could not serve their need, could not bridge the gap the years had made.

She mustn't give way now, she chided herself. She must hold on. She must believe that their lives would improve. Adya would soon find a good job. They'd move to a decent home. She'd make friends. She must keep trying.

But even as she chanted the litany, the black melancholy that stalked her swept over her again, the fear that she would lose her hold on life and be swept away. Leaning her head against the bumpy paint of the kitchen cupboard, she let the silent tears flow free, mourning the life she would not live.

In the middle room, which served the family as dining room, sitting room, and my bedroom, I could not find relief in tears. From under my daybed in the corner I pulled out the box that held my playthings. This corner was my only "own space" in the cramped flat. Here I slept, kept my things, read and daydreamed. On the bed sat the new doll and teddy bear Papa had waiting for me when I arrived. I patted the bear sadly. Poor Papa, trying to make up to me for Mishka's loss. He couldn't understand that no other bear would ever be Mishka to me.

Shaking my head to empty out the sad thoughts, I took Papa's English reader and settled down to copy words. I promised myself that by the time I went to school in January I would be ready to speak to people in my new language. But my thoughts soon wandered. Staring blindly at the schoolbook, I tried to imagine what school would be like. I could start after the Christmas holidays were over, Papa said, but it was hard to wait. In all my life I had never gone to school, and was always wishing I could.

There were so many new and exciting things to look forward to. How happy I could be here if only Papa wasn't always angry and Mamma always sad. Oh, Papa, why can't you see that I don't want to be disobedient or rude. I do forget rules sometimes, but I don't mean to. I just want to find out about things, to go to school, to learn and make new friends. I just want us to be a family again.

But we're not a family yet, we're only three people who don't know each other very well. Please, Papa, be patient until I learn how to please you, until I learn your rules. Tired and troubled, I pulled off the faded brown cover of the daybed and prepared to end the unsatisfactory day, impatient to start a better one tomorrow.

❦ 11 ❧

Mean Streets

New York, 1923

EARLY the next morning, eager to enjoy the snow that had appeared overnight, I inveigled Mamma into letting me play outdoors. "Just by the steps, I promise."

I stood shyly on the stoop, feeling awkward in my long black European coat, watching the children throw snowballs and slide down the hills of snow left along the curbs by the street cleaners. I was fascinated by these new ways to play with snow, especially the sleds improvised out of cardboard cartons by enterprising boys. If only I could do that. My longing must have telegraphed itself. A boy looked up at the stoop, stopped his play and stood studying me for a long moment. Then he came up to offer me his cardboard.

"Want to slide?" he asked.

"Slide?" My vocabulary was still short on action verbs. "No English, me." I smiled in embarrassment.

The boy held out the cardboard again, made a long glide in the air. "Slide. See? Slide on snow," pointing to the nearby mound. "Come on. It's fun."

Thus casually my new world embraced me.

Soon I was sliding and shouting with friends who supplied me with words as each need arose. Every day I felt more at home in the dingy street, stayed out playing longer and worried my anxious mother more. As the holidays progressed, so did my English. With the easy mimicry of childhood, I spoke it with a Bronx accent, leaping at once beyond my father's hard-won facility in the new tongue.

After the New Year Papa took me, numb with excitement, to the public school three blocks away. School at last. To my enthralled eye, the ancient red brick, with its sooty carved stone trim, was more beautiful than the gilded domes of the Kremlin. I was not even downcast to be put in the second grade, a full year below my age level. I was thrilled they would take me at all. The school records officially endowed me with a new American name, Nora, because Papa said Niura didn't sound American. He now spelled his own name Adolph Lourie for the same reason.

So the new year brought progress to our small family. Papa's earnings had picked up during the holidays, and so had his self-confidence. He even began to have hopes of finding a better job as the economy began to rise out of its slump and his English improved. Only Mamma was still drooping, refusing to meet neighbors, to learn English, to like anything.

I was reveling in my new status of schoolgirl, making friends, gobbling up knowledge as fast as it came my way. I knew enough English now to read the primer and copy out the sentences. My years as an avid bookworm in Russia stood me in good stead. Reading was half of living for me. All I needed was a new language to read in, and I was rapidly acquiring it. Papa worked hard to gain the fluency he vitally needed for his livelihood, but he was frustrated by his inability to overcome his guttural Russian accent. He was torn between pride and envy as I smugly paraded my newest accomplishments at the dinner table each evening.

"Speak Russian, Niurochka," Mamma would plead. "I don't understand."

"But Mamma, I want to practice my English," I would grumble, reluctantly repeating my news in Russian. "Why don't you go to night school with Papa? You have to learn English. You live in America now."

I'm afraid I was irrepressible in any language. When you're eight, pride easily conquers modesty. "Miss O'Reilly said my reading was very good today," I would boast. "I read a whole half page. And I got 100 in arithmetic again. I love arithmetic."

The tidy black-and-white world of numbers, where when you were right you were absolutely right, strongly appealed to me. I suppose it satisfied a deep need for the ordered universe I'd lacked during the years of chaos, when nothing was stable or dependable or steadfast. How good to deal with figures that ranged themselves correctly in response to firm rules. Once you learned the rules, you could command the figures unequivocally.

School became my mecca, a cheerful haven where I was approved.

My flighty memory, which retained facts perfectly, found Papa's arbitrary edicts easy to forget. His way of discipline was so new and different, I couldn't get used to it. Babushka's slap as she bustled by, Aunt Sonya's grave lectures, even Mamma's sad disappointment at misbehavior were correctives I could understand — emphatic but soon over.

But Papa had a grimmer weapon. When he sensed his anger rising to uncontrollable pitch (and in these frustrating days it often did) he refused to give vent to it, as if he feared his own violence. Instead he retired behind a wall of silence that chilled the household like an iceberg in our midst. This was a punishment I could not bear, because it went on and on. Papa dealt out silence in measured lengths. For an hour, an evening, even a whole day, the life of the family congealed under its stony weight.

One afternoon he walked into the kitchen and found me climbing up the tall built-in cabinet for a cookie. Sternly he ordered me down and forbade me to climb again. "You will fall and hurt yourself," he warned. "I have no money for doctor bills. I've told you before — "

"But Papa — " Agile as a monkey, I was supremely confident of my ability not to fall, and my ability to convince anyone of anything.

"No buts. When I say don't, you don't. I will not have argument from you. You must learn to obey, and no buts about it. Now remember, daughter. If you disobey me again, I . . . I will not speak to you for a month. I cannot have a willful, disobedient child."

Not speak for a month. The idea was unreal. I had lived with grownups who threatened, scolded, occasionally spanked, perhaps put me in a corner for fifteen minutes, but whose anger cooled as quickly as my own tears dried. I could not take seriously such an interminable sentence as a month. Papa couldn't really mean it. But only three days later I found out.

I came home from school on a dismal day of cold rain, and found Mamma lying down with the headache that was becoming an almost daily event. An uninteresting-looking dinner was simmering on the stove. My homework was quickly done. It was too nasty to go out to play. Restless and at loose ends, I roamed the flat looking for something to do, something to eat.

I spied some bags and boxes on a high shelf in the kitchen and wondered if they held anything delicious. Without further thought, I was up on the cabinet, rummaging, when . . .

"Niura!"

For an instant I lost my grip on the high shelf and almost fulfilled Papa's dire prophecy, but grabbed hold again in time. Numbly I turned to see my father's furious face. Stammering excuses, I was compounding my sin in my confusion.

"Papa. I didn't mean . . . I didn't know you were home . . . I'm sorry."

"Didn't know I was home. So now you think a rule is to be obeyed only when you can be caught? Are you becoming sneaky as well as willful and disobedient? Very well. You know what I told you. You must learn that when you disobey you will be punished. Get down from there. Good. Now. I will not speak to you again for one month from today."

He turned away and left the room, his face and his clenched knuckles white with rage.

Crushed and penitent, I slunk about the house. Unable to bear the weight of guilt, I retreated to my bed corner and the solace of a favorite book. At dinner I tried vainly to get food past the lump in my throat, careful not to look at Papa's cold face. Mamma's helpless misery only heaped more coals on the fire.

"My teacher said we're going on a field trip next week. Will you sign my permission slip, Papa?" I decided to be sneaky if I had to. Papa always asked about anything special that was happening at school.

But he turned to Mamma and spoke without any sign that he'd heard me. "I heard about a job that's opening up pretty soon, that I might be able to get, Olya. I think when spring comes, things might get better for us." He rose and went over to the armchair where his newspaper waited.

The unhappy day came to an end at last. With my diehard optimism, I fell asleep sure that things would be better tomorrow. Papa couldn't really have meant a month. But as the days went by Papa went on ignoring me. Not answering my questions, indifferent to my tales of triumph at school, only showing he was aware of my existence when he told Mamma to reprimand me for a fault.

Eventually my misery and longing for pardon hardened into a stubborn determination not to be broken. I would match my father's will with my own. If Papa had stopped loving me — Well, I would just have to live with that loss. I would find other roads to happiness. I stayed outdoors longer, playing with my friends, came home only when called to supper, sat in the kitchen with Mamma in the evening, ran off to school early.

"Adya," Mamma complained, "you must stop ostracizing Niurochka this way. She hardly ever comes home any more, except to eat and sleep. Surely she's learned her lesson by now."

I'm certain Papa too was sick of his edict, but his will could not bend. "I'm sure she has, Olya," he admitted. "But I have to keep my word, or she won't believe me next time. I know it's hard on us all, but I said a month."

Only panic succeeded in suspending the sentence after a mere three weeks.

That afternoon I was outside playing with the kids. I had made a new friend in school and discovered that he lived at the other end of my own block. Freddie was a tall spindly kid with curly dark hair and an engaging smile. His charm had earned him the post of monitor. Each day as he passed out papers in class, his radiant grin warmed my bruised heart and earned him an answering smile. Soon we were playing tag at recess and walking home together. Freddie began to linger at my end of the street to play stoop ball or hopscotch.

A February thaw had kept us children outdoors for days, but that day it ended abruptly. The low afternoon sun retreated behind surly clouds and an Arctic wind swept down on the city.

"Brr, it's getting so cold." Freddie shivered in his thin coat; his bare bony knees were turning purple. His uninsulated frame could not stand much chilling. "Let's go up to my house and get my mother to fix us some hot cocoa."

"Good idea. I love cocoa." I was ready for a treat anytime.

Freddie lived in an apartment house on the corner, three flights up in a flat whose tall windows faced the avenue. Before long we were happily sipping warm cocoa, nibbling sugary cookies, and staring out at the crowds hurrying to get out of the wind. Freddie's mother asked me lots of questions about Russia. Freddie brought out his favorite games. Soon we were deep in a Parcheesi contest. Then we spent a happy hour looking at pictures in the stereopticon.

I was turning the pages in big picture book when Freddie's mother came in from the kitchen to ask, "What time does your mother expect you home for supper, Nora? It's getting late. We would have eaten long ago, but we're waiting for Freddie's father. He's working late today."

Supper. Suddenly I remembered that Mamma didn't know where I was. "Oh, I must go home right away. I didn't know it was so late."

I'd barely gotten my arm into my coat sleeve when Johnny Kelly, who lived in my building, burst in, yelling.

"Hey, Freddie, guess what! The police are searching the block. They say there's a lost kid — "

His voice stopped suddenly as he caught sight of me in the hall. "Hey, you're her. Your folks are all upset. They have the police out looking for you. You better get home fast."

"I was just going." I scrambled into my galoshes as fast as I could, my heart thumping wildly at the thought of Papa's anger. "Thank you for the cocoa," I barely remembered to say. "I had a nice time."

As I rushed down the three flights I wondered what would happen now. This was real disobedience. Papa probably wouldn't speak to me for a year. But it was the thought of Mamma's terror that made my heart sink. She'll be sure I'm kidnapped or dead, I agonized, knowing all too well Mamma's habit of expecting the worst to happen.

Dashing down the block, my open coat flapping wildly behind me, I could see a crowd in front of our stoop, framed in lamplight. There was Mamma in tears, Papa trying to comfort her. Two policemen and a ring of neighbors stood around them, all talking at the same time.

"I'm here, Mamma." I began shouting. "I'm not lost. I was just — "

Papa turned at the sound of my voice. As he caught sight of me his drawn face bloomed into a smile of such joy that I could not make another sound. Still running on, panting in great gasps that hurt my chest, carried by momentum rather than conscious will, I ran blindly into Papa, who was already rushing toward me.

"Niurochka!" He swept me up into his arms, hugged me so tight that I lost what little was left of my breath. "Dushenka. We thought you were lost. We were afraid — "

Gulping air so I could talk, I could only gasp, "I'm here, Papa. I'm sorry. I love you, Papa." My arms tight around my father's neck, I burst into violent sobs — fear, relief and love exploding in me all at once. Mamma could only put her arms around us both and weep.

After Papa's apologies to the police were brushed away, "Don't worry, we get these false alarms all the time. We're glad she's safe." and Mamma tried to thank the sympathetic neighbors with gestures and broken words, everybody retired within their own walls as the street emptied into its usual winter-night quiet.

"You see, Olya, they are good people after all," Papa commented.

Our mutual outpouring of relief and joy washed away so many bitter feelings and brought the family close at last.

"I'm really sorry, Mamma, Papa." I tried to explain, aware for once how much my thoughtlessness had grieved and frightened my parents. "It got cold in the street and Freddie said to come up and have hot cocoa at his house. It was so nice there, and I didn't know how late it was. His mother gave us cookies, and he has lots of games. We started playing, and his father was working late and — "

"All right, dushenka, all right." Papa said gently. "We know you didn't mean to be naughty. But you must understand that you can't go away without telling — "

"Oh, yes, Papa. Really, I do understand. I just do things without thinking sometimes, and it's been so sad here at home . . . and . . . " I could see this was getting me into deep water and began again. "But I'll try harder to think, to remember."

"Good." Papa closed the subject. "If you learn that, this trouble will be worthwhile. Now let's eat our supper and be happy."

Even though I didn't always remember to be good, and Papa didn't always succeed in tolerating my growing independence, still he was more careful with his ultimatums and I also tried harder not to provoke them.

As the clashes between father and daughter died down and comradeship burgeoned, I found to my delight that Papa was learning to talk to me as Mamma always had, like a person, not like a child. To his surprise, I think he was finding that those divided years, when Mamma in her need had turned to me for fellowship and courage, had given me a strength and perception far beyond my few years.

Once he learned that it was unnecessary, even futile, to try to shield me from his worries, Papa gratefully found that he could share his perplexity over Mamma's health and her state of mind. He could even depend on my help, since I was long accustomed to propping up my mother in her low moments.

Through February frost and March bluster, life in the dingy flat settled into a kind of normalcy, except for Mamma's growing melancholy. Even the hint of spring in the air, as the equinox brought a taste of warm days to come, failed to rouse her sagging spirits or send color into her sallow cheeks. More and more she was withdrawing into a lonely sadness where we could not follow. Except for doing the most necessary household tasks, she now spent most of her time lying down. Her lack of English provided her with an excuse to leave the shopping to Papa. When a last-minute need arose, I would run to the corner grocery for her.

Papa and I had no idea how to cope with this retreat from life. He was prepared to wait patiently for Mamma's energy to return with rest and tonics. He never knew when the black moods would possess her. Sometimes, in sheer frustration, he would lash out, desperate to force his wife back into the real world, even tried to rouse her to anger. That would at least be better than this passive letting go.

"For God's sake, get hold of yourself," he stormed one day when he came home and found her on her bed, with nothing done. "You have to get up and *try*, Olya."

She looked up at him with mournful eyes, her cheeks wet with tears that flowed unbidden and unchecked. "I can't, Adya. I try, but I just can't make myself move. What's wrong with me?" she would plead in panic. "*Help* me, Adya."

He caught her in his arms, as frightened as she was of the black shadow reaching for her. "I will, darling. I don't know what's troubling you so. Tell me what I can do."

She shook her head helplessly. "I don't know what anybody can do." Her eyes overflowed again. "It's no use, my dear." In a dead voice she said, "I am dying of loneliness. Alone and in a strange land I am dying."

It was more than her husband could bear. Gripping her arms till she cried out, trying to reach her, no matter how, he shouted, "Don't you dare say that! I am here with you. *Niura* is here. We love you! Why are you shutting us out? Why can't you talk to us and let us help you?"

The wet shadowed eyes stared back dully, the weary voice was flat. "You don't understand, Adya. I love you too. I love Niurochka. But this life is impossible for me." A passion of longing roused her, she gripped her husband's hand and pleaded, her voice now vibrant with emotion, "Let's go back to Europe, Adya. Please take me back to a world I know. If we could live in Europe I know I would get well. Anywhere! Germany, France, Latvia, I don't care where. I'd be so happy."

The desperate husband, torn between love and reason, turned away helplessly. "Olya, you know that's impossible. We have no money, no place to go. I must earn a decent living first. This is a good country we've come to. Give it a chance. I'm sure I'll get back on my feet in a few months."

She smiled sadly, fell back on her pillow, turned her head away in despair. "In a few months," she whispered, "I'll be dead."

Unable to combat such irrational melancholy, Papa could only make the most of the time between attacks. He concentrated on keeping life bearable, occasionally pleasant. Despite his wife's pleadings to go back to Europe, he still believed that when he got a decent job, when they had a better home, there would be an upturn in her condition. He had no experience with chronic depression and no money to take Mamma to doctors who might have recognized it as a disease.

Trying to get her more involved in life, he schemed to get her out more, to meet people. His cousins kept inviting us to Brooklyn. They were eager to meet Papa's family. But the thought of a two-hour subway ride to Ocean Parkway terrified Mamma. Finally one Sunday, Papa, ashamed of neglecting the people who had been so good to him, insisted that we pay the obligatory visit.

I was enchanted by the subway train that went so fast through the long tunnels, as the colored lights flashed by. But Mamma sat listlessly, only gripping Papa's arm when the train whipped rocking around curves. When we arrived at the Saldins' brownstone, the whole tribe was gathered to meet us. A hearty, noisy family with numerous children and grandchildren, their loud chatter overwhelmed Mamma. While I ran upstairs to play with assorted cousins, she sat, barely responding to kind questions and sympathetic comments about her "terrible time in Russia," nibbling listlessly at the rich party foods pressed on her from all sides.

Seeing his wife visibly drooping, Papa made our

excuses early, pleading the long trip home. On the ride back, he turned to Mamma expectantly. "Weren't they nice, Olechka? Wasn't that a pleasant home?"

"How vulgar the new styles are," was Mamma's comment. "With her heavy arms, for Morris' wife to wear little short sleeves with slits! They have no taste in America."

How sad, I thought. I had enjoyed my new cousins so much, it felt so good to have family in America. But the evening had given nothing to Mamma

As the weather got warmer, Papa and I began to spend many weekend hours outdoors. Papa, always a walker, now discovered the joy of a daughter who loved walking too. We rambled through nearby St. Ann's Park, glad to be off pavements and under trees, watching birds and squirrels, climbing small hills and running back down to collapse in giggles on the grass.

Our pleasure would have been complete if only Mamma would come too. But she could never be persuaded. "I'll only slow you down," she said, shaking her head against all our coaxing. "I just don't have the energy today."

The best we could do was coax her to sit out on the stoop on sunny days, absently smiling back when neighbors passed and nodded. Though at first she had occasionally walked down to see the stores full of things she couldn't afford to buy, to look at the Christmas decorations, it had long been nearly impossible to get her out of the house.

At least her absence gave us a chance to share our worries.

"What can we do, Papashka?" I would ask more and more often. "How can we make Mamma better?"

But Papa had no answer for me. He just shook his head sadly and said, "I wish I knew, dushenka.

We just have to give her time. She needs to rest, to recover her strength."

But as the weeks went by, neither of us could believe any more in the help of time. We could see that time was pushing Mamma downhill, not up.

One day I came home from school and heard the sound of Mamma's weeping. I was frightened. I had gotten used to seeing her at her work or resting with tears pouring silently down her face. But this was different. This was the sound of heartbreak, and it shocked me. For the first time the thought came: Mamma will never get better, only worse and worse until . . .

That Saturday, a bright day late in March when the park was burgeoning with buds, Papa and I dropped down on a bench, warm and winded after a romp. I slumped cozily against Papa's shoulder. Quietly we breathed in the spring, enjoying tree buds swelling in the sunshine and scrawny squirrels emerging from winter holes to fluff their fur and scurry in search of stray acorns. If only Mamma could enjoy it with us.

"We must do *something*, Papa. Mamma is getting worse all the time. Why is she always so sad? We're back together now, she should be happy. I don't understand."

"I don't either, darling," Papa admitted with a sigh. "I've tried everything I can think of. I know the hard years did her health a lot of harm. But she's getting plenty of good food now. She's taking a tonic. Yet nothing seems to help." Almost to himself he murmured, "I haven't seen her smile in weeks."

"That's the worst thing, Papa. Yesterday when I came home from school, Mamma was lying in bed with tears just pouring down. Her pillow was all wet. But when I asked if anything was hurting her, she said No, nothing. What is it that makes her so sad? Can't we do *something* to help her, Papa?"

My father stared at his outstretched toes through a long silence, then sat straight up in sudden resolution. Taking my hand in his, he nodded. "Yes, dushenka, there is something we can do. And I've finally decided we must do it, even though it will be hard.

"Mamma is very unhappy in America. She is lonely for the kind of life she knew before the war. She just doesn't seem to have the strength to stand living this way until I can get back on my feet. So — " He paused as if reluctant to commit himself to the fateful decision. "So, I've decided we should go back to Europe."

"Back to Europe!" I was aghast. "But Papa, you love it in America. We both do. You're always saying how wonderful it is here, where we can be free, not afraid of — "

"I know, I know, my child. But Mamma doesn't love it. She's miserable here. And I'm afraid . . . " He stopped himself, then began again. "I'm afraid her homesickness is keeping her from getting well. She needs friends, company that she can enjoy. She could have that in Europe."

He marshaled arguments, for himself as much as for me. "Mamma has school friends in Switzerland, relatives in Latvia and France. She knows people all over Europe, people who could keep her from being lonely."

"But she has us, Papa. How can she be lonely when we're finally together?"

"In Europe she could have the friends she enjoys. Maybe we could live in Riga near her cousin Amelia. Or in Germany, where I have business acquaintances. I can probably get better work where I am known. It could be a good life."

"But to cross the ocean again, Papa? Mamma was *so* seasick — "

"I know how much she hates the sea. But I guess she hates America even more. She wants to go. She says so all the time."

"When we were at sea, she kept saying that nothing would ever get her on a ship again."

"This time you would go on a bigger ship. An English ship that only takes five days to cross the ocean. I don't think she'd be so seasick this time."

"But Papa. To leave America?"

"Yes, it will be hard to leave. You and I are the kind of people who are made for America. But we're strong, darling. We can live anywhere."

"But America is better than anyplace. How can Mamma not see that?"

"Mamma is not like us. She needs a place where she can feel at home. Someday, when Mamma is well again and I've made some money, maybe we can come back to America, eh?"

Such a "maybe" was small comfort to me. I had embraced the independent spirit of my new country wholeheartedly.

"But Papa, how can we go to Europe? It costs a lot of money for three tickets, doesn't it? Or are you going to sell the diamonds Mamma and I brought?"

Papa laughed. "No, dushenka, those diamonds were sold long ago, just to buy food and pay our rent. I'll have to borrow the money. There's a bank called the Morris Plan, which is very helpful to immigrants. I'll borrow the passage money from them, with a bit more to keep you going until I can send you more."

"Keep *us* going? Oh, Papa, you don't mean we have to go without *you?*"

"I'll work hard. And as soon as I've paid off the loan, I'll come and join you wherever Mamma decides to live."

This was the final blow. To be separated again? After all that time apart?

"Oh, Papa!" The full weight of the coming ordeal descended on me. I burrowed my head in Papa's armpit and wept.

He was shocked at the violence of my feelings. "Darling, dushenka, don't cry. Don't. It won't be long, I promise. It's not like in the revolution, when I couldn't come home. This is just a matter of earning some money. It'll only take a few months. I'll give up the flat, and stay with Cousin Barney. I won't need to spend any money. In three months, maybe four, I'll pay off the loan and have enough for my own passage. You'll see. I'll be there before you even miss me."

I looked up into my father's face, shook my head mournfully. "Oh, no, Papa. I miss you already!"

In my mind's eye I saw the sad months in Moscow, the terrible days on the ship, the endless despair that I had to battle for Mamma's spirit. I remembered the glorious day when we arrived in New York and Papa's rapturous face loomed over Mamma's shoulder, when I knew I could hand my worries over to him. Papa would make everything all right, and I could be a child again. But none of it had happened.

I looked up pleadingly, willing Papa to say, I know this will be very hard on you, darling. Maybe we shouldn't think about it. But the only thing I saw was his hopeful face, smiling with the joy of having found a solution to our terrible problem. I felt my shoulders bow unconsciously to the coming burden.

Sniffing back the sobs, I rubbed my face on Papa's shirt to dry my wet cheeks. "If we have to go, I suppose we have to," I conceded. "For Mamma's sake."

With a heavy sigh, I accepted the inevitable. "But, oh, Papa, it will be hard to take care of Mamma again all by myself."

❧ *12* ❧

A Springtime Fall

New York/Southampton, 1923

EVEN TODAY I can remember my desperate hope that something would happen to prevent the coming parting — that Papa wouldn't be able to get the loan, that he would convince Mamma to stay in America, that she would remember how terrible her last ocean crossing was. But in only two months my luck ran out.

Squeezed next to Mamma by the crowded rail, I waved frantically to Papa across the widening water. My heart sank as I watched his face and flailing arm grow small and indistinct while the big white ship was slowly tugged away from the pier.

Oh, Papa, you shouldn't have let us go! I cried to him in my heart. How will we manage to live without you? What will happen to us? I could feel Mamma trembling beside me. It took so little nowadays to bring her to tears and so much to stop them. Again the burden of responsibility sat heavily on my skinny shoulders. Grimly I set myself to be cheerful.

"What a gorgeous day. Look, Mamma, how calm the water is. In this lovely weather you won't be seasick. Papa said it only takes five days to get to Europe on the Homeric. Isn't it a beautiful ship, Mamushka? And so big." I babbled, trying hard to distract my mother, whose face already wore a mask of melancholy, so out of tune with the holiday gaiety that rippled along the deck.

The sparkling day, blue and gold trimmed with lacy clouds, seemed to hold the essence of May. In the busy harbor small boats left a glittering wake as they scooted around ponderous freighters loaded with the world's cargo. The soft air blowing from the land held a promise of flowers, mingled with the tang of salt rising from the water. America flaunted its beauty for Mamma as she fled its squalor.

When Papa announced his willingness to live in Europe, Mamma grew deliriously happy. Having set her heart stubbornly against the alien new world, returning to the familiar old one seemed the panacea for all her ills. Her spirits soared and energized her languid body. At first it looked as if she was really recovering her health, both in body and mind. Her husband's qualms about the wisdom of their plan faded in the face of his wife's new pleasure in living.

Ironically, just as our family was about to break up again, it was beginning to take on real life. Now Mamma made valiant efforts to take part in family doings. She often came along on our excursions, and tried to participate in our fun, though she tired very easily. Papa and I were glad to temper our steps to hers, in our joy at having our circle complete at last. We strolled together under the blossoming trees in the park, window-shopped along the avenue. On one memorable occasion my father indulged us to the extent of buying tickets to a movie. Mamma was intrigued by the oversized figures moving on a screen in the flickering light beam. I was awed by the magic and became a lifetime addict.

In the new euphoria my parents began to draw physically closer. As their spirits rose, their bodies came alive and regained their old comfort in each other, responding to the rising sense of spring. Now she worried that our departure would threaten this growing bond.

As the day of parting neared, Mamma's doubts resurfaced. The reality dawned — she would be on her own again, responsible for her child, without a husband's strength to lean on. As her trepidation returned, so did her violent mood swings, keeping the household in constant upheaval. She wanted desperately to go — but she was terrified of going. Papa found it impossible to accommodate himself to her ups and downs. A decision once made, in his rather rigid mind, was final.

Still he tried to bend with the wind of his wife's shifting moods. Twice he suggested that the trip be canceled, or at least postponed. "You are just beginning to recover, Olenka. Wouldn't it be wiser to wait till you're stronger? Then I wouldn't worry about you so much."

But whenever Adya doubted, Olya grew surer. Each time she convinced him that she should go. She so longed to return to a familiar world that in the end she made herself believe she could endure the trip and win through to the life she dreamed of.

"'If I could get us out of Russia and survive those two terrible weeks on the winter sea," she assured him, trying hard to believe it too, "I can certainly manage an easy five-day crossing in good weather and a train trip to Paris. And once we get to Aunt Manya's, I'll be able to rest. I'm sure we can stay there until you come. I could give piano lessons . . . If we can just get there . . . ."

So set was she on leaving that Papa curbed his arguments and stifled his fears. Olga kept hers

locked in her heart, to gnaw away in silence. I tried
to plead for delay, for more time together in the happy
state we now enjoyed, reminding her of her agonies
on the earlier crossing, But my pleas seemed only
to feed her obsession. I could only hope that the joy
of returning to her beloved Europe would help
Mamma to face the trip.

Now we stood at the rail, watching America grow
small and misty. As we left the sunny harbor for the
open sea, I saw the realization of what Mamma had
done flood over her. She had actually left her husband. Once more she was alone with her child, and
on the unfriendly sea. All her stifled terrors now came
pouring to overwhelm her failing body. Blindly she
turned from the rail and pushed through the crowds
on deck and down unfamiliar corridors, seeking sanctuary as the storm of regret broke.

I followed her helplessly. I recognized the familiar symptoms, and knew how little I could do to
relieve them. So closely had I shared my mother's
life for four hard years that in spite of the lifetime
between then and now I can still read her troubled
mind and relate to her bewildered feelings.

Stumbling down a companionway to our deck
Mamma tripped, and might have fallen but for a tall
young man in staff uniform who was standing at the
bottom. He reached out for her as she teetered precariously. Guiding her down the last steps, he could
not help noticing her tears and distress.

"Is anything wrong?" he asked sympathetically.
"Can I be of help in any way? I am Emanuel Golding,
the ship's interpreter."

Mamma, choked by sobs, could only shake her
head, her dark eyes drowned in tears, her soft mouth
set in tragedy.

I came clattering down the staircase. "My

mother doesn't speak English," I explained. "We're from Russia."

Mr. Golding repeated his question in excellent Russian, but Mamma was too distraught to speak. Again I stepped into the breach.

"Mamma is upset because we left my father in America. She's very nervous about getting seasick, too. She was very sick when we came to America last year. Maybe if she could lie down and rest . . . "

The kind young man saw us to our cabin. "A sedative would probably help her relax. I'll get Dr. Nelson and see what he recommends," he said.

By the time the ship's doctor arrived, Mamma's hysteria had mounted alarmingly. She had used up the last of her emotional reserves. Now she was shut up in a dark pit of regret and terror that no ray could penetrate. How had she dared leave Adya and launch herself back into the world with no strength to sustain her? She sobbed into her pillow. What would happen to her poor child?

I waited anxiously for the doctor, stroking my mother's back, crooning futile comfort. "Don't, Mamushka, please don't cry so much. You'll make yourself sick. You'll see, it'll be all right. In just a few days we'll be in Europe. You'll get better, you'll be happy. You'll see. Please, please don't cry any more."

Sitting on the edge of the bed, I saw to my horror a dark stain spreading across the cover toward me. I leaped up, screaming. "Mamma, you're bleeding. What is it? Are you hurt? Mamma, answer me." I shook the wailing woman, but without response. Olga's heart had long been bleeding, and from deeper wounds.

Dr. Nelson, arriving with Mr. Golding, found much more to deal with than a simple case of nerves. Mamma was hemorrhaging. She had not even known she was pregnant. She was miscarrying again, losing blood in dangerous amounts. They rushed her to the ship's hospital on a stretcher, while Mr. Golding tried to get answers to the doctor's questions, most of which I had to supply.

Finally, calm returned. Olga — examined, cleaned up and medicated — was half comatose, half asleep. Now Mr. Golding could turn his attention to me, sitting huddled in a corner.

"You haven't had any lunch yet, have you?" he said. "Neither have I. Come along and let's get some. It will do us both good. Your mother will be sleeping for quite awhile." He took my hand with a warm smile. "Do you know I've got a little girl just about your age? Now you can keep me from missing her."

The tight band of fear around my heart eased a notch. "Is Mamma going to be all right?" I asked as I trotted along trying to keep up with Mr. Golding's strides. "What's the matter with her?"

"She's pretty sick right now," he admitted. "But Dr. Nelson will take good care of her. She'll need to stay in bed for awhile, and get lots of rest. Now, what shall we have for lunch?"

What a nice man Mr. Golding was, I thought as I gobbled down my lamb chop and mashed potatoes, suddenly aware how hungry I was. His long narrow face and dark curly hair reminded me of Aunt Sonya's friend Leonid. So did his helpfulness. His brown eyes behind dark-rimmed glasses were kind. Now that Mamma seemed to be in good hands, and would have the care she needed, I could turn my mind to enjoying shipboard adventures, and getting to know my new friend. I was full of questions.

"Tell me about your little girl. Where do you live? What does an interpreter do?"

Throughout the trip, Mamma lay sad and somnolent in her hospital bed, far down on the lowest, most stable deck, too depressed even to notice the gentle motion of the summer sea.

Knowing she was in a safe place and getting kindly care, I felt free to roam. I explored the broad decks and red plush salons. I was well cared for by a kindly steward and attached myself to Mr. Golding whenever I could. I took the stories about his little daughter as permission to substitute for her temporarily. I sat with him at meals and listened as he talked about his family.

"You'd like Miriam," the fond father told me. "She'll be ten this fall, and she loves dancing. Last year she began ballet lessons, and she's practicing all the time."

I wondered wistfully if some day I too might live in a pretty cottage where Mamma could grow roses, as Mrs. Golding did in Southampton, and where I could take dance lessons like Miriam.

"I wish I could see your house," I said, "and meet Miriam. But we're going to go on to Cherbourg, Papa said."

"Well," Mannie Golding hesitated, probably wondering how much he could safely tell me. "I'm afraid your Mamma will not be well enough to travel for awhile. We'll have to take her to a hospital in Southampton, where the White Star Line has its headquarters. We could not leave you in Cherbourg, where you have no one to meet you."

"But, Papa — "

"We'll notify your father."

"Oh, good. Papa will know what to do. I've been worrying about what would happen when the trip is over."

In my visits to Mamma I could plainly see that even walking would be impossible for her, let alone traveling to Paris. She lay exhausted on her pillows, tears seeping slowly from under her closed lids. Now and then her thin fingers would clutch nervously at the covers, as if vainly seeking protection against the disaster she knew she had brought on herself. Not only had she taken her daughter away from her father, but she had lost the new child who might have survived in America.

As I stroked her hair and crooned the old litany of comfort, the heavy lids would slowly open and the tear-drenched eyes would gaze at me with heartbreak. Then Mamma would slowly shake her head, denying the possibility that "Everything will be all right, you just have to get well."

I awoke late to find the ship at anchor. As I dressed hastily, my friend the steward came to pack and collect my luggage.

"Hurry, child, they are waiting to take you ashore," he said as he pulled open each drawer." I've been so busy this morning I forgot to wake you."

"I'm hurrying," I said. "I'll be ready in a minute, and we'll go get Mamma."

"Oh, your Mamma has gone already. They took her in an ambulance. She's too weak to walk. She's probably at Shirley Warren Infirmary by now."

"Already? But why didn't they wait for me? Now they'll have to make another trip."

"Oh, they couldn't take you there. You can't stay in a hospital. You're not sick."

"Not stay? But I have to stay with Mamma. She'll be upset. She can't speak English. I *have* to take care of her."

"Don't worry, child," the kind old man comforted me. "She'll be taken good care of. And so will you." He closed the suitcase and hurried me, still vainly protesting, up on deck. I looked around for Mr. Golding; but he was nowhere to be seen. Helpless, I was firmly turned over to the driver of a battered van.

In just a few minutes we arrived at a large walled park and turned in through wrought-iron gates. It was more than half a century later that I discovered to what sort of place I was being delivered. Passing several red brick structures under tall oaks, we stopped before one of the larger buildings. At the sound of our horn, a woman in starched blue cotton and high-topped shoes came to the door.

"Come along, come along." she commanded briskly, pushing me into the big front room.

I stared in surprise at the assortment of females who occupied it. Young and old, large and small, all wore the same uniform: starched cotton dresses in pale blue and white stripes, covered with stiff white aprons. Thick brown wool stockings and high black shoes completed the outfit. The younger women were busy dusting, polishing or scrubbing; the older ones sat over their mending or knitting. There was not an idle pair of hands to be seen.

I was turned over to a stout woman who led me to a linen room and outfitted me with the same coarse uniform. To my amazement it included a boned cotton corset, as foreign as armor to my skinny unformed figure. The rough muslin underclothes, two sizes too large but the smallest ones to be had, bunched up under the wasp-waisted corset. It soon rubbed red spots on my back and under my arms, and set me twitching and scratching.

"Why do I have to wear these ugly clothes?" I complained to anyone who would listen. "They don't fit me. They hurt and make me itch."

But the only ones who would answer were as helpless as I was. "Everybody here has to wear them. It's all we have," came the sharp retort.

"But I have my own clothes. Why can't I wear them? At least they fit me."

"Oh, no. Everybody has to wear the uniform here," was the impassive refrain. "It's the rule."

I soon learned that the odd establishment lived wholly by its rules. Working, eating, sleeping, keeping clean, everything had to be done "the way we do it," and any query earned only one reply, "It's the rule."

I felt I was being squeezed into a straitjacket of rules, of inflexible routine. Up at six, shiver through a cold bath, and then the bed had to be made and the dormitory tidied. After a breakfast of lumpy porridge and cold toast, everyone worked at their assorted tasks till noon. I was given aprons to hem. On my hard wooden chair I fidgeted over the unfamiliar task, sweating in the starched cambric, the scratchy wool stockings, wanting to be running outdoors instead.

At midday came a hearty English dinner: shepherd's pie or pork pasties or boiled mutton, always heavy with grease, served with cabbage or turnips. In the warm days of late spring the starches and fats lay in my stomach like so much sludge, nauseating and constipating, relieved only slightly by the cups of strong tea I washed it down with. My finicky digestion was totally unequal to this ordeal. I soon fell back on bread and butter and an occasional potato. Only the dessert that sometimes embellished the plain fare, the custard or trifle or gooseberry tart that marked Sundays, provided any real pleasure at the table.

After dinner there was a free hour, but real rest was impossible, since the upstairs dormitories were off limits between breakfast and bedtime. Tired women sat nodding around the big common room downstairs. Only a few walked about under the trees. I took full advantage of the time to get away by myself, to stretch out on the grass and make believe I was free and not cooped up.

Soon it was time to take up work again, until the day ended with a cold supper and an early bedtime. Undressing by my cot and wiggling inside my tight covers to make a little extra room for my toes, I wondered numbly how I had fallen into this narrow box and if I would ever manage to get out.

It didn't take long for inertia to give way to impatience. I might be trapped in this incomprehensible place with its irrational rules, but I would still fight for basic rights. The chief of these was my right to take care of my mother.

After four days with no news of Mamma, I went looking for the head matron. "I want to see my mother," I demanded. "How is she? Why doesn't someone tell me anything about her?"

"Your mother is at Shirley Warren Infirmary. She is very sick." The woman tried to be patient and curb her annoyance at being challenged by a child. Children were supposed to be seen and not heard. "She needs a long rest and absolute quiet."

"She may need a rest," I contradicted boldly. "But she also needs me. I've been taking care of her since I was four, when my Papa went away. She depends on me. She can't speak English. You have no right to keep me away from her. She needs me." My voice rose shrilly. "You must take me to see her. I have to make sure she's all right."

The prim Englishwoman stiffened in shock; she could not believe her ears. For a child to intrude in this rude way upon the concerns of grownups, to make demands . . . She clamped her thin lips firmly on her rage and pushed me out of her office.

"You can't see your mother till she's better. Now go back to your hems."

For several days this contest of wills went on, with me constantly demanding to be taken to see my mother. The matrons who ran the workhouse — for this refuge for society's rejects was where the White Star Line had chosen to warehouse the child left on their hands by a passenger's collapse — could only repeat and repeat that they couldn't take me to the Infirmary.

Finally my small stock of patience ran out. I was never going to see Mamma, I decided, unless I went by myself. Once the idea flashed into my head, it became my compelling goal, the answer to all my vexing problems. I would just go and find Mamma by myself.

I had already discovered that making a nuisance of myself helped me to get ignored when it mattered to me. Everyone was glad when I went out to play in the grounds and left them alone. No one cared whether or not I hemmed aprons as long as I stopped my nagging.

I wandered about near the gate, idly picking daisies and buttercups, taking note that the deaf old gateman as often as not left the heavy gate ajar after letting a delivery van pass. That afternoon I found it easy to slip through as soon as the gateman went back inside his tiny house. Running around the corner, I set off down a long avenue, looking for a likely passerby to ask the way to Shirley Warren Infirmary.

It was the uniform that undid me. The plump lady I spoke to, who looked kind and motherly, stared at me suspiciously. "Aren't you a workhouse child?" she demanded, squinting in the bright sunshine. "What do you want at the Infirmary?"

"Workhouse?" I stumbled over the unfamiliar word. "I don't know. My mother is — "

"Of course you are." The plump lady was in the full flow of righteousness. "I know that uniform." She took me firmly by the arm and propelled me back along the street. "Do they let you wander about the city alone? How lax."

My protests, my efforts to pull loose, did no good. The plump lady was determined to deliver the wayward child back to authority along with a piece of her mind. When at last I managed to wrench my bruised arm out of the iron grasp and turned to flee, I ran right into the legs of a tall bobby and was inescapably trapped.

Yet my abortive rebellion did produce results. Berated for defiance of rules, I stubbornly insisted on my right to see my mother, and refused to promise to be good. Eventually the frustrated head matron responsible for my safety had to capitulate.

"If I take you to see your another, will you promise not to run away again? We don't want to keep you apart. It's only that she's very sick, and they don't want to upset her,"

"I *won't* upset her," I assured her ingratiatingly, smelling victory. "She'll feel better if she sees me. And I won't run away. I didn't before. I only went to visit my mother. I'll be good, as long as I get to see Mamma."

But the visit to Shirley Warren proved more worrying than reassuring. Walking down the white corridor, eagerly anticipating Mamma's pleasure, I heard the familiar voice raised in a mournful wail.

"I'm dying! You are torturing me. I can't breathe. I'm going to die . . . "

Rushing toward the sound, I found my mother in bed in a small room, her long dark hair loose over her face, her hands feebly plucking at the neck of her hospital gown. Her face was tear-strained, her eyes enormous in their dark shadows.

"Mamma. Mamma!" I cried, throwing my arms protectively around her. "Don't cry, Mamushka, I'm here. I'll take care of you. No one will hurt you. Please don't cry any more."

"Niurochka!" Mamma's arms gripped my shoulders. "Oh, my darling, I thought I'd never see you again. Help me, dushenka, save me!"

I held her tight, my thoughts whirling in confusion. I had often seen my mother worried, sad, anxious or depressed. But this irrational terror was a thing unknown. How was I to deal with this new Mamma, in the grip of a torment far beyond reason?

"Please, Mamma," I pleaded, rubbing the quivering shoulder, smoothing back the tangled hair. "Please don't get so upset. You have to rest and get well, so we can go home. So we can be together again. There's nothing to be frightened of, Mamma. No one is trying to hurt you. They are trying to make you better."

I turned to the matron and the nurse who had followed us into the room. But the two, seeing that my presence seemed to be calming the distraught patient, wisely decided to leave mother and daughter alone for a brief visit.

Olga's fearful eyes followed them. As they left the room, she clutched me closer, whispering, "You must get me out of here, Niura. They will kill me here. They watch me all the time. They don't let me sleep. They leave a bright light shining all night, and they bang loud drums right outside my window. They — "

"Hush, Mamma. *Please* don't upset yourself like this." I tried to stem the rising tide of hysteria in my mother's voice. I couldn't believe anyone could be doing such terrible things, yet why was Mamma saying them? *Could* somebody be trying to hurt her? Was it possible? "You must try to be quiet, Mamma, you must rest and get your strength back, so we can leave here and get back to Papa. Nobody wants to hurt you. Please, Mamushka."

Perhaps the soothing murmur of the beloved voice, perhaps the consoling closeness of the small familiar body, or her own waning strength, subdued the haunting fears, let reason return. With a sigh of infinite sadness, the tight-tensed body relaxed and my mother fell back in exhaustion on her pillows.

She gazed at me mournfully.

"My darling child, what will happen to you when I die? What will you do here, all alone in this cold English city? Oh, how could I have taken you away from Papa?"

"Mamma, don't talk like that." Trying to convince us both, I could only repeat the litany of hopes that sounded hollow even to me. "I'll be fine, Mamma. You just have to get better, to rest and not get upset. Don't be afraid. You won't die. Just try to sleep now."

Mamma's eyes closed wearily in obedience, but her head slowly nodded, as if to say, "Yes, I am going to die. You'll see, you'll see."

The nurse came in and pulled me away, with a finger on her lips. Outside, she spoke softly. "You must go now and let her rest. She'll sleep now. She's very weak. She lost a lot of blood."

"But why is she so frightened? She says she's not allowed to sleep, that bright lights shine all night and drums make noise."

The nurse put a gentle arm around me. "You must understand that your mother is very ill. Her mind is affected, she has delusions — "

"Delusions?" I stared at her in shock. "You mean she's . . . she . . . ?" I could not bring myself to say the awful word.

"No no." The nurse tried to reassure me. "Not really. When she's stronger, I'm sure her mind will steady."

"But she's so *afraid*, and so lonely. She needs me. She can't speak English. Couldn't I stay here with her? I could sleep at the bottom of her bed. I could talk to her, quiet her — "

"I'm sorry, child. That's impossible. Your mother is getting the best of care. Perhaps you could come and see her again next week." Just then the matron appeared and took me back to the walled park, turning a deaf ear to all my pleas and demands.

The visit raised my anxiety about my mother to an obsession. Somehow I had to manage to be near Mamma, who needed my support more than she had ever needed it 'in fear or famine, in seasickness or homesickness. This time she needed my strength and comfort in a struggle for actual survival. I could sense how low Mamma's fires had sunk, how easily she could slip over the edge to oblivion. Bursting with vitality as I was myself, I felt in my mother the draining away of that vital force to a dangerously low level, and it terrified me.

A remedy suggested itself that night when I was lying on my cot, trying to muffle my sobs in my pillow. In the crowded dormitory it was impossible to make any private noise, even though my cot was the last in the row, next to a partition that ran across the long room. Just past the foot of my bed a door led into the area beyond the partition. I had never gone inside, but I had glimpsed pale women lying in beds there, as attendants passed in and out with trays or bedpans or linens.

"What's the matter, little one?" came a whisper from the neighboring bed. Bridget was a thin bony Irishwoman, with a crippled hip and a useless right leg. All knobs and angles, she radiated the warmth of a plump pillowy motherwoman. She had soon taken me under her scrawny wing, and had already helped me through some discouraged moments.

"Oh, Bridget, I don't know what to do," I whispered back, sniffling. "My Mamma is so sick, she needs me so much. And they won't let me see her again till next week. I've been thinking and thinking, but I don't know what to do."

Bridget's sympathy was copious and healing. "It's too bad, it is, to be 'eld away from yer own mum, and she ailin'. Me own mum was sick for three year

afore she died, and it was sich a comfort t' me, to be
nearby all that time. They let me tend her hair, and
plump her pillers. Sometimes I'd sing 'er an hymn
— " She rambled on, clutching the comfort of memories, till I broke in.

"Oh, if I could only do that. Mamma loves it
when I brush her hair. But here — "

"It *was* 'ere," Bridget assured me. "Me Mum
was in the infirmary 'ere, jist next door. They'd let
me in to see 'er soon's I come up to bed the night."

"Here?" The solution broke over me like a di-
vine revelation. "Is that why those people next door
stay in bed all the time? Is it an infirmary? Why can't
Mamma come here too, and stay next door? And I
could take care of her." My voice rose in excitement.

"Sure ye could. Now hush," Bridget warned.
"Don't be wakin' up everybody, child. Best quiet down
'n' git to sleep now."

I tried hard to be quiet, having learned the
wisdom of not annoying people from whom I wanted
a favor. But it was hard to wait till morning to begin
asking. I fell asleep planning my campaign to have
Mamma moved next door. I knew it would be hard to
accomplish, but I was prepared to nag as long as it
took to achieve my goal.

I was surprised to find, however, that the idea
of bringing Mamma here to be near me was less impossible than I feared. The time between the head
matron's first "Preposterous! What an idea." and the
final "Well, it might do. If it will stop your pestering
it's worth looking into. I'll speak to them at the Infirmary and see . . . " turned out to be only a few days.

Mamma's condition was hopeless, I later discovered. In 1923 pernicious anemia was incurable.
There was no known treatment that could check the
steady deterioration. Until they heard from my father, custodial care could be as easily given in one

infirmary as another. The hospital was happy to be rid of a hysterical woman with whom they could not speak. It also made sense to have her near the daughter who could interpret for her and knew how to calm her, as well.

I could hardly believe it when the head matron sent for me one afternoon and announced, primly pleased to be conferring a boon, that my mother had arrived while we were at dinner. Mrs. Lourie was in the infirmary. Nora could visit her that evening as soon as she was ready for bed.

I was a rapturously happy child as I snuggled into my narrow cot that night. Mamma lay drowsing beyond the partition, equally happy to be near her Niurochka, languid and pale but coherent, apparently relieved of her terrors. When I found her in the third bed left of the aisle in the infirmary, Mamma hugged me tight and wept joyful tears over me.

Perhaps the nearness of her child might prove to be the elixir she needed against the crowding terrors that tormented her. My warm little body pressed against her, the familiar voice whispering comfort and love in her ear, eased her tense limbs and stilled the unbearable thoughts. At bedtime, assured that I would be just on the other side of the partition, she was satisfied to let me leave, to close her eyes and let sleep in. And I in my turn, clutching the happy thought of a morning visit with a Mamma who would be next door tomorrow and every day, also surrendered to the sandman with a long sigh of content.

I was deep in sleep, in a dream where I was back on board ship, walking the rolling deck. The wind was stirring the waves to whitecaps that slapped hard against the side and sent spray over the rail. I was excited by the wild weather and happy knowing that we were sailing back to America — back to Papa. Suddenly, far ahead, I saw Mamma's tall slender figure trying to balance on the pitching deck, sliding downhill as the ship tilted.

"Mamma." I cried in alarm, running hard to catch her. But no matter how fast I ran, Mamma seemed to be just as far away as ever, slipping lower, not bracing herself, just screaming "Niura, Niura, help me." as she slid closer and closer to the rail that dipped perilously low to the waves. As in a slow-motion movie, even as I ran I watched my mother slip under the rail, still screaming, "Niura. I am dying. Help me."

Shouting "Mamma. Mamma. I'm coming. Hold on." I awoke to the sound of my own voice, my heart thumping in terror. Suddenly I realized that Mamma *was* screaming. The sound was not in my dream but just beyond the partition.

I scrambled out of bed, fighting the entangling covers, as an infirmary attendant came running through the door.

"Get back in bed, child," she whispered. "Your mother is just having a nightmare."

But I was not easily subdued. "Mamma is calling me. She's frightened. I can help her. Please let me go to her!"

Fighting off the restraining arms, I tried to reach the nearby door, to reach Mamma, who needed me. The noise of our scuffle brought out the charge nurse.

"Hush. You'll wake everybody up," she warned. "Be quiet and go back to bed. We're taking care of your mother."

"No, no." I wouldn't be hushed. "Mamma needs me. I must go to her. I can talk to her. You can't. She's afraid. Please let me see her. She's calling me."

My pleading did not soften the stony face of the nurse. Nor could she soften my resolve; denial only hardened it. If my pleading didn't succeed, I would demand.

"I *have* to help my Mamma. She depends on me. You have no right to keep me away from her. She's calling me. Can't you *hear* her? I *have* to go to her." My childish treble must have taken on a menacing tone. "What are you doing to my mother that you don't want me to see? If you don't let me see her *now*, I'll go to the police tomorrow and complain. You have *no right* to keep me from my mother."

I realize now that the harassed nurse was in a quandary. She knew there was nothing to be done for the distraught woman next door, whose oxygen-starved brain was failing under the trauma of pernicious anemia. How could she tell a small daughter that her mother was having an acute attack of melancholia, with delusions of persecution? But she couldn't let a child rouse the whole dormitory either.

"Nora, I cannot let you create a scene in the middle of the night. You'll wake everybody up. I promise you can see your mother in the morning. We're not doing anything to her, just trying to quiet her."

I struggled in her grasp and tried to speak.

"No, don't interrupt. If you insist on seeing her now, you will not be able to see her tomorrow. We'll move you out of this building and you won't see her again. You can't stay here if you're going to upset everyone."

I sensed a crack in the defenses, and clutched at my chance. Tomorrow would take care of itself. Right now my only object was to get to Mamma.

"Yes, I *do* insist on seeing my mother now. I don't care about afterwards. Just let me see her now!"

As the startled attendant loosened her hold, I slipped by and through the half-open door outlined by the dim light inside.

I could not see Mamma; cloth screens had been set up around her bed, but I could hear her wailing. "I'm dying . . . you are killing me . . . help me."

Rushing around the screen, I stopped in shock at the sight of the haggard woman in the bed. Her face was as pale as death under the tangle of raven hair, her eyes wild, her mouth twisted in agony. Her limbs strained against the attendant who held her.

"Mamma!" I ran to kneel beside the bed, clasped the clutching hands, laid my warm cheek against the cold arm. "Mamma, I'm here. I'll help you. You won't die. Please, Mamma, don't be frightened."

Shaken by a terror beyond any I had ever felt, I burst into tears that fell hot on my mother's clammy, saqllow skin.

Slowly the rolling eyes focused on the tousled head, the tormented voice hushed, the brow knitted in anxious thought as the dying brain struggled to command memory.

"Niura?" She grasped my arm with a desperate grip. "Niurochka. My darling, help me. Oh, I don't want to leave you."

She stared suspiciously up at the attendants standing uncertainly about the bed. Pulling my head close, she whispered secretly, as if the nurses could understand her Russian words.

"Dushenka, I'm dying. They don't let me breathe. Look how they tied this gown so tight — it's choking me. And they just gave me an injection. It will kill me, I know. Oh, Niurochka, my *darling.* I don't want to die."

"No, no, Mamma. You're not going to die. No one wants to hurt you. You're just imagining it." Desperately I pulled at the tie at the back of the hospital gown, but it was already open. "See, Mamma, your gown isn't even tied. You mustn't be afraid . . . "

My mother looked at me with infinite sadness, as if from an enormous distance. "So you are against me too, Niura. But you will see. Tonight I am going to die. I know. I will never see you again, my daughter. Remember me, dushenka . . . Tell Papa . . . "

As the sedative took hold, her voice sank low. With her last strength, my mother took my wet face between her hands and kissed my sweaty brow tenderly. "I am so tired . . . Goodbye, Niurochka. I love you. Don't leave me . . . " The shadowed eyes were veiled by the heavy lids, the pleading voice faded to silence, the hands lay flaccid on the sheet.

"She'll sleep now." With a sigh of relief, the nurse tried to raise me up. "And you must too. Mary, take Nora to her bed."

"No, no, not yet." I fought against the attendant's strong grip. "Let me stay with her a little longer. She said she was going to *die*, that she would never see me again. I can't leave her now."

I crouched like a puppy beside the bed, gripping Mamma's hand in both my own as if to hold her back from her fate.

But soon, I imagine, as tension relaxed in the now quiet room, my heavy head sagged against the mattress, and exhaustion closed my eyes. The nurse nodded to Mary.

"Take her to the little cottage," she ordered. "And Maud, gather up her clothes and bring them along. I'll see to setting things to rights here." Shaking her head she bustled off, muttering, "We can't have this sort of thing. It just won't do."

❧ 13 ❧
A Park But Not a Garden
Southampton, 1923

CREAK-CREAK, creak-creak. A monotonous sound drew me from a well of sleep, deep as death, scratching on a nerve like a nail on glass. I floated up reluctantly, unwilling to return to life. My eyes opened on a wall, but it was the wrong color. Instead of the flaking whitewash on the familiar wooden partition, I faced soiled tan plaster across which ran a long rattail of damp stain. Surprised, I sat up in bed, turned — and froze in horror.

Half a dozen wrinkled faces stared at me. All the witches of my fairy tale books, it seemed, sat about the small room, waiting expectantly to meet the little girl who had materialized in the corner daybed. My fearful eyes locked on the nearest head, bobbing to the rhythm of her creaking rocking chair. The face was long and wizened, with lank white hair hanging about it in thin strands, myopic pale blue eyes squinting. Three long hairs sprouted from the moles on her chin, exactly like the picture in my old book of Baba Yaga, the Grandmother Witch who ate children.

"Good morning, child." The face split into a broad smile, revealing two long brown teeth.

"Good morning," nodded the companion heads.

With a terrified whimper, I turned my back and burrowed as deep as I could into the thin mattress, pulling the covers over my head. For the first time in my life I knew the consuming fear that paralyzes the will and prostrates the spirit. Lying trembling in a corner of an unfamiliar house in an unknown country, surrounded by ancient crones who personified the malice of a hundred folk tales, without the power to think or reason or feel anything but blind panic, I felt utterly abandoned. I hardly even noticed the warm stream that dampened the mattress under me. Cowering in my cocoon like a beaten animal, I lay in a daze of despair until exhaustion returned me to oblivion.

The high summer sun had already started down from the zenith when consciousness returned, and with it fearful memory. But now, forearmed against shock, reason began to stir, battling panic. Still unwilling to face the room, I lay still, remembering last night's threat of exile, working out how I'd gotten here, what must have happened.

I had made a bargain to be allowed to see Mamma, and they had kept it. While I slept they must have moved me into this awful place. I struggled to recollect the confused alarms of the night. What happened to my mother? Behind my shuttered eyes rose the picture of Mamma, ashy gray against her pillows, the fading voice murmuring, "Tonight I am going to die."

Against the total conviction in that voice, the heartbroken farewell in the closing eyes, what were all the kind promises of nurses that "She just needs rest"? My burdened heart rejected them all, accepted the finality of that midnight scene. Mamma was gone, she must be packed away in the attic where I kept other lost loves — Babushka, Mara, Aunt Sonya,

Nyanya, even Mishka — all the beloved figures of a cherished and irretrievable past.

Much as I longed to remain forever in the shelter of the steamy covers, my face to the wall and my back resolutely to the room with its terrifying gargoyles of Baba Yaga, into my heavy heart sank the inescapable fact that I couldn't. Sooner or later I'd have to force myself out of the bed. Did I really wet it? I wondered in mortification. I hadn't done that since I was two. I'd have to face the grinning heads, even speak to them, to ask for food and drink and dry sheets and the way to the bathroom.

As reason reasserted itself and roused initiative, I faced the truth of life — that no lover-prince or father-king would come to rescue the princess in the grim tower. In the narrow soiled cot I grew up and accepted the end of the fairy-tale dream that had sustained me in all the bad years.

Life *didn't* always have a happy ending. In the end it was up to me. Life had to be faced alone. But oh, what a desolate word that was: Alone. It shut the door on a lifetime in which, through war, famine and exile, I had lived sheltered in the arms of those who loved me.

So, painfully, I made my peace with the present, cleaned myself up, found my clothes, got dressed. I performed the necessary functions, ate the dreary meals brought to the cottage from the main kitchen, slept and woke. I spent my days leafing idly through old magazines piled on a table, or sitting in the sun outside the door. I even found paper and pencil in a desk and went back to drawing last year's jagged cornflowers.

Pretty soon I had to admit that my ancient companions were harmless, even friendly. Eventually I made myself answer when they spoke to me. But I never lost the shiver of fear that ran down my back when a Baba Yaga face leaned close and grinned at me in greeting. And I could never find the courage to do battle against my misery. For the first time I accepted my fate passively.

I lived in a shell, shutting out both joy and sorrow. Only at night, when I had the sitting room to myself, would the tears come to melt a little of the protective ice around my bruised heart. I'd cry myself to sleep thinking of Papa, of Babushka, of all the faraway arms that would have held me tight and comforted me. Strangely, I did not think of Mamma. I needed comfort, but thoughts of Mamma would bring only desolation. My mind shut a door on the unbearable memory of that last visit with her.

The long days dragged away one by one, in a daze of discouragement and loneliness so deep that I barely distinguished day from dark, or sun from rain. Until I could be set free from this barless prison I was as inert as in a dungeon. The child who had always lived on springs, who never walked when she could run, or sit when she could bounce, who had been curious and eager to take note of every nuance in the world of sight and sound and smell, now sat unnoticing in the sun like her companion crones.

It must have been nearly a week before a ray of light shone into my darkness. One afternoon I was lying on my cot, idly turning the pages of an old *Illustrated London News*, hardly aware of what I was looking at, when the gateman popped his head in the door.

"There you are, little one," he said. "I've brought you a visitor. Ta ta."

Stepping back, he ushered in a young woman who entered uncertainly, blinded by the change from blazing sunshine to soft shadow, then smiled as she saw me.

"Hello," she said, coming forward with outstretched hand. "I'm Manny Golding's wife, Ruth. He asked me to look you up and find out how you're getting on."

As I stared at her dully, the cheerful smile faded to concern. "Are you all right, Nora? Have you been ill? You remember the interpreter on the Homeric, don't you? He's my husband."

I collected my scattered senses and got up to welcome my caller. "No, I'm not sick," I said. "How do you do, Mrs. Golding?" Remembering old lessons in manners, I added, "Thank you for coming to see me. Won't you sit down?"

Ruth Golding glanced around the fusty room, the ancient heads nodding in their chairs. "No, thank you, dear. It's such a fine day, why don't we take a walk in the grounds? Too nice a day to be shut up inside."

The warmth of the voice and the smile reached into my benumbed heart, stirred the supine spirit.

"Oh, yes," I agreed, taking the outstretched hand and pulling her out the door. Sighing as at the easing of a load, I nodded, blinking in the sudden sunlight. "Oh, yes, this is much better."

Ruth Golding's heart hurt for the pale drooping child standing beside her in the hot clumsy uniform. How sad to see a youngster bowed under the weight of such care and sorrow! She thought of her own saucy romping daughter. How different this child seemed from the one her husband had described with such enthusiasm.

In her interview with the head matron she had learned a little about the mother's condition and the child's banishment from the dormitory. But she was not prepared for the dejected figure beside her. This child seemed almost as drained of life as the old women in whose house she lived. Something would have to be done.

"Tell me how you're getting on, Nora," she said. "I have to give Manny a full report, you know. He was so sorry he didn't get a chance to come himself. The schedules are so hectic now, with the new American quota, and the pileups at the ports. They've just transferred him to the South American run. I hardly get to see him myself these days."

I looked up at the sweet cheerful face, the nicest thing I'd seen for days. I tried a smile in reply, but it came out crooked and stiff. "Mr. Golding was so nice to Mamma and me," I said, trying not to let the tears come at the thought of our happy lunches aboard ship. But the memory was too much for me. "Oh, I wish he could come to see me," I burst out. "I wish I could talk to him."

Ruth Golding heard the despair in the quivering voice; her mother's heart rushed to meet a child's need. She pulled me down on a garden seat and put her arms around me. "Tell me your trouble, darling. Perhaps I can help you."

How wonderful it felt to rest my head on a kind breast, to feel the comfort of sheltering arms. My heart thawed in the warmth, the tears flowed, as I sobbed out all my miseries.

Cradling my shaking body, Ruth Golding sat appalled, visualizing her own child left to endure such desolation. Definitely something would have to be done.

"My poor child," she crooned. As the sobs subsided, she dropped a kiss on my unkempt head, wiped my streaming eyes. "Be patient, my dear. I'm sure things will get better soon. In the meantime, how would you like to come and spend the afternoon at my house and play with my Miriam?"

"Your house?" I stared, eyes wide with glad surprise. "Oh, I'd love it. How wonderful. A whole afternoon away from here. Oh, thank you, thank you."

That fervent "Thank you" stabbed Ruth to the

heart. My ecstasy at the chance to spend just a few hours away made crystal clear the depths of my unhappiness in this place. Ruth set her pretty mouth in resolution. A way would have to be found to effect a rescue. And suddenly it occurred to her what that way might be.

It was a magic afternoon for me. The bus dropped us off at a street of cottages, each with its dooryard garden rioting with summer bloom. Indoors, chintzes took up the flowery theme. Miriam's first disdainful stare at my dowdy attire was quickly squelched by her mother, who pointed out that their guest was in a uniform not of her own choosing, that her mother was quite ill, and that she needed cheering up.

Her sympathy roused, Miriam took me up to her pretty room to play games and have a tea party for her dolls. The tears started up again as I remembered my own tea parties in the yellow house, with my lost Mishka in the seat of honor. But I brushed them away, unwilling to spoil this joyful day. Soon we were playing like old friends.

"Why don't you dance for Nora," Miriam's mother suggested, "while I get the tea ready?"

She took me back to the living room to wait until Miriam called "Ready," then put a record on the phonograph.

More magic. As Miriam, in a pink tutu, came through the door *en pointe* and pirouetted gaily to the music, I sat entranced. When the dance ended and Miriam dropped coyly into a low curtsy, I clapped my hands in delight.

"How pretty. You're just like the dancers in the 'Blue Bird,' that Mamma and I saw in Moscow," I gushed, as Miriam beamed.

All too soon it was time to leave. Full of scones and jam and cambric tea, I reluctantly boarded the bus with Mrs. Golding for the return trip.

"Oh, Mrs. Golding, I had such a happy day. It was just like being home again." A heavy sigh escaped me. "If only I didn't have to go back to that place." At the thought of it my eyes filled once more. "Oh, Mrs. Golding, couldn't you please do something to get me out?" How I longed to say, "Couldn't you let me stay with you and Miriam?" but I didn't quite dare.

Ruth Golding hugged me tight, whispering, "I will. I promise I will. Just be patient a little while longer, and I promise I'll do my very best to get you moved."

As she turned me over to the gateman, with a last quick hug she said, "Remember, I promised. Just be patient. And don't be sad. It won't be long."

Strangely, the pleasant outing, instead of cheering me up, only made my heart heavier. By contrast with the Golding cottage, in flower inside and out, and its sunny occupants, the little house of the Baba Yagas seemed even more dismal. Afraid to believe in Ruth's promise, I shrank back into my shell of numb endurance. I retreated into memory, lying for hours on my bed or on the bench outside the door, retelling myself the stories I loved. Crying over the trials of Little Eva or Sara Crewe kept my mind off my own troubles.

Relief, when it came, was as unexpected as it was sudden. The head Matron appeared one morning with a bundle under her arm.

"Here, put these on," she ordered, unrolling the bundle on my cot. My face lit up at the sight of my blue dress.

"My clothes! You're going to let me wear my own clothes?"

"Yes," snapped the matron. "You are leaving. Get dressed. I'll be back for you in ten minutes."

I was ready and waiting in five. All the energy

that had lain buried under the weight of sorrow and fear leaped free at the magic words "You are leaving." The gates of my prison had opened, and I was eager to fly. My body, at home in my familiar clothes and unconfined for the first time in weeks, tingled with expectation and release.

Only one thread still bound me to this place. When matron came for me, though I knew I asked in vain, for the first time I asked, "Can I see my mother before I go?"

The matron shook her head. "Your mother is not here, Nora. She was very ill, as you know. She needed more expert care than we could give her."

"She's dead, isn't she," I said softly. It was not a question.

"No, child," the shocked matron replied. "Whatever gave you that idea? But she's too sick to have any visitors. Come along. The bus is waiting."

I desisted. Convinced the matron was just saying what people usually said to children to keep from telling them the harsh truth, I said no more. Locking Mamma away in my heart, I turned eagerly to a new chapter in my life. It didn't occur to me to ask where I was going. Wherever it was, it was bound to be an improvement over the Baba Yagas, whom I left with scarcely a goodbye, though my smiles of joy may have cheered the old women who had wanted to love me.

A bright red bus bearing the legend "Atlantic Park" took me north out of the city into the open downs of Swaythling and delivered me to a place stranger than any I had yet encountered. In a wide meadow two huge metal-and-glass hangars loomed above an assortment of small buildings like a pair of elephants among a herd of motley sheep.

Like the scar of an old wound, the grounds of Atlantic Park Hostel showed bald in the green hair of the downs. Around the two tall hangars of the wartime airfield, with their attendant hodgepodge of outbuildings, the yard had been trodden by countless aimless feet into a dusty pavement where no grass would grow. The place still wore a discarded air, though it had been housing thousands for over a year, I later discovered. After being abandoned by the Americans after the Armistice, Swaythling Aerodrome had stood derelict until its recent conversion into a Hostel for Transmigrants.

Everywhere about the trampled lawns and dusty paths of the compound I saw people — people of all ages, shapes, dress and condition. To the local cooks and clerks and waitresses who kept the place running these people must have looked foreign. But to me, trying to look in all directions at once to take it all in, they were a homey and welcome sight. These boys with shaven heads in skimpy black jackets, these buxom women in shawls and kerchiefs, these bearded men in flat Russian caps, looked like the people on the streets at home. In this familiar world of the dispossessed, my battered spirit warmed again into its natural buoyancy. Soon I was chattering and asking questions in my usual rapid-fire fashion.

It didn't take me long to worm my way into the good graces of the staff. Waiting in the admitting office to be assigned a billet, I eavesdropped with interest on the struggles of the nurse whose duty it was to get all new arrivals bathed, deloused and fumigated. As the nurse tried to explain the procedures to a new batch of Russians in peasant dress, nervously clutching their bundles, incomprehension was clearly written on their blank faces.

"We only want to *fumigate* your things," the nurse repeated over and over. "Disinfect . . . we'll give them right back . . . Oh, *where* is that dratted interpreter? I'm not getting anywhere. Now listen . . . "

Oh, the poor things I thought, watching the scene, remembering my own first days in America. They're so frightened. And they have no idea what they're supposed to do. With me, as usual, to think was to act. I went over and explained in Russian what the nurse wanted, and was amply rewarded by the relieved smiles that broke over the anxious faces, and their readiness to give up their bundles.

"They understand now," I assured the nurse, who stood amazed at the sudden resolution of her difficulties. "Where do you want them to go? They're willing."

"You speak English," the nurse gasped.

"Oh, yes," I assured her airily. "I've been to America. What shall I tell them now?"

"How wonderful. And you know Russian too. Nancy." She turned to the admitting clerk who was entering each new record on her roster. "This child speaks fluent English — and Russian as well. She says she's been — "

"Yes," the clerk nodded. "I know. That's the child from the workhouse, the one whose mother . . . " Her voice trailed off lamely. But the nurse turned the awkward moment aside.

"But she can talk to these people. What a help she can be. Those interpreters are never on hand when we need them."

Thus, catalyzed by a kind woman's response to a child's desperate need, my life made an abrupt flip-flop from despair to delight. The contrast between the regimented desolation of the workhouse and the cheerful confused bustle of the migrant hostel could hardly have been more striking.

Everyone soon heard about the little girl so sadly left on her own. Everyone wanted to cheer me up, to mother me and love me. With spirits rebound-ing from unnatural depression, full of interest and curiosity about the many lives around me, I bounced about the barracks, petted and indulged by all.

To attach me to a family group, the clerk assigned me to Mrs. Mosskin's upper bunk. Little Jerzy Mosskin usually woke up during the night to go to the bathroom, his mother explained to me as we got acquainted. "I wouldn't let him sleep where he could fall out and hurt himself," she said indignantly. "So I keep him on a pallet on the floor beside my bed — when he isn't curled up with me." Mrs. Mosskin was happy to offer me his unused bed.

Though I slept there, I quickly acquired friends and playmates in every corner of the big sleeping barracks. Dizzy with sociability after my long bout of solitude, I flitted about, chatting and asking questions, lending a hand with fussy babies, running outside for a game of tag or ball, and always eager to offer my linguistic talents whenever the medical staff needed help.

Within a few days I was even able to expand my services. Just down the aisle from the Mosskins slept a large family whose daughter Masha was just my age. We soon became buddies, and Masha would tag along when I reported to the admitting office.

When I was stymied by my inability to communicate in Polish, Masha, quick to size up the situation, stepped into the breach.

"I know Polish, Niura. In our town everybody had to learn Russian at school, but we all spoke Polish at home. What do you want to tell these people?"

Thus spontaneously the peewee interpreter team was created. The nurses would issue their instructions to me in English, I would transmit them in Russian; and when Poles were involved, Masha would be briefed by me in Russian and explain the proceedings in Polish. The overworked medical staff welcomed two new volunteers. Their official interpreters were often inadequate to cover the needs of the hostel's swelling population.

Atlantic Park was a remarkable place, and an answer to prayer for thousands of immigrants, as I discovered many years later when I was reading about its history in the newspapers of that period. The exodus from a devastated postwar Europe had sent hordes of exiles flooding into the Channel ports, only to be bottlenecked there by the new American immigration quota. Struggling to cope, the three major British steamship companies joined forces to transform the unused hangars and buildings at Eastleigh into a holding tank for emigrants waiting to cross the sea, where they could be kept healthy and made more fit to pass the rigid regulations at the American entry ports.

In the past thousands of diseased and disabled immigrants had been turned back at those ports and sent back to Europe, at enormous expense to the shipping companies, and incalculable grief and hardship to the rejected. Their plight had prompted the establishment of elaborate health inspection procedures at the embarkation ports, to weed out the unacceptable cases before they futilely crossed the ocean. Those charged with carrying out these procedures needed all the help they could get.

Naturally Masha and I reveled in our celebrity status and were always ready to respond to any plea for help. A growing contingent of migrants would call on us whenever some problem required an appeal to the staff. In this way I became privy to many of the family dramas in the suspended lives at Atlantic Park. Love stories of any kind provided particular grist for the gossip mill, a welcome respite from the featureless waiting of barracks life.

The Jewish contingent was now becoming the dominant group of long-term residents, coming as they did from the countries with the worst conditions and the lowest quotas. Wherever the women gathered to gossip the names heard were Shaina Smulewicz and her Dov Mendelson.

Dov was an unobjectionable young man, a tailor from Minsk. Shaina's mother, a widow emigrating with her two daughters to a brother in Cincinnati, had nothing against an eventual match, when they were all in America and Dov was earning a living. But the lovers had been impatient, and matters had now reached a crisis.

"How could you do such a thing to me?" hissed round little Mrs. Smulewicz after Shaina's reluctant confession. The mother was trying not to let neighboring bunks hear the shameful news, yet was unable to control her helpless rage. "How can I bring you home to Izzy in such a condition? Maybe they won't even let me into America with a pregnant daughter who's single. Such a disgrace. Such a *shame.*" On and on the verbal blows rained on Shaina's bowed head, and always the refrain. "How could you do this to me?"

Useless for the weeping girl to protest that Dov loved her, that they wanted to marry right away, that the baby would be cared for. It all fell on deaf ears. The mother could not imagine a proper wedding in this outlandish place. No home to hold a celebration, no money to provide the obligatory feast, no wedding clothes, no canopy to stand under. The whole idea was impossible. Mrs. Smulewicz, exploding with the repressed sorrows of years, wallowed in the misery of her daughter's disgrace, and would not listen to anything Shaina had to say.

Sensible Dov, sheepish at the scandal he had caused, was determined to set things right. He went to the rabbi who regularly visited Atlantic Park to conduct services and counsel the perplexed. It was the rabbi who had first interested the Jews of Southampton in the problems of their brethren in Atlantic Park.

As its population swelled and stories of their plight spread through the town, Atlantic Park became the chief social service project for the concerned women of the local congregation. They were now paying regular visits to the hostel, bringing clothes, holiday foods and small comforts to cheer the exiles. Since many of the emigrants were from the *shtetls* of eastern Europe, and were unfamiliar with city living and suspicious of new ways, the locals tried to instruct them in the modern amenities of western urban life. Ruth Golding's mother, Hannah Moses, was deeply involved in this work. It was through her that Ruth had been able to arrange for my transfer to the Park.

When Dov laid his troubles in the rabbi's lap, the story was quickly passed on to these women, whose sympathies were stirred by the lovers' dilemma. As usual, Mrs. Moses became a leader in planning a happy solution. It took only a few days to arrange an orthodox ceremony in the local synagogue, obtain a license, even provide wedding clothes and a buffet lunch in the spacious Moses home. That valiant lady even succeeded in convincing Mrs. Smulewicz to put a good face on the matter, give her consent and participate in the festivities.

The radiant couple and their families were invited to spend the night before the wedding as guests of Mrs. Moses and her neighbors. After an ample dinner, the hostess took the bride's mother and sister into the guestroom they were to share. She lit the gas jets, unaware that this was an invention unheard of in their small village in Lithuania. When the two were ready for bed, assuming the jets were an unfamiliar kind of lamp, they blew them out and went to sleep.

This time tragedy was averted. Luckily Shaina came early in the morning for a final prenuptial visit and found her family unconscious. They were revived in time, and were recovered enough to see Shaina married and her baby legitimized.

These kind English women and their rabbi were a godsend to the Jews at the hostel. They influenced the management to arrange a separate kitchen and dining area where the orthodox could prepare and serve kosher food, and even encouraged the creation of some small apartments where at least a few married couples could carry on some semblance of family life. They gave English lessons, planned outings for children, and occasionally invited young people to visit them in their homes for a bit of socializing.

Having settled Dov and Shaina's difficulties, talk now turned to the growing attachment between young Ivan Petrov and pretty Rachel Popkin. No one in our area missed out on this choice item of gossip, and the rising tide of Mrs. Popkin's fury was gauged daily by a widening circle.

After the galling confinement of the workhouse, I savored the heady wine of liberty. Masha and I wandered about in the blossoming fields and cool shrubberies that stretched behind the barracks and reached toward the rolling downs on the horizon. Here the grass had not been stamped flat by a thousand feet, as on the mangled lawns around the buildings.

I often saw the two timid lovers strolling together, hands straying to touch when they thought themselves unobserved, eyes eloquent with longing. And talking, always talking. They had two whole lives to share, and so little time. I heard a lot of gossip about them, and my inventive mind imagined the rest of their story.

One sleepy summer afternoon Rachel's mother lay on her bunk, her heavy brows set in their usual scowl, her bowels churning with anxiety and rage — her familiar spirits. The supine position, imposed by doctor's orders to rest, was alien to her fierce energies, her furious will to fix, to arrange, to control.

Her small meek husband offered no challenge to her passion to rule. They were barely mated before his pacific spirit abdicated permanently. And their daughter Rachel was just like him — shy, sweet, submissive. Mrs. Popkin thought longingly of her son Joshua, far away in America. In him she had bred a worthy antagonist, and in the years before he emigrated — to find a broader scope for his gnawing ambition or get away from his mother's driving lash — the two had often come close to maiming each other and the family with the fury of their contending wills.

When we get to America, Mrs. Popkin daydreamed, Joshua will find Rachel a rich husband. He had already written them about his boss at the necktie factory, who was so friendly and helpful in arranging the family's passage papers. A recent widower "only in his forties," Joshua wrote. "I think he's looking already, and I know he'll like Rachel. She wouldn't want for a thing." (And neither would we, he didn't say.)

Thank God their names were on next month's quota, thought Mrs. Popkin. They'd better get out of this place soon. She was worried about Rachel and that young *goy*. How could a nice Jewish girl like Rachel, raised so Orthodox . . . ?

She should go and look for Rachel, she thought, not leave her alone with him. But it was so hot out in the sun, and anyway, where could they go? The doctor had warned her sternly about her blood pressure. "You *must* get a lot of rest and you must *not* get excited," he warned, "or I won't be responsible. Do you want to have a stroke?"

I'll just shut my eyes for ten minutes, she promised herself, struggling to relax. After all, we'll be leaving in a few days. The balmy summer air drained her will, sank her at last into troubled sleep.

Outside, Rachel was walking with the "young goy" in the sunlit field behind the barracks. Her tender brow in an anxious furrow, her brown velvet eyes pleading, she was trying to convince Ivan that they could not go on meeting. This was the excuse her heart always gave her head for one more stolen tryst.

"You must stop coming to the women's barracks, Vanya," she entreated. "It makes Mama so angry. And it makes me so sad. We'll soon be leaving for America now, and then we'll never see each other again. So what's the use of making ourselves miserable? The sooner we forget each other the better. Don't you see?"

"Forget each other? The sooner the better? How can you even think such things. Never mind say them." Ivan lashed out in a fury of protest. "I can't say about you, but I can tell you I'm not going to forget you. Or lose you either. Rachel, sweetheart, you know I lost everybody I loved, everything. My whole life was gone. And then I saw you . . . Darling, you *are* my life now. I couldn't live if I lost you too. I just couldn't stand it, to be alone again.

"Yes, I know," as Rachel tried to interrupt, to reason. "I know we can't do anything about it now. You *have* to go to America with your family. I *have* to wait for my number, and then try and find my uncle in that Buffalo. I'll have to learn English, to get a job. But I don't mind all that if only you'll be waiting for me. If you tell me where I can find you when I get to America. If I know that at the end of all the waiting we can be together — "

"But Vanya, that's just it." Rachel was desperate; she had to shut out the unendurable picture of a future she couldn't have. "We *can't* be together. Not ever. You're not Jewish. And besides, you know I have to marry a rich man, for the family. So they can live well in America. Joshua wrote Mama about his boss already — "

"But you don't *care* about him." Vanya couldn't bear the thought of a rich man — or any other man — having his Rachel. "You don't even *know* him. They're just selling you, Rachel. To an old man you don't even know. How could you . . . when you love me . . . ? You said — "

"I do love you, Vanya. I'll always love you. But I can't ever marry you. The family is depending on me . . . our whole future . . . Mama said — "

"Mama said!" Vanya shouted, so loud that several nearby strollers turned in surprise. This old refrain was too much for him. Desperate for privacy, the couple turned away from the barracks toward a line of willows.

"How can you decide your whole life — *our* whole life — by what *Mama* said?" He dropped his voice but not the passion of his pleading. "You're not a child. You're talking about marriage, about grownup things, but you talk like a child. 'Mama said I can't come out to play'," he mocked. "That's what you sound like. Rachel, it's *your* life."

Vanya stopped and took her hands, facing her to look into her eyes. "It's *our* life . . . the life we could have together in America. Free, in a free country. Our children. Our home — " His voice broke, but he took a deep breath and made a great effort not to sob. "Rachel, you *can't* throw it all away just because Mama says No."

This rosy future was more than Rachel could bear to contemplate. She tore her hands loose and ran blindly away from the barracks, away from Vanya and his impossible dream. Nearby the grassy bank sloped down to a brook. She was going to cry, and she couldn't do it anywhere in the barracks. In all this space there was scarcely a corner where someone could be alone with a sorrow — or a joy. Privacy was a luxury no migrant could enjoy.

Ivan could not let her go like this. Conscious of interested eyes on his back, but uncaring, he ran after Rachel until he found her lying beside the brook behind a fringe of brush and willows.

Throwing himself down beside the sobbing girl, an arm across her shaking shoulders, Vanya tried to comfort her. "Rachel, sweetheart, don't cry so. I love you so much. I only want you to be happy. Please, Rachel, don't make us both so miserable. Only give me your brother's address in America. That's all. When I find you, you can make up your mind what to do. Just don't get married before I come. All I want now is that you should wait for me, and tell me how to find you in America. That's all."

On his fair Slavic face all his sorrows and hopes were traced — his cheeks flushed bright red, his china blue eyes wells of tenderness. How different the two were — in looks, in breeding, in lifestyle — and how alike in sweetness, in innocence, in their need to give love and feel joy. In this little backwater world of despair, of life suspended and hopes repressed, they shone like two small sunrays in a sad gray sky.

"Ra-chel!" Her mother's harsh screech reverberated through the drowsy day, sounding almost beside them instead of where she stood in the barracks doorway.

Rachel jumped up in panic, whispering, "I've got to go."

But Ivan pulled her down urgently. "Wait, darling. You've got a minute or two; she doesn't know where you are. We *have* to settle something."

His words were racing, trying to get everything said in the last few moments of safety. "Listen, I know it's hard for you to meet me, but you see how it is. You *know* we belong together. Don't deny us, Rachel. Just meet me one more time, give me your address, tell me you'll wait. Don't let them sell you. That's all I'm asking. Please, Rachel. *Please.*"

"I don't know." Rachel was wild to get away before her mother found them together. "Let me go, Vanya, please. I'll . . . I'll be here tomorrow afternoon," she gave way to his pleading eyes. "Same time. We'll talk tomorrow. I *must* go now."

Looking down at the flushed desperate face, the cornsilk hair falling over one eye, love for a moment mastered her panic. She bent quickly to kiss him, whispered a goodbye, and was gone before he could move. Even in her fright she thought to run alongside the brook, to climb the bank past a bend so anyone meeting her would not see Vanya behind her. Only then did she call, "I'm coming, Mama."

The boy was hardly visible in any case. In the sudden letdown he felt empty, limp with exhaustion. He stayed sprawled on the bank, tension slowly draining from his nerves and muscles while his head still pounded. His mind was whirling with Rachel and their quandary.

He had known from the beginning how totally Mrs. Popkin dominated her family. To Rachel the idea of following her own desires, not her mother's demands, was unthinkable. He remembered once asking, "What does your father say about it?" and Rachel's surprise at the idea of asking her father's opinion.

But she did ask, and reported, "He said, 'Do what your mother says.' He always says that."

How could anyone fight that kind of brainwashing? Ivan wondered despairingly. His spirit sank at the hopelessness of the struggle he faced to win

Rachel away from her family. In the speckled shade of a young willow, he tried to imagine a world without Rachel. His fevered mind reached back with longing to boyhood days in his village. While he was starving in a Siberian forest as a conscript in the Red army, his father was taken away for hoarding, his farm was burnt to the ground, his mother and sisters disappeared — everything was gone when he finally found his way home after the civil war ended.

Vanya couldn't bear to stay where everything was a painful reminder. His uncle Vassily had run away to America years before to escape conscription. All Vanya knew was that he lived in a place called Buffalo, but the lonely boy decided to go to America to look for him.

Vassily's letters to his sister had gone up in smoke with the farmhouse. Vanya knew how improbable were his chances of finding one man without a real address, in a strange city — but what else did he have to do with his solitary life? He missed his people like the loss of an arm. Selling the few possessions his friends had saved for him, Vanya set off across Europe. He hitched rides in wagons when he could, walked when he had to, worked at odd jobs for food, slept in barns and haystacks and abandoned villages. Carefully hoarding and hiding the needed passage money, he scrounged and starved his way westward to reach the sea.

Close to his goal at last, wandering solitary among the crowds of refugees in Atlantic Park, he saw Rachel. Her soft dark beauty was different from the fair sun-bleached girls he had known, her *shtetl* Russian was strange to his ears. But something tender and wistful in the fringed brown eyes, something unconsciously maternal in her patience with small fretful children, something defeated in her quiet submission under the lash of her mother's waspish tongue, touched his empty heart. He had found a polestar.

Even before he mustered up the courage to speak to her, the intensity of his attention had magnetized a like interest in the shy girl. Each lonely youngster felt the sudden warmth of being cared about, the heady joy of sharing unspoken feelings and innate sympathies. By the time they became acquainted, they were already almost friends, already nearly lovers.

I won't let it happen to me again. Ivan promised himself as he lay alone on the bank. This time I'll fight, I won't let everything be lost again. I'm so tired of being alone . . . I'll find a way. I'll make Rachel see.

His head was beginning to throb again; his skin felt hot and tight. He stumbled up the bank and headed for the recreation lounge, where he sank gratefully into an old overstuffed armchair. His head was spinning now, his temples pounding; his throat felt dry and scratchy. Could I be getting sick? he wondered anxiously.

On this drowsy summer day the lounge was more than half empty. Only the regulars were in their usual places, the card addicts who stopped playing only to eat and sleep, the ardent pundits endlessly debating the world's condition, the inveterate readers with no jobs to keep them from their books, the desperate letter writers detailing their plight to one more distant cousin in America.

Fighting to steady his mind, Vanya tried to concentrate on the talk around him, but it ran in and out of his dizzy head like wind, leaving no impression until a random phrase about health inspection penetrated. The greatest dread of the hostel's inhabitants, to say nothing of the medical staff, was of an epidemic. Any hint of an infectious disease was automatically a bar to admission into the United States. Immigration authorities would turn back whole boatloads at the port rather than risk infecting their own population with one of the plagues reported to be raging in the war-devastated areas of Europe.

If I'm sick they won't let me into America, Vanya realized, panic-stricken. I've got to see the doctor right away. I've got to get better before my name comes up in the quota. He staggered out to the little medical office, a building that looked as if it had been knocked together out of old airplane wings, which to some extent it had.

The card players watched the boy's shaky progress. Paul Popkin gloomily shook his head. "That boy looks drunk, look at him. That's the boy my Rachel's been talking to, no?"

"Where would he get anything to get drunk with, around here?" Boris Mosskin was watching Vanya too. "He looks sick to me. Maybe he's catching something, God forbid! In a place like this, you know, it wouldn't take much to start an epidemic."

"Don't borrow trouble," growled Max Gruenwald. "It's probably a touch of sunstroke or something. He just came in from outside a few minutes ago. We have enough to worry about without an epidemic to keep us out of America."

Mosskin's worry was well grounded. Vanya had come down with scarlet fever. He was immediately placed in strict quarantine.

❧ *14* ❧
Waiting to Live
Southampton, 1923

EVEN ALL these years later, I get a warm feeling around my heart when I think of Atlantic Park. Despite the heartaches it held, it was an Eden of release from my misery at the workhouse. With so much going on around me, I was too busy and interested to spend much time brooding about Mamma. As the days passed with no news of her, my conviction grew fixed, that my mother had really died. What I most wondered about now was how I would get back to Papa. Without Mamma to push him to return to Europe, I was sure he would want to stay in America. Of course he would send for me, but when? Yet now that I was in a place I enjoyed, on the whole I was content to wait until he did.

Life became even more fun when I made friends with Michael Gruenwald. Because he reminded me of my darling Mara, I hung around him until he noticed me. Though Michael (originally Mikhail, but now answering only to Michael) was nearly twelve, it was easy to spark his interest because I had already been to America and had even learned its language.

"Tell me about America," he would say. "I want to know all about it." I actually didn't know much myself, but it was enough to impress Michael. Or he would pop up and demand: "Talk English to me. I want to learn more words."

Soon he began to include me in his games with other boys and, always the tomboy, I cheerfully followed him into every escapade. After a Rugby team from nearby Eastleigh came over for a game with the Park boys, Michael conceived the idea of visiting the village. Hearing of the project, I demanded to go too. Despite the groans of his companions about "bringing a kid along," Michael let me come.

"She can talk better to the people in the town," he pointed out.

I loved the picturesque village with its neat rows of red brick and gray stucco houses, each with its peaked and gabled roof, its friendly front porch, its small bright garden in the fenced dooryard. The streets looked cozy and inviting, so different from the cold rows of square apartment houses in New York or the drab war-stained cities of Russia.

Tagging after the boys as they explored, I kept lagging behind to admire the fanciful roof ornaments, like tiny gargoyles, and the carved trim curled around the little porches. These quaint cottages, so like the pictures in my old fairytale books, fascinated me so much that I nearly got lost several times; or would have, if Michael hadn't remembered to look back and shout at me before the boys turned a corner.

We pooled our scanty funds to buy ice cream, a rare treat, and wandered about until the setting sun brought home the anxious thought that we would be late for supper. Rush as we might, the mile back was much longer for our tired feet than the easy mile that had brought us to Eastleigh. But it was a wonderful day, worth even the sharp reprimands we all earned for going off without telling anyone.

Soon after, I found the crowded hostel all astir. The new annual quotas were opening up. Many of the families I knew would be leaving for America at last. In the first contingent went the Popkins, with an unhappy Rachel who had to leave without a last goodbye for poor sick Vanya, still in quarantine. All she could do was leave him a note with Mrs. Mosskin.

I watched Rachel's woebegone face staring out of the red bus as it rolled down the road south to the great docks. Poor Vanya, I thought. How terrible he'll feel when he gets better and finds Rachel is gone. I knew how painful loneliness could be. Now I was learning that being in love could be just as hard. Often it seemed to make people more sad than happy.

I'm glad I'm not grown up yet, I decided. Grownups have so many problems to deal with. It will be a long time before I'm ready for them.

As my friends disappeared in the red bus one by one, I grew restive. When was Papa going to send for me? Why hadn't he written? Did he even know where I was? Once more loneliness began to gnaw at me. When Masha's family got ready to leave, being left behind seemed too much to bear. I went to say goodbye with such a woebegone face that I saw her mother's eyes fill as she gathered me to her ample breast.

"Don't be sad, little one," she consoled. "You'll be leaving one of these days, you'll see. Just be patient a little longer."

"Can I see you in America?" I asked eagerly, hoping to preserve at least one friendship. "Where are you going to live?"

"We're on our way to Pitts-burgh," Masha's father said the strange name proudly. "I'm an iron-worker, and my cousins write me that Pitts-burgh has many steel mills. I hope to get work there."

"Pitts-burgh?" I repeated uncertainly. "Is that near New York, do you think?"

He shook his head doubtfully. "I don't know. I don't think so. It's in the state of Penn-syl-vania."

Masha's mother hastened to change the subject. "I have a present for you, Niurochka. We bought the children English straw hats for the trip. Would you like to have Masha's blue silk hat, for a remembrance of your friend?"

Masha's blue silk hat! It had a wreath of tiny pink silk roses around the navy crown, and a ruffle around the brim. I had admired it ever since we became friends. I hadn't owned anything so dressy since I was four.

"Oh, yes, I'd love to have it," I said. "It's so pretty, and it will remind me of Masha. I'll wear it when I go to America."

With old friends gone, I lost interest in new arrivals and old gossip. I moped about, wishing for the letter from Papa that would end the suspense about my future. Even Michael could hardly rouse my interest in new escapades. Had Papa forgotten about me? No, that was impossible. But suppose something had happened to him too. I knew now that Mammas and Papas were not indestructible. What would happen to me if Papa died too?

Once more my comfort lay in books; the library corner in the lounge became my haven. I was there when the mystery of Papa's silence was finally unraveled. One of Michael's buddies came hunting me.

"So this is where you're hiding out," he grumbled. "Hurry up, the rabbi wants to see you."

I looked up. "See me?" I asked. "Why should he want to see *me*?"

"How should I know?" The messenger shrugged his shoulders. "He's got three of us out looking for you. Hurry up."

Arriving out of breath at the rabbi's small office, I was amply repaid for my exertions. He had a letter from Papa, with the news I'd been waiting for.

"Your father wants you to come back to New York," the kind man was happy to report. "He's sending a ticket for your passage."

"At last." A vast sigh of relief escaped me, as I sat down to hear Papa's message.

"He had some trouble finding where you were, he says. Actually, we also had some trouble finding him. It seems he was staying with relatives, and didn't know for some time of your mother's illness. We didn't know his address until he finally got in touch with the White Star Line. But now he has a new job, and will be sending your ticket shortly. So you'll be leaving soon — probably in the next two weeks."

"I'm so glad Papa found me." I thanked the rabbi and dashed off to share my good news with Mrs. Mosskin.

At Mrs. Golding's request, the rabbi had written to Adolph Lourie about his wife's miscarriage and collapse, the pessimistic diagnosis, and his daughter's plight. But the letter had to be forwarded twice before it reached him. Olga had his cousin Barney's address, but he had not thought to give it to the steamship line when he bought the tickets.

In later years, when I was a teenager, Papa talked to me about this terrible time. His shock when the news finally reached him was almost more than he could bear, he said, his eyes growing moist at the memory. He had already started to worry when the expected letter from Olga in Paris failed to arrive. But the reality was far worse than anything he had imagined. After all the years of separation, after the debacle of his business venture, after the discouraging reunion with his wife, and the reluctant second parting, how could he absorb this terrible blow?

And how was he to deal with the new problems it created? A trip to England was impossible for him. His new job as assistant manager of a large home for the elderly included room and board, so he could save most of his pay. It was too precious to risk, even if he had the money to go. The job was making it possible for him to pay off his debts and reestablish himself.

The rabbi's report told him that his wife's condition was incurable and always fatal. The pernicious anemia had driven her into irreversible melancholia, and she was now deeply withdrawn. She had retreated from her dread of persecution into a silence where nothing seemed to reach her. The medical consensus was that there was nothing to be done for her except to keep her as comfortable as possible for as long as the dregs of her vitality were able to sustain life, which was probably only a matter of months. She was being well cared for in a sanitarium for chronic cases.

How bitterly Papa now regretted his weakness in giving way to his wife's longing to leave America. It was likely, he now realized, that she was already fatally ill in the months before she sailed. That would explain her chronic fatigue and depression. Desperately searching for an escape from her incipient breakdown, she might well have put the blame for her misery on the new country rather than on her own failing constitution.

What fatal haste! If she had waited only one more month, when he got his job, she would have found the congenial companionship she craved. Many of the staff jobs at the Home of the Daughters of Jacob were filled by refugees from eastern Europe like themselves, who spoke her language and shared her background. And once she knew about the coming child she certainly would not have risked a sea voyage. At the Home she could have had medical care, release from the burdensome housekeeping chores, and the sense of community that he found warm and healing. Olga might even have been able to carry the child. We might have had a son at last. How tragic that his wife had missed it all by just those few weeks.

Now his daughter was all he could salvage out of the wreckage of the life that ten years ago had held so much promise and joy. With his first month's pay and an advance on the second, he scraped together the price of a third-class ticket, and waited with impatience to hear from the White Star Line when his child would be arriving.

Across the sea, I too was waiting. On the day that Ivan Petrov was released from quarantine and wandered about searching everywhere for Rachel, I was sitting in the sunshine, happily thinking of America and Papa. Seeing Vanya shamble by, I suddenly remembered.

"Rachel left you a note," I said. "Did you get it?"

"A note." The sudden light in his eyes was dazzling. "Where?" His heart fluttered in his chest like a caged bird.

"Mrs. Mosskin has it. Come on, let's go get it."

But when he held the precious note in his hands, begging me with a shy smile to read it to him — "I can read print," he confessed, "but handwriting is harder, and Rachel's is so small" — the red balloon of hope quickly collapsed, leaving him more crushed than before.

"I wish I could have said goodbye," Rachel had written. "I will always remember you, Vanya. But you must forget me, because there could never be a future for us . . . " Here the ink ran a little, where a tear might have fallen. "Go to America, find a nice wife. Be happy. I will try to be happy too. Goodbye.

Good luck in America."

It was the final straw. Blindly he rushed out and away from the barracks, heading for the willow where he had held Rachel in his arms, where he had lived his last happy moment. I can imagine his agony as he lay under the willow, unaware when daylight faded and night fell. His mind must have ranged back longingly into the lost years, ahead to endless uncertainties, to an alien world he could not face alone. When daylight came, the bank was empty. Life had stolen all its promise, and Vanya rejected it.

The next day stands out sharply in my memory still. It was a day that I recognized with a sharp stab of homesickness — a Russian summer day, hot, still and enrvating, like the summer days of all my life. A day for lazy joys, a day to wade in a cool brook, or to read a favorite book under the speckled shade of the big willow that bent over the pond at our dacha.

As the sun grew stronger and the air hotter with the approach of noon, longing for those lost happy days washed over me. The willow, I thought. The trailing willow by the brook. Under it I could lie and dream that I was back at the dacha, with the family who'd shared all my summers. I turned my back on the gray bulk of the barracks and started off across the trampled yard toward the greener downs.

Below a bank of shrubbery and venerable beech trees ran the stream. It lay beyond a meadow, its green starred with bright wildflowers, where small white butterflies dipped and fluttered. I chased one, then was distracted by a dragonfly refracting the sun through its iridescent wings. But the sun was merciless. I hurried on toward the shade of the tallest beech. Taking its lofty crown as my landmark, I plunged into the wooded slope and down to the brook. Beside that beech was my willow.

Intent upon my path, I plowed through the underbrush until I neared the big beech, then — Shock braked me so abruptly that my feet, skidding on the lush carpet of leaves, shot out from under me and sent me sliding down the slope into the tree. Frozen in horror, I lay staring up at booted legs dangling above my head.

In the women's barracks the languorous day had stifled the usual aimless bustle. The babble in which most of Europe's tongues could be heard was for once hushed to a mere hum. The odor of humanity hung heavy in the dense air. Under its blanket of heat the barracks drowsed and dreamed. This was a day to escape into sleep, into a cloudless past in some lost homeland, or into an imagined new world, far from the hollow squares of double-decker bunks filling the enormous room.

Bubbling snores rose from the ranged bunks; the more wakeful young played quietly, whispered in out-of-the-way corners. Dov Mendelson was coaxing his bride to come outside. Little Jerzy Mosskin idly bounced a ball down the aisle. Cot springs complained as a fat woman turned in her sleep. Flies droned round the footboards where drying underclothes steamed in the heat.

Plump Mrs. Mosskin moaned softly in her sleep, deep in a dream of her Boris, of his arms around her, their bodies flowing together in the love-dance so long denied her. In a life tuned only to survival, the act of love was her one great joy, her only escape from dismal reality. In their bed she had lived her real life, a life now proscribed by the arbitrary social arrangements of Atlantic Park's barracks, where husbands were exiled at night to the men's section. Twice Boris managed to steal into her narrow bunk on moonless nights, but the unprivacy of

the crowded dormitory blunted the joy of their reunion. These days Mrs. Mosskin's pleasure came
mostly in solitary dreams.

As she clasped her pillow close, limbs tensed
to the coming of fancied fulfillment, a sudden cre-
scendo of voices shattered the drowsy peace of the
barracks. Heads popped up from damp pillows.
Startled little ones ran crying to throw themselves
on their mothers. Babies screamed in response.
People tumbled from their bunks half awake to search
out the clamor.

"Dead?"

"Who's dead?"

"Dead? Where?"

"What do you mean 'dead'?"

Many voices shouted as I came running and
screaming, "He's dead. Up in the tree. Vanya's dead."
I was trying to talk and sob and catch my breath, all
at once.

"Vanya? Dead?" A murmur of disbelief ran
through the crowd as the news sank in.

But it was true, I told them between gasps and
sobs. I had hauled myself up to see the face on the
body that dangled from the beech. The gray face and
the awful staring eyes, the limp body, were unmistakable.

During the famine, I had often seen dead people
lying on Samara streets. Now I had to pass the terrible fact on to others, get rid of it somehow. I had
scrambled back up the slippery slope, run pell-mell
through the flowery meadow, frantic to be back with
the living. Vanya. Only yesterday I'd been reading
him Rachel's letter.

The news of the suicide ran like a shock wave
through the camp. Most of its people had known loss
and despair; many had lived through times when
they too longed for death, perhaps even prayed for

it. But to take it with your own hand . . .

Mixed with their sorrow for Vanya, and an un-
defined regret that someone had not done something
(nobody quite knew what) to save him, was a personal fear. Could life become so unbearable, people
thought, that *I* could do such a thing? The event
translated into a sort of cataclysm that shook the
foundations of all our lives, like an earth tremor that
moves the ground and momentarily creates a doubt
that it will ever again be safe to walk on.

For me, Vanya's death was incomprehensible.
In this place filled with people struggling to stay alive,
to win through, to keep a hold on the remnants of
their lost lives — for one of them to throw his life
away, give up the struggle so early.

Oh, Vanya. Why? My mind could not encom-
pass the act.

Life here was already so full of complexities. I
didn't want to deal with all the conflicting impressions. It was all too much, too hard. How I longed for
the day when I could leave Atlantic Park and go home
to Papa, and be little again! I wanted to have a home
and go to school, and read and play and not have all
these complicated things going on around me.

That day the bunks in the barracks stayed
empty. The shattering event drove the Park's inmates
to gather in groups that buzzed with chatter, explored
the news from every angle, worried it endlessly. They
could not let it go. In the lounge, knots of chairs
were filled with men and women twittering like cov-
eys of uneasy birds. Even the men whose endless
card games stopped only for meals and sleep couldn't
concentrate on their pinochle.

At a table in the corner, near the lumpy arm-
chair where I had taken refuge with a book, Solomon
Ellenbogen was getting peevish as talk kept inter-
rupting the play in their marathon game. A small

swarthy man, timid with his domineering wife, ineffectual as a father, unprosperous in business, he was a bellicose and passionate cardplayer. It was only at the cardtable that he succeeded, that he felt sure of his own worth. Solomon Ellenbogen had small patience when balked in his favorite pursuit.

"Are we playing a game or not?" he demanded sulkily. "Whose turn is it anyway?"

The newest member of the foursome, taking the rebuke to himself, stammered his apologies. Lev Zabelski was anxious to ingratiate himself. His strange pale eyes moved deferentially around the group. "Sorry. We are here only a few days, you know . . . such a terrible thing . . . and Mr. Gruenwald . . . " He took a breath and began again. "I have so many questions . . . He and I were acquainted in Odessa, you know . . . "

Gruenwald, the clique's self-elected leader by force of past social status, was less conciliatory. A merchant and banker in Russia, he loved to exercise any remaining shreds of power whenever an opportunity arose. "Don't be rude, Sol," he snapped. "An awful thing like this death is bound to upset everybody. We'll play pinochle later, no? Are we going somewhere, maybe?" he spread his arms eloquently. "We have such busy schedules?"

Boris Mosskin, anxious to preserve peace, chimed in support "Sure, Sol. Let's stop for awhile if Mr. Zabelski wants to talk. You've come to the right place, Mr. Zabelski. Gruenwald always has all the facts and figures. What do you want to know?"

Ellenbogen subsided sulkily, overruled, and grumpily tossed in the best hand he'd held all day.

"Mr.Gruenwald is a genius with facts and figures," Zabelski agreed unctuously. "I did business with his bank in Odessa, you know," he added, basking in reflected importance. "These barracks are so big . . . look more like for airplanes than people."

Mosskin applauded. "You got it. That's just what they are — airplane hangars."

"Remarkable." Zabelski was impressed. His glance swept the bookcases in the library corner, the open door to the dining room where the long tables were already being set for supper. "We've been on the road for months. We stayed in a lot worse places than this, I can tell you."

"It's not bad." Boris Mosskin agreed. "They separate families, but I guess they can't help that. There are only a few private rooms for couples — a drop in the bucket." He shrugged. "But if you *have* to wait before you start living a regular life again, this is a lot better than what we could afford to rent. You know, we aren't allowed to work in England. Can't take jobs away from the locals. You get food, and baths, even medicine if you're sick. All paid for by the shipping companies. A real mitzvah, what they do."

"How can they afford it?" Zabelski wondered. "Don't some people stay here a long time — weeks, maybe?"

"*Weeks*?" Ellenbogen snorted in derision. "*We* are here five months already. Gruenwald even longer. And who knows how much longer it'll be before we can leave."

Zabelski's eyes opened wide, and his hand hit his cheek in eloquent surprise. "*Months*? But how do you get along? All that time. What do people *do* here so long?"

"Do? Do, he asks." Ellenbogen's shrug was eloquent. "We play cards."

Boris Mosskin tried to supply a more serious answer. "*That's* the whole problem, Mr. Zabelski. We don't do anything. We just pass the time."

"People find different ways," Gruenwald added. "Nothing is real, nothing is important. You don't live

— you just wait. And who knows for how long?"

"Some people can't take the waiting. Sitting there helpless, not knowing what's going to happen. Or when." Sol Ellenbogen shrugged his shoulders despondently. "That's why things happen sometimes. Like with this Vanya today. He just couldn't take it. A couple of months ago an old man went berserk and tried to kill his family with a knife. They had to send him to the asylum. *He'll* never get to America."

"It's the women who have it the hardest, I think," Boris Mosskin said. "It's hard for the men, sure, but the women are really lost. They don't have a home to take care of. Their family is in pieces — men separated from women, children running wild, daughters getting in trouble. No center for family life, no routine." He shook his sandy head and repeated dolefully, "The women are the lost ones."

Lev Zabelski's optimism dictated a hopeful reaction. "Yes," he countered, "but it's safe here. At least we're not starving, like in Russia, or getting beat up on the road, or our things stolen — "

"Or getting shot for nothing. Like my brother in Kishinev," put in Max Gruenwald bitterly. "Whatever it takes to get to America, it's better than staying in Russia, where God knows what can happen any minute. Zabelski and I lived in the south during the civil war. He'll tell you. One day the Reds come in, start shooting people for running a bank, or for hoarding food. The next week, the Whites push them out. Then *they* start shooting people. For selling food to the Reds, or holding office in the local soviet. Whatever they think of, God knows. And then the Reds come back, and the whole *megillah* starts all over again. Right, Zabelski?"

"My God, yes." Lev Zabelski held his head at the memory of the terrible past. "Anything is better than going back to that."

Boris Mosskin felt the need to say something helpful. "I heard that in the old days people had to wait on the docks until they could go on board. They lived that way for days; slept right on their bundles, even in bad weather. Ate whatever they could buy on the street. Imagine."

"The rabbi told me they even did vaccinations out on the docks then. They had no place to put anybody. Of course," Ellenbogen said. "that was before the quota. Then they only stayed a few days at the most. It wasn't so hard to get into America then. *Now* — anything can keep you out.

"Grossinger was telling me about a group of 250 who got here from Poland with their passports not filled out right. He said they had to go *back* to get them fixed."

"I heard about them," Mosskin said. "But surely they had no money. How could they afford to go all the way back, and then back here again?"

"The rabbi said that Otto Schiff formed a committee in America that arranged for them to go back and get correct passports."

"Otto Schiff?" Zabelski asked.

"I heard." Gruenwald said. "Schiff is that rich banker in New York who's been helping Jews in Europe. Imagine! I wish somebody had done that for me when I needed it."

Mosskin turned to Zabelski. "Did you know Mr. Gruenwald already went to America? But he had to come back."

"Had to come back?" Zabelski's pale eyes opened wide. "You don't mean it. How terrible. You got all the way across? And then they wouldn't let you in?"

Gruenwald nodded, glad to have a new audience for his favorite catastrophe. "And for what? Because we were criminals? Because we had cholera or

typhus, or were full of lice?" He paused to under-
score the dramatic effect.

"God forbid." Zabelski was the perfect straight
man. "But what . . . how could they? What *was* it?"

"You wouldn't guess in a million years. Because
the ship was late."

"You're joking." Zabelski felt an obligatory
snicker was indicated — but he didn't see the joke.
The other two men leaned back in their chairs, grinning with anticipation.

Gruenwald, having milked the story, was ready
for his finale. "Because the ship was late. Over five
hundred people, almost a ship full. Sent back because of bad weather. First we hit a storm, then we
ran into heavy fog. In the end we were over a day late
getting in. The trouble was, it was the *last* monthly
quota for the year. Ships from Trieste and
Constantinople brought in a lot of Russians from the
Crimea. They filled the whole Russian quota before
we got there."

"Oh, my, my." Zabelski couldn't believe his
ears. "But . . . something couldn't be done? A whole
ship full of people? Just on account of fog?"

"Oh, they landed some Norwegians and
Czechs, and others whose quotas weren't filled yet.
But all the Russians had to go back. A lot of Irish
too," Gruenwald added. "Lots of quotas fill up in just
a few days. So the steamship lines try to bring over
as many immigrants as they can in the early part of
the month. They try to beat each other to land before their quotas are filled. It's a terrible mess over
there. Terrible."

"So many people are trying to get into America,"
Mosskin said. "I guess they just don't know how to
handle it."

Gruenwald was not ready to give up center
stage. "We sat in New York Harbor for more than a

week while they argued about what to do with us. A lot of people, especially the Jewish community, fought hard to get an exception, but it was no use. We had to go back."

Zabelski was stunned. "Sat in the harbor? They never even let you land? You stayed on the ship all that time? With New York right there in *front* of you?"

Gruenwald was basking in sympathy. "We couldn't even land on Ellis Island. It was already over-crowded. They had no place to put us."

"What a terrible thing." Zabelski mourned. "To be so close, and not even set foot — "

"That's just what happened," Ellenbogen chimed in. "He went to America all right. But he never got *into* America." He guffawed.

Gruenwald glared as his partner stole his favor-ite punchline. "So here I am, stuck in Atlantic Park for God knows how long. Now . . . I don't know . . . " Suddenly his self-assurance seemed to evaporate. "Sometimes I think we'll never get to America. And even if we do . . . How can I make a life again? After all these years of . . . " His voice trailed off dismally.

Mosskin and Zabelski spoke together, each anxious to dispel this glimpse of the black abyss of the future. "Nonsense," Mosskin boomed in his hearty baritone. "Of course you'll find a way. A man like you . . . " as Zabelski turned to Ellenbogen, trying to ignore his hero's moment of weakness. "Let's play cards."

American intentions to pass a more stringent quota law the next year (one that would be particu-larly exclusionary for people from eastern and south-ern Europe), were profoundly disturbing. Haunting the immigrants was the specter of having to spend months, maybe even years, in the limbo of Atlantic Park, wait-ing to get through the narrow portal of hope while teeming thousands crowded in behind them.

The impatient ones, especially those without relatives in the States, decided to head instead for Canada or South America. Fearful in the face of a still greater unknown, they were yet determined to take any expedient route out of Europe. They left as fast as the steamship companies, desperate to relieve the expense and problems of growing congestion at their hostels, could pack them into ships.

Brazil and Argentina, taking advantage of the bottlenecks created by U.S. intransigence, offered to pay one-way fares west, exploiting a cheap way to develop their thinly-settled interior regions. This offer was a boon to the thousands of indigent migrants who had struggled across Europe and had exhausted their slender means along the way.

The rush of response to the South American offers created traveling conditions little better than those endured by the early settlers of the new continent. To make more room, cargo space was converted for human freight, as Manny Golding, newly transferred to the liner Andes, was probably amazed to discover. In two holds, one for men and the other for women, three tiers of shelves were used as bunks, with a straw mattress and a blanket provided for each traveler. When the ship unloaded in Buenos Aires or Rio, the cheap mattresses would be thrown overboard and the holds filled with profitable Argentine beef for Britain. Many years later, a retired interpreter whom I talked to in Southampton described the scene for me.

Though a great many immigrants altered their plans in order to escape the lengthening delays at the European ports, many more, especially those with family ties in the United States, remained. They were obsessed by "The Promised Land," and determined to wait it out, however long it took to get there.

With a sigh, I tried to turn my attention back to *Uncle Tom's Cabin*, an old friend from home re-discovered among the dog-eared books in the hostel's hodgepodge collection. At eight, I had already read it three times in Russian. Each time I'd wept floods of tears in sympathy with Eliza and Little Eva and patient Uncle Tom. I didn't read English nearly as well as I spoke it, but the story was so familiar that I could follow it fairly well. In its pages I could almost forget that I was uneasy and frightened, sweaty and itchy, and in need of a mother's lap.

But not today. Too much had happened. Though I needed the book's comfort more than ever, it paled beside the real-life stories around me. I couldn't stop thinking about Vanya and Rachel when I saw them, shyly smiling at each other. How sweet they had been together. Rachel's frightened eyes always looking around to see if fierce Mrs. Popkin was watching, shrinking at any loud voice, fearing it might be her mother's demanding bellow. Yet she turned like a flower to Vanya's sunny grin, blooming under the admiration in his eyes, the tender way he said her name.

Rachel knew she had no hope of any future with Vanya. But she could no more deny Vanya her presence than she could reject food. Fate took a hand and parted them. I could still see the young lover's stricken face yesterday when he emerged from the isolation ward and learned that Rachel was gone. But no one had suspected the depth of Vanya's despair.

I forced my mind away from Vanya's body hanging on the tree. I could not give way, wallow in grief like so many. I lived largely in the present, cheerfully bouncing through whatever the day brought, eager to participate in the life around me. Only in desolate moments would I retreat to visions of my happy baby world, milking memories for comfort.

Sighing, I put down Uncle Tom. No use trying to read now. I went to stand in the doorway in hope of a rising breeze, stood looking out, beyond the trampled yard, the overgrown old runways barely visible in the distant grass, beyond the English countryside to another place, another time, another life. As I leaned pensively against the jamb, kind Mrs. Mosskin came to stand by me, put a comforting arm around my drooping shoulders.

"What is it, Niurochka?"

"I wish I could see Mamma."

"You know your Mamma is still very sick, darling. As soon as she's better I'm sure you'll be able to see her."

I sighed. I knew Mamma would never be better. "I wish I could have Mishka."

Sarah Mosskin was puzzled. "Who? Who's Mishka, child?"

"My bear. He's lost. I'll never see him again."

"Lost? Where? In Russia?"

I nodded sadly. Against my will tears filled my eyes. I put my arms around Mrs. Mosskin's plump waist. "I wish I could go home."

My friend held me close, her own eyes filling.

"None of us can go home, darling. We must forget home, forget Russia. We must think of America."

My heart contracted in pain. Forget Russia? Forget Samara, my Volga, my family, the yellow house where I was born, where I was happy? How?

⚹ 15 ⚹
Going West
Southampton/New York, 1923

MY TIME in Atlantic Park was relatively brief — two months at most, my immediate future much more certain than many, since I was returning to my father and was thus outside the quota. Yet I could not help being caught up in the anxieties of the immigrant families, whose entire lives might hang on an error in a document, a wayward bacterium, the whim of an immigration clerk — any random chance that might tip the balance for or against them. It has given me a lifelong reverence for the momentous randomness of things.

Once my ticket arrived, it was only a matter of getting my transit arranged, and finding a chaperone for the voyage. I was put in a cabin with the three Davidoffs, a young couple with a little boy. At last I was one of those waving goodbye from the red bus on its way to the port.

As it happened, I sailed on the Homeric again. Staring once more at a dwindling shore from the familiar deck, I thought of the time when this ship had brought Mamma and me to England. That was only three months ago, though it seemed more like years.

Now I was returning alone, leaving friends I would never see again, leaving Mamma behind in an alien land.

Like all those lost souls warehoused at Atlantic Park, I had been snatched up by the scruff by a capricious fate, shaken and tossed about like a puppy, then dropped casually back to the parent hound. My early inner sense of being special and lucky — my conviction that for me everything would always end with a "happy ever after" — had been badly shaken. Now I had learned the difference between life and fairy tales. Now I knew that even when life did get better, when finally people got what they yearned for, the cost could be hard to bear. It was a very grownup feeling for an eight-year-old, and I didn't like it.

But my spirits soon rebounded. The sunny summer sea sparkled, the air was salty and sweet. The cloudless sky shed its loving blue like a blessing on the ship filled with eager yet anxious immigrants finally on the brink of their heart's desire. I romped through the fair days, chattering with old acquaintances, making new ones, racing around the decks with other children, asking endless questions of the staff, milking the bottomless reservoir of kindness my orphan state generated. Though Manny Golding was gone to the booming South American run, there were still some in the crew who remembered my traumatic eastward voyage.

The fine weather stilled contrary winds and speeded the crossing, until rising fog offshore slowed us not far out from Ambrose Light. As the first sightings of the coast faded out in the white mist, the captain sent word around that we would anchor in the outer harbor overnight and disembark the next morning.

My euphoric anticipation had grown into hectic excitement by that last day. I felt restless and feverish;

my body seemed to be sending out vague signals of discomfort that I could not interpret. But I put it all down to impatience, and tried to ignore them.

Yet by evening I felt really unwell. Though the ship lay quiet in a calm sea, my dinner sat uneasily in my stomach. The decks and salons rocked with gaiety through the evening hours, as the excited passengers vented their accumulating tensions in dance and song and chatter. But I found myself unable to enjoy any of it. Periodic waves of heat surged up into my head, making it throb, and it hurt to sing, or even to talk.

Was I getting sick? I wondered anxiously. For weeks I'd been eavesdropping on horrifying stories of immigrants rejected at the ports for failure to pass the health inspection, or put into quarantine for weeks. The old nightmare returned, of being taken back out to sea while Papa was left despairing on shore. Could I have come this far only to be denied America at the last moment? And if I was, where would I go, alone?

A gleam of reason ordered me to curb my rising panic and fight the final battle. I left the partying above decks and retreated to the quiet of the cabin. Out of my sweaty clothes and into my cool nightgown, my hot face and arms refreshed by dashes of cold water, I felt a little better. Comforting myself with the thought that by this time tomorrow I would be safe with Papa, I climbed into my upper bunk and fell almost instantly asleep.

Throughout the night I woke and slept in restless rhythm. At times dimly aware of Mr. Davidoff's snores or little Davy grinding his teeth, I would drop back into a world of confused dreams from which I would suddenly start awake, then sleep again. Toward morning, awaking bathed in sweat, I felt a welcome relaxation in my heavy limbs. Mopping myself dry on a corner of the sheet, I fell into a deep well of exhausted sleep, sinking down and down into a sea of silence.

It was broad daylight when I finally came awake, struggling to the surface like a swimmer in heavy surf. I opened my eyes briefly to bright sunshine slanting into the porthole. Still half asleep, letting consciousness seep slowly back, I was jolted by two simultaneous thoughts: this was the day of arrival, and the cabin was eerily quiet. Where was everybody?

I sat up abruptly. A sudden wave of dizziness rocked me back on my pillow. Lying still to let the spasm ebb away, I tried to integrate the several messages my mind was signaling:

The cabin was empty; the Davidoffs were gone.

The ship was barely rocking; it must be in the harbor.

I felt very hot, more feverish than last night. My head pounded when I raised it.

I had to hurry and get dressed and find out where I was supposed to go.

I had to pass a health inspection, and I felt really really sick.

I was afraid.

I had to do something. I had to fight. I had to get back into America. I must not give up.

Letting myself gingerly down to the floor, I found that the dizziness gradually passed as my equilibrium slowly reestablished itself. Filling the little sink with cold water, I plunged my arms in up to the elbows, splashed my face over and over, felt the chill run deliciously up my arms into my body. Refreshed, I felt encouraged that I might manage to cope.

Minutes later, carefully dressed in my best clothes, the blue silk hat perched on my throbbing head like a talisman, my papers clutched in my hot hand, I emerged up on deck.

I was directed down to a lower level, where lines of people were already waiting to go through a cargo door into launches that would ferry them to Ellis Island. As a third class passenger I was to be one of them. Nearby loomed the enormous Liberty, on her own island. This time the statue did not seem welcoming — but stern and somehow searching. I turned away from the sight, as if hoping to escape her notice. Taking my place at the end of a line, I drained my mind of everything but the effort to remain upright and inconspicuous.

I managed both. The fresh harbor breeze cooled my flushed cheeks and the sunlight dancing on the little wavecrests raised my low spirits. Soon the launch docked at the island landing. Long lines of immigrants wound up the path to one of the sprawling brick buildings that dominated the island. Striped in dingy white, the weathered red brick was eerily reminiscent of the fancy Victorian houses in Eastleigh, though swollen to monstrous size.

Inside the building I found myself in a cavernous space under a high ceiling. Across one end of the enormous room hung a row of placards. In large letters they divided the long queues according to their nationality. At the direction of clerks who checked their papers and herded each into the proper fenced-off area, they joined lines of earlier arrivals from other ships.

The lines crawled slowly toward blue-uniformed health examiners. Each face, clouded with worry as its owner approached the final barrier to the magic land, bloomed into joy as the inspector approved and returned papers, and waved the accepted one into America. Here and there the hunched shoulders of a questionable case moved anxiously into an upstairs office for a more searching investigation by a higher authority. An occasional despairing soul, rejected outright, sat dejectedly waiting to be sent back.

Behind a wire partition at one side were the relatives and friends, waiting for the reunions to come. I looked around anxiously for Papa, but could not find his face in the crowd pressed against the wire. Where was he? I worried. What would I do if he didn't come? I needed his support so desperately now.

I took my place in line, clutching my papers nervously, taking deep breaths to cool my hot throat. How could I keep the inspector from seeing how sick I felt? On the Polish line I saw the Davidoffs, trying to keep little Davy from climbing up the wire partition, but my fuzzy mind did not think of waving.

My own line inched its way forward. I moved numbly with it, trying to focus on surviving the endless minutes till my moment came. As I neared the front, I strained to hear the questions, to see what the inspector looked at, what made him frown or smile. I concentrated on looking cheerful and healthy. Though I could not help looking around for Papa every few minutes, I tried hard not to think about his absence. One problem at a time was all I could deal with right now.

My turn came at last. Advancing with all the assurance I could summon, I smiled shyly and volunteered a "Good morning."

"You speak English?" This was an unusual immigrant. "Are you American?"

"Not yet," I replied pertly, offering my papers. "But I have been here before. I'm coming back to my Papa." I looked around again. "But I don't see him," I couldn't help saying anxiously.

"He might have been held up at the ferry," said the inspector. "If he's late, you can wait for him in that room," pointing to a door behind him. "Now let's get you passed through. Let me look at you. Take off that pretty hat."

I turned my face up confidingly, willing myself to seem untroubled.

"What red cheeks you have. Do you feel all right?"

"Oh, yes," I answered airily. "But it's so hot this morning."

"It sure is," the man agreed. He checked my ears perfunctorily, ruffled my hair, nodded. "Let me see your hands."

I extended them, turned them over palms down, and was aghast to see a rosy rash sprinkling the backs of both hands.

"Is that a rash?" The man's attention was alerted. "What's that from?"

Think fast. I told myself. Be careful.

"Oh, that. I get it sometimes when I eat strawberries and things. It goes away in a little while. Or it may be from the heat." I smiled.

"Yeah, that's probably it." The inspector nodded, relieved not to have to hassle an engaging child. "It sure is hot," he repeated. "Okay." He set the stamp of approval on my papers. "Here. Now you can go in there and wait for your dad."

Smiling my thanks, I made a beeline for the door into a large waiting room where various people, alone or in groups, were sitting about. I had done it! I had gotten back into America.

Now it was up to Papa. I couldn't hold up my aching head any longer. Looking around for some place where I might collapse without attracting attention, I saw a pile of sacks in a corner. Gratefully I curled up on them and closed my eyes.

Papa later said it took him quite a while to spy the limp little bundle in a corner, fast asleep. Catching me up in his arms, he was shocked to find me burning hot.

"Dushenka," he murmured in my ear. "Are you all right? Were you worried? I'm sorry. I was held up in a subway tie-up. My darling child, you're here. You're home."

341

Startled out of a heavy sleep, only half-conscious, I stared dully at my father, my eyes glazed with fever. As awareness returned, I threw my arms around his neck, joy rising above pain.

"Oh, Papa, you're here!" Putting my mouth close to his ear, I whispered, "Oh, Papa, I feel so sick. I didn't let them know, Papa. They passed me in. They didn't send me back." My heavy head drooped on my father's shoulder. "Can we go home now, Papa? I'm hot and my head aches so much." A sudden chill shook my thin body. "Ooh, now I feel c-c-cold. What's the matter with me, Papa?"

My father held me closer, pulled his jacket around my shivering body, terrified that someone might see me. "Yes, darling, I'll take you right home. You'll be all right, you're just having a chill."

His thoughts raced. What to do? How to avoid the danger of discovery? He had to collect the luggage at the pier: Olga's big straw trunk, three large suitcases, all the possessions saved out of the wreck of their life in Russia. Locating them now and getting them transported uptown would take precious time. I was obviously ill. My cheeks flaunted the flags of fever. I had to be removed from the searching eyes of immigration people as rapidly as possible. If someone in authority caught sight of me now, I would be sent to quarantine for weeks, alone and terrified.

Papa knew he had no choice. He scooped me up, wrapped me in his jacket, and carried me, his eyes darting nervously about to see who might be watching, out to the waiting ferry. There he tucked me into a corner and placed himself to hide me as much as possible. Once ashore, he hurriedly commandeered a cab. Even so, it took two anxious hours before I was safe in his small bedroom at the Home and being looked at by the doctor.

With my fever now raging, I was only dimly aware

of the trip. I only knew that my throbbing head was pillowed on Papa's chest, that his arm supported me, that I was not alone any longer.

The next weeks were a confusion of pain and fever and chills and cooling cloths on my head; violent spasms of vomiting and awful-tasting medicine. The daily doses of castor oil were the worst. I had scarlet fever.

All my energies were focused on battling the disease. I did not know when Papa sat by my bed, wondering whether he was going to lose all that was left of his family. I lay in a timeless daze while the inhabitants of my life swept through my fevered dreams in driven gusts. Like the spirits in Dante's "Inferno" with the wonderful engravings that I used to look at in Luba's house, people swept by and were gone and then came again and were swept away. The places of my life came and went like pictures in a magic lantern show: Atlantic Park, the house of the Baba Yagas, the Bronx tenement, Moscow, Samara, the yellow house — they came and went and came again, but always fainter, always farther away . . .

Until one morning I awoke drenched in sweat, clammy and too weak to raise my head. But the head was clear; the throbbing was gone. I felt somehow washed out and clean. Papa, waking in the other bed, came to feel my forehead and smiled his old bright smile.

"At last, dushenka. Your fever is gone," he assured me. "Now you're going to get better."

It was three more weeks before the doctor pronounced me cured, before I could be released from my quarantine, and go downstairs to meet Papa's new friends and learn my way around his new home — the Home. But I was content to wait. The pain was gone from my head and the heat from my body. I could eat again, and begin to put some flesh back on my emaciated body, a body that strangely had been growing rapidly while in the throes of the disease.

I was surprised to find, when I could get up and get dressed again, that my last year's dresses would barely cover my thighs. I could not recognize this long skinny new self.

As my strength returned, I spent my days sitting on the iron fire escape at the end of our corridor on the third floor, obeying the isolation dictum yet enjoying the late-summer air and sun, reading and drowsing by turns. Often my book would lie unnoticed on my lap while my mind ranged back over the months and years.

But like a smelter, the long fever had burned away the past and left me free for a new life in America. All the people and places of my fevered dreams had receded into memory, outside reality. Like well-loved stories I had read, they lived in my heart but not in my life.

When Papa talked of the past, it did not touch me now — not even when he told me about the loss of our luggage. The handyman Papa sent to the pier had found the old straw trunk full of Mama's linens and the valise that she had packed to keep in the cabin. But the two big leather suitcases that held Mamma's furs and her silverware, all the valuable possessions that she had managed to rescue from the Bolsheviks, had both disappeared.

Once I was out of danger, Papa went downtown himself and demanded a search. But it was hopeless; our belongings had vanished without a trace. Papa kept talking about it, blaming himself for not having found a way to get the luggage and save me from quarantine at the same time. He knew he'd had to make a choice, but the loss was a terrible blow for him. It was the last remnant of the life he had built with my mother.

But I could not make myself feel anything. I was sorry we had lost the family photographs, all those dear faces that were beginning to fade in my memory. Otherwise, the luggage had little reality for me. The White Star Line had kept it stored during all my peregrinations, and I had never thought about it. Those things were all part of the past; a past that had cost me so much pain to live, and to leave. A past I could no longer bear.

I had survived. I was back with Papa. I had a new home, and a new life to live in America.

∗⊰ Afterword ⊱∗

I HAVE TOLD the story of three lives in crisis. One was lost; two saved. The reader who has followed them to the end of the book has an interest in them and deserves to know the rest of their story.

By the time I returned from England and recovered from scarlet fever, Papa's life was already set on its lifelong course. His position as assistant superintendent of the Home of the Daughters of Jacob provided him with room and board, so he was able to devote most of his salary to clearing his debts and paying for my mother's care and mine.

Through his Brooklyn cousins he heard of an Englishwoman, the divorced wife of one of the cousins, who was willing to board me. She was already taking care of a small boy and his mother, a divorced schoolteacher, as well as her own two sons. I lived in her household until I was fourteen, when I went to live with Papa at the Home. By that time he had a two-bedroom apartment at his disposal.

Mamma surprisingly lived for a year before her anemia completed the job of destroying her body. Her mind had already failed through the deterioration of her central nervous system, a characteristic

346

symptom of the disease. She was cared for in a sana-
torium for chronic cases, and lost all awareness of
her former life. I remember an evening when Papa
came for his weekly visit. Sitting down, he pulled me
to him and held me between his knees. Hugging me
close, he said softly into my neck, "Yesterday I had a
letter from Southampton. Mamma is dead." I felt his
body quiver as he choked on a sob.

My face buried against his chest, I tried to register the meaning of his words. I found I could not
feel his sorrow, I could not cry. I had done my mourning a year ago in the house of the Baba Yagas. I was
sure then that Mamma had died. Ever since I had
lived as a motherless child. It was only when adoles-
cence triggered wrenching emotional storms and confusion that I longed for my mother, for the comfort of
her arms against the terror I felt at being so small
and so alone in the vastness of the universe.

Three years after Papa got his job at the Home
of the Daughters of Jacob, the superintendent died
of a heart attack, and Papa was appointed in his place.
He kept that position until the night he died of his
second coronary thrombosis, two months before his
57th birthday. He devoted all his vitality and intelligence to the welfare of the 500 or more old people in
his care. During the Depression years, the privately
supported home floundered in a sea of red ink, and
Papa wore himself out trying to keep it afloat.

The achievement that makes me proudest came
when the Social Security program was passed. Papa
spent months lobbying the legislature in Albany for
the passage of a bill that would allow the Social Security pensions of people in old age homes to be
paid to the institution that housed and fed them.
That law provided a stable cushion of monthly support, which assured the continuing existence of the
home.

As its financial position improved, Papa embarked on a series of improvements for the buildings, and also became active in the Jewish community, as well as among the city's agencies. He sat on the boards of Yeshiva University and other public service institutions, and devoted much of his scarce spare time to welfare problems. Out of the wreck of his Russian life, he created an American one that used his abilities well and satisfied his need to succeed.

As long as Papa lived, I periodically had news of our Russian family, because he and Babushka corresponded regularly. A year or two after we left, Aunt Sonya married Leonid, and in due course gave birth to a son, whom she named after Papa. Sadly, only two years later her husband died of diphtheria in one of the recurring epidemics that regularly devastated the area, and she lived the rest of her life as a widow. But as I grew into adulthood, my life became busier and more absorbing, and I did not often think of the people in Samara who had once been my world.

About the time Ara and I were twenty the Samara family sent us a picture of them all, except Zeyde, who had died only a few years after we left there. Everybody appeared so much older, the children all grown up, except for Sonya's son Adik who looked about ten. With it came a solo portrait of Mara, very handsome and impressive in a dark shirt that featured a medallion indicating his membership in the Communist Party. They all seemed strange – not the people I had once felt so close to. I realized with a pang how far apart our lives had become, and how little I knew about them – and I suppose they about me.

It was only after he developed an ulcer at the age of 49 that Papa, feeling the first stirrings of mortality, decided that if he was ever to marry again, it would have to be before he turned fifty. With his rather rigid concept of proper behavior, he assumed that people who married after that age would be thought ridiculous. As I grew up and became more independent in my activities, Papa would often trot out his usual response to anything unconventional or daring: "How will it look?"

So he married for the wrong reasons, and found he had a wife with whom he had almost nothing in common. Like so many men, he had to find emotional satisfaction in his work and friends.

My own life took the usual surprising turns into unexpected paths. In my teens I read voraciously and developed a lifelong passion for Shakespeare, to the point that my professors later accused me of writing all my essays in iambic pentameter.

But I did not know what I wanted to become until my senior high school year. I'd been writing occasional poems since the age of 12. One day, not having done the composition due that day for my English class, I submitted this poem instead, written when I was thinking of Mamma:

> *ALAS, POOR YORICK!*
> *And ever weeds grow tall above our loves,*
> *In lonely graveyards and within our hearts.*
> *The infrequent sun makes puddles on the wall;*
> *Love rots in fading rose leaves. Every breath*
> *Sends drops to wear away the carven stone*
> *Atom by atom, leaving at the end*
> *Oblivion, and in the hearts of those*
> *Whom we forget, forgetfulness as well.*

When my teacher, Mrs. Obear, read my poem aloud in class and said: "This is a poem one would wish to have written," I knew I wanted to be a writer.

At about the same time I was surprised to receive a letter from Aunt Xenia, Mamma's oldest sister. Her own daughter Asya had died at 17, and

Xenia's life had fallen apart. Alone and in despair, she wrote Papa's family for Mamma's address, and learned that she too was gone. Xenia wrote to me as the last link with the sister she had loved.

Her letter moved me deeply. Not only did it make me realize how much I was missing Mamma, but it described a life filled with what to me seemed unbearable pain.

After Asya's death, Xenia's husband divorced her and married a woman who possessed the ultimate asset – a whole apartment. Though Xenia, like everybody else, was working for the state, teaching languages and the violin, because she was a member of the despised *bourjui,* she ranked lowest on the list for privileges, and could not qualify for an apartment, or even a room. Her only home was a sheltered corner in a courtyard, except when a friend would go on a trip and ask her to housesit – a vital service in a city where any empty living space was easy prey to squatters. Once more I felt helpless: someone I loved was suffering and I was powerless to help her.

Xenia and I found great comfort in each other. She needed a daughter, I a mother. My Russian had rusted through disuse; she had no English. But we found common ground in French, in which I'd gained fluency through four years of study. Xenia shared my rapture when I discovered love, my sorrow when I lost it. Until the war disrupted our correspondence, I wrote her the things I wanted to tell my mother about.

Some years after the war I learned that Hadassah, a Jewish social service agency, had set up a program for finding lost relatives, and through them I found Xenia again. Though her life had improved a bit, it was bleak by any standard. She was now retired from teaching and living on an infinitesimal pension in a real room. But she was terrified of any effort I made to help her. Eventually she agreed I might send her a few dollars, but when I stupidly sent the money through (I thought) the normal channel of a Bank Money Order, she replied in an agony of fear. "You must *never* send anything in an official way again," she pleaded. "Just put five or ten dollars into your letter, well wrapped. If I went to a bank to cash money from America I might lose my pension, or even be arrested as a spy." She never went to the bank for the money.

I could not believe such a thing to be possible, but since in her mind it was very real, I had to limit my gifts carefully. I sent her pictures of the children. She sent me advice about starting their musical education. "Study of the violin must be started at six, or it will be too late," she dictated. Once she sent me a lovely little silk handkerchief, folded into a letter without the least lump. She sent a picture of my mother in her teens, and once a tiny wallet sized snapshot of herself, old and very worn. But my mother's mouth was unmistakable.

We only had a few years. Her health was already deteriorating. The day came when my letter brought no reply, and I lost a mother once more.

Halfway through college at Barnard in New York, I met the love of my life, a tall weedy Columbia student who was a promising young poet and turned out to be the matching half of my soul. Like me, he was an only child, the product of a disastrous union between two German immigrants, as ill-matched a pair as one could hope to find: his father was a left-wing radical, his mother basically a monarchist. Herman's psyche, frayed by their constant wars over him, at last found a haven in our total commitment to literature and our love.

The one blight on my happiness was my father's anger at my choice. Herman was not a Jew, and Papa brought up all the classic warnings against inter-marriage. I had long before come to consider myself a humanist, and to believe that assimilation was the best route to human progress, so felt no fear of being abused because of my race. But my father did not speak to me as long as my marriage lasted.

Our five years together were the happiest of my life. We married after I got my degree, settled down to a lifetime of achievement and joy, and decided to start our family. But I had barely become pregnant when my husband was diagnosed with acute lymphoblastic leukemia. In 1939 there was no known treatment. Again my life was wrecked by a disease before a cure for it was found. Within six weeks I found myself a widow.

Afterwards my father and I were reconciled, and he was thrilled when, six months later, he became a grandfather. My son Peter was, finally, the boy Papa had always hoped for. He would visit us regularly one evening a week, and I always kept the baby up for him. It delighted me to watch them play together: the baby crowing in his high chair, Papa on the couch in front of him, running his fingers up the tray to send the child into spasms of giggles.

Peter was ten months old when one evening I got a phone call from the Home. Papa was dead of a coronary thrombosis. His death came just a month after he had received the news of Babushka's death at the age of 81. Thus, by the age of 26, I had lost mother, grandmother, father and husband. It seemed that the Furies that had dogged our family were not through with us yet.

But life, as the saying goes, went on. I raised my son, married another newspaperman when Peter was three, had four more children – all girls. We chose first names that we liked, and middle names from our families. Jane Elizabeth was for both Babushka and Jim's favorite grandmother. Julia Olga (always called Jill) was for Mamma. Laurie Margaret was for Jim's sister. And our last child was named by Jim for me, and by me for him - Nora James. All five grew into interesting and productive people, who make me intensely proud and have always been my greatest joy.

I worked at whatever local jobs presented themselves to eke out an uncertain living. My husband Jim was a man of great charm and intelligence, but thrift and practicality had been entirely overlooked at his creation. Decades went by while our lives were totally devoted to weathering the uncertain present.

Eventually, as the children started off on their own adventuring, I moved to better jobs in New York City, eventually to an editorial career at the American Management Association, and finally was recruited to be Alumnae Director at my alma mater. Since by then we had bought a home eighty miles away in Connecticut, I became a weekend commuter. But after Jim suffered his first heart attack in 1972, I decided I should be nearer home, and a year later took early retirement and became editor of our alumnae magazine instead, working mostly from home.

It was during those years, I think, that my lifelong stirrings of nostalgia first became compelling. As I began to contemplate my early history, I found it eventful almost to the point of melodrama. It soon became evident to me that it was a story which needed to be told – if only for the sake of all the world's displaced families whose lives had been, and were still being, shattered by huge impersonal political movements that took no account of the agonies of the helpless individuals caught up in them. I began to research and read about the period in order to understand more fully the events through which we had lived.

All efforts to find news of my family proved fruitless, and until *glasnost* came, Samara (then Kuibishev) was not an Intourist city. On my first trip to the USSR I could not visit it. So when I eventually heard of a Russian tour that would include Samara, I signed on and looked forward to it eagerly, hoping to find some way to connect with the people I'd lost three quarters of a century before.

By this time my husband had died, all my children had established their own families, and had presented me with eleven grandchildren, and I had retired to the North Carolina mountains, where two of my daughters also have their homes.

As our days in Samara were coming to an end, and I was making my farewells to the kind people who had tried so hard, yet so fruitlessly, to help me find news of my family, I tried to evaluate what I had gained from this adventure.

Though several people called after they saw me on television and heard my story, the only useful news came from an old lady who had known Aunt Sonya. Vera Markova was a retired engineer, not much older than my son, though she looked almost as old as I did. Our interview took place in her apartment, with the young daughter of one of our hosts acting as interpreter.

"I remember your Aunt Sonya Lurye very well," she said. "My mother was also a dentist, though they worked in different clinics. But of course they were acquainted. I remember walking on the street with my mother when I was about seven. We met your Aunt Sonya and they stopped to talk. She had a very sweet face, and I remember that she smiled and patted my head as she stood talking. When I grew up I would see her occasionally, but we never really got to know each other. I know that she worked at the Children's Clinic all her life, until she died at about the age of eighty. I may be wrong, but I don't remember ever hearing that she'd retired."

Vera Markova and I had a lovely visit, and I remember thinking: "If I had stayed in Samara, we could have been friends." Strangely, as I was saying goodbye, she held my hand and said exactly the same thing.

But after that my searches led to a dead end. The fragments I had gleaned from family correspondence in the early years led nowhere at the local records office. There was so much disorganization in the shifting of regimes and authority that no trace could be found of records for the period that concerned me, already more than half a century old. Undoubtedly they are moldering away in some forgotten warehouse, and may not even be in a readable state by now. And my later efforts to track down Aunt Sonya's family in Israel proved equally fruitless.

So I had to go home without having found any connection that might lead me to the younger generations. I had found the places, but not the people, of my history.

Remembering that other "going home" — from Atlantic Park back into America, a trip so charged with mixed emotions — I felt again the comfort that had come when I was back in Papa's arms and knew I was home. All during my long eventful life, I have felt truly at home in my adopted country. Now I could return to my children, my grandchildren, my friends, my garden, my little house in a friendly town — my real life.

Though I had failed to learn the history I yearned for in my old age, I *had* relived so many memories and filled the empty spot in my heart where they belonged. My trip had been truly a coming home to my childhood; and it helped me to let go once again the life I might have lived.

But as I turned away from the past, I discovered that it would not die. Now the people of that lost life had a life of their own for me, so vividly that it became impossible to let them go. So I've had to put them all into words, and bring them back into a world they left too soon. Now when I leave that world, I will leave behind the resurrected people of my stormy early life — not only children, grandchildren and friends, but parents, grandparents, cousins and aunts: the people who made me, as well as those I made.

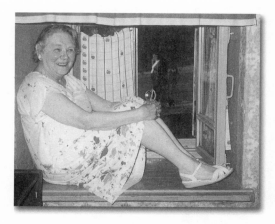

"Here in this shabby hallway, scrunched up in a scanty space, on the other side of the planet and of a century, incredibly I've come home and found . . .myself."

After a long busy life in America, the author felt impelled to learn about the family she'd left in Samara, the city on the Volga where she was born. After *glasnost* she was finally able to return there and find the places, though not the people, of her youth. Her search resurrected childhood memories of revolution, civil war, famine and exile, which she felt impelled to share, "to speak for so many others who have silently endured the loss of all they valued."

Nora Lourie Percival has lived in the United States since she was eight. She grew up in New York City and graduated from Barnard College during the troubled decade before World War II. Her first husband died before their son was born, and this story forms the basis for her book, **Regarding Love**. A second marriage produced four daughters, and she is now the proud grandmother of eleven.

In her busy life of family and work the author's early writing aspirations languished, but in her later years a need grew to record her traumatic childhood, when she was a witness to history. After years of research and remembrance, and the fall of the Iron Curtain, the tale has now been told.

After her husband's death, she settled in the North Carolina mountains near two of her daughters. A version of her first chapter recently won a prize in the Memoir contest of the Asheville Writers' Workshop.

Also from *High Country Publishers:*

Monteith's Mountains

by Skip Brooks

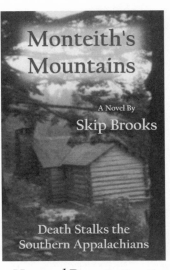

... a suspense thriller set in 1900 ... as real as today."
– *Publishers Weekly*

... extraordinary work. . . . the Smokies and its people come to life. . . . creative, profound and interesting.
– Dr. Bob Hieronimus, Co-Founder of 21st Century Radio

... suspenseful, powerful and arousing read, holding you by plot, character, and the inspiring beauty of its southern Appalachian settings.
– Howard Dorgan, Past President of the Appalachian Studies Association and author of four books on Appalachian Culture.

... dramatic portrait of the Great Smoky Mountains and their people. .. captures both the voices of mountain people and the dramatic landscape of their beloved Smokies in a haunting tale.
– Dr. William Ferris, Public Policy Scholar The Woodrow Wilson International Center for Scholars and Former Director; National Endowment for The Humanities

ISBN: 0971304548
October 2002
Hardcover, 288 pages, $21.95

Also from *High Country Publishers*:

Where the Water-Dogs Laughed
or
The Sacred Dream of the Great Bear
By Charles F. Price

Tusquittee Bald, known in Cherokee legend as the place where the water-dogs laughed, frames this the latest in Charles F. Price's saga of the Southern Appalachians at the close of the 19th century. Hamby McFee seeks out Yan-e'gwa, the great bear that has terrorized and excited loggers and hunters, and finds his own fate in the process.

ISBN: 1932158502
October 2003

Visit our website to learn more about High Country
Publishers books and authors
www.highcountrypublishers.com

HCP books are available through Biblio Distribution, a division of NBN Books to
bookstores, wholesalers, and online retailers.